Three Classic
Silent Screen Comedies
Starring Harold Lloyd

By the same Author

Four Great Comedians: Chaplin, Lloyd, Keaton, Langdon
Focus on Chaplin
The Golden Age of Sound Comedy

Three Classic Silent Screen Comedies Starring HAROLD LLOYD

Donald W. McCaffrey

Rutherford • Madison • Teaneck
Fairleigh Dickinson University Press
London: Associated University Presses

© 1976 by Associated University Presses, Inc.

Associated University Presses, Inc.
Cranbury, New Jersey 08512

Associated University Presses
108 New Bond Street
London W1Y OQX, England

Library of Congress Cataloging in Publication Data

McCaffrey, Donald W.
  Three classic silent screen comedies starring Harold Lloyd.

  "Portions of this book were originally published in dissertation form as An investigation of three feature length silent film comedies starring Harold Lloyd."
    Bibliography: p.
    Filmograpny: p.
    Includes index.
    1. Comedy films—History and criticism. 2. Lloyd, Harold Clayton, 1894-1971. I. Title.
PN1995.9.C55M33   791.43'7   74-4993
ISBN 0-8386-1455-8

Portions of this book were originally published in dissertation form as *An Investigation of Three Feature Length Silent Film Comedies Starring Harold Lloyd*, © 1962 by Donald W. McCaffrey

PRINTED IN THE UNITED STATES OF AMERICA

Dedicated to a scholar who has espoused and fostered clarity in thinking, speaking, and writing—Professor Donald C. Bryant

Contents

Acknowledgments

When an author's dissertation is published, he is, naturally, grateful to the institution that had awarded him a doctorate, in this case, the University of Iowa in Iowa City, Iowa, and to the committee that assisted him in developing the study: Donald Bryant, Chairman; Oscar Brockett, David Schaal, and Charles Wood.

For this revised version of the treatise, I would like to acknowledge the assistance of the Faculty Research Committee of the University of North Dakota. From this same institution I obtained excellent photographic reproductions through the efforts of Jerry Olson. From the early years (late fifties) of the investigation of silent-screen comedy, Murray Glass of Em Gee Film Library in Encino, California, has been most helpful by coming to my aid with films and photographic stills. More recently, Richard Simonton, Jr., of North Hollywood, California, has provided many of the rare stills that appear in this book.

Since there are many special production problems in publishing a work of this type, I am grateful for the guidance I received from Mathilde E. Finch, Editor-in-Chief, Associated University Presses, Inc., and copyeditor David Redstone.

Without the professional skills of my wife, Joann, this study would not have been realized. She has never been merely the average proofreader of the manuscript—a task by no means minor. She has been the writer's best critic and a second editor for this study as well as three other major works.

Introduction

On March 9, 1971, the *New York Times* printed a front-page obituary of Harold Lloyd, who died on the eighth at the age of seventy-seven. The next day, the tenth, an editorial in the *Times* lauded this famous film comedian as a man who brought the spirit of optimism to the comic drama. Recognizing his well-known character as a lampoon of the success story, this commentary maintained the view that Lloyd's comic portrait was one of hope, a vital part of the American spirit of the past, that had faded away in the modern, pessimistic theater of the absurd.

With the death of Lloyd in 1971, only Charles Chaplin lived on as the last king of comedy of the silent screen and a reminder to those who still see such films that the twenties was an age when some of the best motion-picture comedy of the twentieth century flourished. Both Lloyd and Chaplin received popular and critical acclaim for their silent and sound films. They also received stronger financial gain from their movies than the other two master comedians of the period, Buster Keaton and Harry Langdon. Revivals and re-releases of Chaplin's and Lloyd's films in the sixties revealed that, even forty years after creation, their works could draw millions of dollars at the box office. In 1941 *Newsweek* reported that Lloyd's films had grossed more money than any movies by another male actor—over $30,000,000.[1] Because Chaplin has had many successful releases since this date, it is likely that his films have equaled if not surpassed Lloyd's in total box office receipts.

Interest in Lloyd's comedies was revived when he came out of retirement in 1947 to play the lead in *The Sin of Harold Diddlebock* (later retitled *Mad Wednesday*), a picture written and directed by

1. Review of *A Girl, a Guy and a Gob*, *Newsweek*, 17 (March 17, 1941): 63.

the famous film director of sophisticated comedy, Preston Sturges. In 1950 the comedian released his 1932 creation, *Movie Crazy,* and in the sixties he released compilation works which used scenes from his features, *Harold Lloyd's World of Comedy* (1962) and *Harold Lloyd's Funny Side of Life* (1966). The 1962 movie contained scenes and sequences from both silent and sound films: *Safety Last* (1923), *Why Worry?* (1923), *Girl Shy* (1924), *Hot Water* (1924), *Feet First* (1930), *Movie Crazy* (1932), *The Milky Way* (1936), and *Professor Beware* (1938). The 1966 release contained the full-length 1925 feature, *The Freshman*[2] plus portions of *Girl Shy, Why Worry?, For Heaven's Sake* (1926), *The Kid Brother* (1927), and *Speedy* (1928). Both of these compilation features were successful ventures. In a June 1965 interview, Lloyd told this author that his *World of Comedy* had grossed over $3,000,000. He also was greatly impressed by the enthusiasm of the audience for the film when it was shown at the Cannes Film Festival on May 12, 1962.

During his life the comedian received other recognitions for his films. He was given an Oscar (on which was inscribed "To a Master Comedian") by the Academy of Motion Picture Arts and Sciences in 1952. More in response to his fame as a movie star than because of the position to which he was elected, *Time* magazine featured him in a cover story for its July 25, 1949, issue. The story was sparked by his election to the position of Imperial Potentate of the Shriners.

It is not, however, the main purpose of this exploration to investigate the life of Harold Lloyd. The focus of the examination is on three of his silent-screen features, *Grandma's Boy* (1922), *Safety Last* (1923), and *The Freshman* (1925). Completed in 1962 and revised in 1973 through 1974, this study is a thorough investigation of the structure, characters, and comic techniques employed in these works. When this project was completed in 1962, scholars had attempted to develop detailed, in-depth studies of serious films—for example, the works of D. W. Griffith and those of Sergei Eisenstein, but the film comedy had been neglected or usually confined to overall views of the life and work of the comedian—a traditional biographical approach. One of the best of this type of study was Theodore Huff's *Charlie Chaplin,* published in 1951. While collecting information on the silent-screen period,

---

2. Through correspondence the author urged Lloyd to release a complete feature. During a week of interviews in Beverly Hills, California (June 1965), the comedian presented a special screening of *Harold Lloyd's Funny Side of Life* before its commercial release. He asked the author, his wife, and two daughters for their reactions to the work.

the author unearthed another type of study: contemporary (1920's) explorations on the structure and character of the screenplay, which were intended to instruct aspiring screen-wrights. Scott O'Dell's *Representative Photoplays Analyzed* and Frederick Palmer's *Technique of the Photoplay*, published in 1924 by the Palmer Institute of Authorship in Hollywood, California, assisted in giving historical perspective into the way some of Lloyd's and his contemporaries' films were analyzed.

By far the most important step in preparing this treatise on silent-screen comedy was the direct study of the three films by a 16mm editola. Each film was viewed in detail through the construction of a shot-by-shot scenario as a record of the most minute actions in the movies. Each work was viewed at least six times, often with a small audience. From complete runnings of the motion pictures at sixteen frames per second (silent speed), a timing on parts of the film was registered to give data on the overall structure and sequences of the works.

Also important to this investigation were journalistic reviews of the twenties, present-day reflections, and basic comic theory. These areas of research helped flesh out a thorough examination of period film comedy.

On May 25, 1973, a little over two years after Harold Lloyd's death, his fabulous twenty-acre estate with its large mansion became a museum to depict a way of life enjoyed by motion-picture stars of a bygone age. Daily tourists now visit a shrine to one of the greatest comedians in film history. But his artistic worth is not enshrined in the memorial, as impressive as it is to those who dote on this type of nostalgia. It is in Lloyd's creations, the films themselves, which give the final testimony of his great contribution to our culture.

Three Classic
Silent Screen Comedies
Starring Harold Lloyd

1
Historical Background

Born in 1893, Harold Lloyd entered a world with vaudeville in its infancy and the motion pictures in an embryonic state. According to John Montgomery, the first comic films were brief works produced by the laboratory scientist—works like Fred Ott's *Sneeze,* a film produced in 1894[1] that ran long enough to show one sneeze.

When Harold Lloyd was still in grade school, vaudeville became a popular form of entertainment. According to Bernard Sobel, vaudeville entered a golden age from 1900 to 1910.[2] The comic tramp became a favorite on the American stage in this era. Some reflection of the stage in the movies can be seen in 1901 when the tramps, Weary Willie and Happy Holligan, were featured in films that were only fifty or seventy feet long.[3] By 1915 many film comedians had some variation on the tramp-clown as the basis for their comic characters. Charles Chaplin, Ben Turpin, Roscoe "Fatty" Arbuckle, and Charles Murray were some of the comedians who had played this type of character in the comic film when Lloyd turned to comedy in his film work. With writer-director Hal Roach in 1915, Lloyd developed a series of one-reel comedies featuring a tramp-clown called Willie Work, a character with all the physical characteristics of the stage tramp. With only a slight degree of sophistication, Lloyd then created a comic character called Lonesome Luke, a clown who was also in the tramp tradition.

1. John Montgomery, *Comedy Films* (London, 1954), p. 18.
2. Bernard Sobel, *A Pictorial History of Burlesque* (New York, 1956), p. 101.
3. Lewis Jacobs, *The Rise of the American Film* (New York, 1939), p. 18.

Three years before he formed a strong alliance with Hal Roach to develop a comic tramp character, the comedian appeared in a number of serious bit roles. The year was 1912. The Edison Company came from New York to San Diego to shoot on location, and Lloyd witnessed his first motion-picture company at work. While attending high school in San Diego, he had played a number of roles in local stage stock companies as well as roles in school plays, and now he was intrigued by this chance to act in movies. He received his first bit role—a Yaqui Indian.[4] If John Weaver's listing of credits for Lloyd's early work is correct, this film was called *Naked Yaqui*.[5] A year later, in 1913, his family moved to Los Angeles, and he began to make persistent efforts to break into the movies. While working as an extra for Universal Studios, Lloyd met Hal Roach. They both struggled as extras, often working in the same film. No clear, detailed evidence of the films in which he appeared during these two years has been unearthed, although both he and Roach obviously worked together in a period drama called *Samson*.[6] The comedian's future was assured in 1915 when Roach inherited money and began to produce one-reel comedies. For a period of about ten years he was featured as the lead in many films produced by Roach.

Lloyd's Predecessors and Contemporaries: Possible Influences

While Lloyd made his fledgling movie-acting effort as an Indian, Mack Sennett had established his directorial skills working under the tutelage of D. W. Griffith for Biograph. After signing a contract with movie producers Adam Kessel and Charles Bauman, Sennett launched his own company, Keystone. According to Kalton Lahue and Terry Brewer the first creation of the famous comedy director was two half-reel comedies released September 23, 1912, called *Cohen Collects a Debt* and *The Water Nymph*.[7] From the Keystone Company came a steady stream of one- and two-reel works; the company was the fountainhead for the major comedians of the 1910's. Charles Chaplin, Ben Turpin, Ford Sterling,

4. William Cahn, *Harold Lloyd's World of Comedy* (New York, 1964), p. 31.
5. John T. Weaver, *Twenty Years of Silents: 1908-1929* (Metuchen, N. J., 1971), p. 215.
6. Cahn, p. 22. (A picture, mislabeled *Damon and Pythias*, of the two extras and good friends appearing startled as they stand in the background of a scene in this movie provides an interesting illustration for Cahn's book.)
7. Kalton C. Lahue and Terry Brewer, *Kops and Custards* (Norman, Okla., 1967), p. 33.

Harold Lloyd (center background) and Hal Roach (left background) as bit players. J. Warren Kerrigan (foreground) in the 1914 production of **Samson**.

Roscoe "Fatty" Arbuckle, and Charles Murray were all products of Mack Sennett's "school" for comedy in the Keystone Company.

Most of the works ground out in three days or a week by Sennett dealt in broad, fast-paced slapstick. The producer-writer-director had been influenced by the wild farces from France and Italy that were imported during this decade, but he added his own touch—a comic drama with more bizarre characters and more outlandish situations. To this exaggeration of earlier material he added the frantic pace of the chase and the fight which occurred in the last one, two, or even three hundred feet of his films.

The four major comedians of the twenties, Charles Chaplin, Harold Lloyd, Buster Keaton, and Harry Langdon were strongly indebted to the pioneer efforts of Mack Sennett. He developed a tradition of slapstick comedy that influenced the creation of very effective features even though the Keystone entrepreneur himself was not to be credited with a major work of merit in the 1910's and 1920's. His full-length film *Tillie's Punctured Romance* (1914) can be labeled as a first—the first feature-length (six reels) comedy—but the work survives only as a curiosity. When he produced such features as *Mickey* (1916-1918) starring Mabel Normand, these motion pictures seemed to lack enough of the vigor of his one- and two-reel works to give them a place in history. But he established a tradition that was to influence all the comedians of the period.

Charles Chaplin, a predecessor of Harold Lloyd, had a great influence on the development of the comic film. A product of the English school of pantomime which was derived from the London music halls, Chaplin introduced a skill and subtlety of gesture and character portrayal which influenced all the budding comedians in the formative years of motion-picture comedy. When Chaplin, working for Sennett, reached stardom in 1914, his success invited imitation. Since one of the first steps a young comedian would take was to develop a comic wardrobe or, more specifically, collect incongruous attire, Lloyd tried to avoid imitation by reversing some of the characteristics of Chaplin's "little tramp" costume. Of his own and his father's attempt to create a comic costume he wrote:

> In a haberdashery dad found a black-and-white vertical-striped shirt and bought out the stock. The coat of a woman's tailored suit, a pair of very tight and short trousers, a vest too short, a cut-down collar, a

cut-down hat and two dots of a mustache completed the original version of Lonesome Luke. The cunning thought behind all this, you will observe, was to reverse the Chaplin outfit. All his clothes were too large, mine all too small. My shoes were funny, but different; my mustache funny, but different. Nevertheless, the idea was purely imitative and was recognized as such by audiences, though I painstakingly avoided copying the well-known Chaplin mannerism.[8]

Lloyd also states that Chaplin's method of building a series of high-quality gags instead of relying on one or two main gags, which was the practice of Mack Sennett and actor-director "Fatty" Arbuckle, influenced the story construction of his later one- and two-reel works.[9]

Lloyd's early work, however, had many of the characteristics of Arbuckle's and Sennett's pioneer efforts. His films, like theirs, were created around only one or two main gags, used a tramp-clown as a leading character, and were replete with implausible situations and gross slapstick. Before he perfected his comedies, he evidently used these ingredients poorly. A short, scathing review of his first major comic film in 1915 points out the inferiority of his work:

> JUST NUTS (Pathé)—An exaggerated slapstick comedy that the title fully describes. It is neither funny nor original and has little to recommend it in any way. The incidents are exceedingly disconnected and are not in themselves funny.[10]

The author, doing research on silent screen comedians in New York in June of 1964, viewed an excellent print of *Just Nuts* at the Museum of Modern Art Film Library. Lloyd's comic character in this one-reeler illustrated the way in which he was employing some of the techniques of Chaplin. The Lonesome Luke character had not been established but was only a month away from its creation. The comedian used big shoes, large pants and a somewhat small felt hat that was not a derby. The character achieved much of its comedy through the incongruity of being both a tramp and a masher—a relentless, obnoxious fellow in pursuit of a woman.

As the above review indicates, the incidents are disconnected. The plot seems to be contrived in an off-the-cuff fashion, as was the practice in most "park comedies." Lloyd and Roach obviously

---

8. Harold Lloyd, *An American Comedy* (New York, 1928), p. 92.
9. *Ibid.*, p. 94.
10. Review of *Just Nuts, The New York Dramatic Mirror* 73 (April 21, 1915): 35. (Lloyd's view of this film appears in Appendix C.)

A 1915 picture of the Rolin Company with Lloyd seated center. Immediately behind him, Hal Roach, to the right, Harry "Snub" Pollard, and in front of him, Bebe Daniels.

got a camera and film, a few actors (a girl and a man to play the policeman), and found a park. There they started shooting. In a fantastic gag, the masher is shown following a woman with such concentration that he gets run over by a car; as if he were made of rubber, he immediately jumps up and continues his pursuit. He takes what he wants in every situation. From a sleeping man who is on a park bench, he steals a paper and the man's glasses in order to read the news.

When *Just Nuts* switches incoherently to a dance sequence in a large tavern, the comic protagonist helps himself to a drink from a tray carried by the waiter. Getting into an altercation with the police, the obnoxious fellow seems Chaplinesque as he eludes the

Part of the Rolin Company "gathered in Westlake Park for the second Lonesome Luke one-reeler" according to Lloyd's autobiography.

law. In a final crowd fight the tramp-masher is the center of the struggle, but he loses in his attempt to gain the affections of the girl—the policeman leaves with the woman he desires.

The Willie Work one-reel films which followed *Just Nuts* and the Lonesome Luke series showed a degree of improvement over this first major venture into the comic film. The new comedy character, Lonesome Luke, was instituted the same year that the primitive *Just Nuts* was produced. According to a review, better material improved Lloyd's work slightly:

LONESOME LUKE (Pathé)—written by "Tad," the well-known cartoonist, this split-reel comedy, though entirely lacking in originality and utilizing time-worn features still has several amusing parts. A bear escapes from a menagerie and a prisoner in jail is offered his freedom to don a bear skin and enter a cage with a lion. He enters the cage, but immediately becomes afraid, and escaping into the audience causes consternation, until he is finally captured by an alleged comedy police department.[11]

This brief synopsis and evaluation of the film reveals a fantastic situation in the Mack Sennett tradition, a tradition of comedy which incorporated the violent and the absurd. The use of a "comedy police department" also indicates an imitation of the famous Keystone Cops.

Although many of the Lonesome Luke films are no longer extant, reissued titles like *Harold the Cinema Director* (probably the 1916 *Luke's Movie Muddle*) from a French print, show the development of the economically profitable comic character. In this work he also has strong inclinations toward women as he runs a movie theater, and he gets into a fight with one indignant husband. Comedy is created by Luke's scurrying around trying to sell tickets, take tickets, and usher people to their seats—all by himself. His projectionist (Snub Pollard) proves incompetent as he seems eternally entangled in movie film. Luke fights with him and tries to take over his job. When a fire is thought to be started in the auditorium, the audience rushes out, trampling poor Luke. Lloyd executes a clever comic dance in his dazed state. A final slapstick fight between the projectionist and the manager brings the lively one-reeler to a close.

Luke's Movie Muddle, a minor work, nevertheless shows an attempt to develop a character that departed from that of Chaplin's. Luke is more aggressive and obnoxious than Chaplin's little tramp. There is also a dash, a flair, in his pantomime that gives the character distinctively merry and lively personal facets.

Harold Lloyd, it should be noted, was employed by a producing group that imitated, as did other producing groups, the successful split-reel,[12] one-reel, and two-reel comedies of the day. The use of the comic chase became a stock situation for many films. John B. Kennedy quotes Lloyd's evaluation of the overuse of the chase:

> Our record week's output was three. Wide, heavy slapstick on the simplest theme—eight hundred feet of so-called plot. Whatever the plot, the picture always ended with two hundred feet of chase.[13]

---

11. Review of *Lonsome Luke, The New York Dramatic Mirror* 73 (June 9, 1915): 39.
12. Many short comedies, like the above-mentioned *Lonesome Luke,* were not a full reel in length. The producer often filled out the reel with brief travelogue or "nature study" material. The term applied to this incongruous combination was a "split-reel comedy."
13. John B. Kennedy, "It Pays to be Sappy," *Colliers* 79 (June 11, 1927): 12.

Following the prolific production precedures of his contemporaries and predecessors, Lloyd turned out numerous Lonesome Luke films from 1915 through 1917. During these two years he appeared in over sixty films using the comic tramp character.

Harold in the dress of a woman for **Spit Ball Sadie** (1915).

Most of these works were one-reel films, but about ten were two-reel creations. Chaplin was a worker of considerable vitality and tenacity, but during these same two years he cut his production for Mutual to twelve two-reelers. He worked with more care and made some of the best short comedies of the silent motion-picture era. Lloyd began to be more concerned about quality than quantity by the end of 1919, and instead of following the Sennett practice of developing a one-reel in three days and a two-reel in a week, he began to take twice as long to create a film. In 1920 he cut his output to only five two-reelers.

During his one- and two-reel period, Lloyd was one of the most prolific of the major comedians. Nelson E. Garringer tried to list

In the 1916 **Luke's Double**, with Gaylord Lloyd (the comedian's brother) on
his knees. Bebe Daniels and "Snub" Pollard on the bench.

his early works in *Films in Review*,[14] and even though some of these films are not on the copyright records, Garringer was able to set down the titles of over 125 one- and two-reel comedies. Kalton Lahue lists 172 short films[15] by filling in the period Garringer does not handle—one-reelers of 1915 and 1916. It is quite possible that from ten to twenty-five of his creations have not been uncovered because reviews and copyright procedures were very erratic at this time.

On the eve of his switch away from the tramp-comic portrait, partly out of mere boredom with the role and partly because he wanted a more original, distinctive character, Lloyd received praise for his work in *The Dramatic Mirror* of August 1917. Evidence of his growth as a comedian was revealed in a review of *Lonesome Luke's Wild Women*.[16] While the reviewer notes the use of "rough slapstick" in this film, he also comments on the cleverness and originality in the pantomime which Lloyd incorporated into this two-reel work. He prophetically adds that Lloyd's use of "farce-comedy" might prove successful in a five-reel, feature-length work.[17]

But Harold Lloyd continued with one- and two-reel works even after he had abandoned the Lonesome Luke character. In order to develop a new comic character with fresh material, he directed and starred in a one-reel work, *Over the Fence*, a movie released in September immediately after his successful *Lonesome Luke's Wild Women*. By the end of this year, 1917, he had switched to his best-known comic character, an eager young man with horn-rimmed glasses. In order to perfect the portrait, he made a number of one-reelers. As he indicated in an interview conducted by Kevin Brownlow, the character had to be established[18] in order to sell it effectively to the public. The majority of his films (more than sixty) released in 1918 and 1919 were one-reelers.

A November 1917 one-reel release, *All Aboard*, revealed the way in which the comedian was developing his character during this transitional period. His protagonist was shown as a clean-cut,

14. Nelson E. Garringer, "Harold Lloyd Made a Fortune by Combining Comedy and Thrills," *Films in Review* 13 (August-September, 1962): 420-22.

15. Kalton C. Lahue, *World of Laughter: The Motion Picture Comedy Short, 1910-1930* (Norman, Okla., 1966), pp. 202-8.

16. Review of *Lonesome Luke's Wild Women*, *The Dramatic Mirror* 77 (August 25, 1917): 21.

17. Critics and reviewers of this time assigned a genre classification of "farce-comedy" to a work that exhibited strong plot and character development. The use of improbable situations in comedy was being frowned on by the critics.

18. Kevin Brownlow, *The Parade's Gone By . . .* (New York, 1968), p. 460.

well-dressed young man with an air of confidence in appearance and manner—nearly the opposite in demeanor of the tramp-clown figure. But even in the first scene when he is caught flirting with a girl (Bebe Daniels) by her parents and another suitor, Harold turns on his rival and kicks him into a garden pond. Pos-

An early "glass character" one-reeler, **The Flirt** (1917).

ing as a baron, this adversary receives a tomato in the face as he struts in front of the girl. As the young man winds up to heave another missile, he accidently knocks off the hat of a passing policeman. Clearly his character had some of the deviltry of the tramp-comedian of the Sennett tradition.

The fourth scene in *All Aboard* shows the two sides of his "glass character" (as Lloyd called his creation—because of the use of horn-rimmed glasses). Becoming seasick during dinner, the girl's mother collapses, and the well-mannered Harold hurries to help her to her feet. As the ship rolls back and forth,[19] the ample body

19. The pitch of the boat receives comic exaggeration similar to that in a scene of Chaplin's *The Immigrant,* a June 1917 release. If Lloyd received some stimulus for his scene from Chaplin's, he changed the material to fit an upper-class dining room. Chaplin shows the plight of European peasants on board a ship.

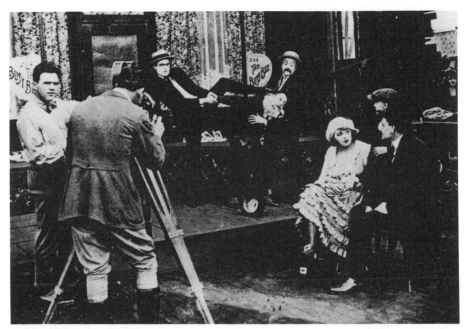

Hal Roach (far left) directing **Spring Fever** (1917). The struggling dwarf between Lloyd and Pollard is Sammy Brooks.

of the mother not only trips the protagonist twice, but becomes entwined with him in a rug. As the dwarf captain of the boat (grotesque in the Sennett tradition), comes to the aid of the indignant, embarrassed matron, she shoves him on his back as he helps her up and strides out of the room. The complaining captain then not only gets pushed over by Harold; he gets a kick in the chest that sends the little fellow out the door.

A 1918 one-reel work, *Back Stage,* also reveals a curious hybrid in the comedian's comic character. As a happy-go-lucky stagehand, Lloyd's character wears a derby, baggy pants, and large comedy shoes; but the character also wears the now-famous horn-rimmed glasses. He has some of the same overeagerness and naiveté of his later characterizations. A loosely constructed work, *Back Stage* is in many ways a throwback to earlier comedies. There are many broad slapstick routines. Some of the routines, however, are cleverly executed by Lloyd in a style that is similar to Charles Chaplin's 1917 work in two-reel films. At one point in the film the comedian appears to run down a stairwell. He comes "up" again and folds up the "stairwell" into what is really a stage flat. The stagehand also assumes the role of a Hindu snake charmer to get a snake out of the room in the theater. Such routines are reminiscent of the English music hall theater; an examination of Charles Chaplin's 1917 output reveals similar pantomime incidents.

The year after *Back Stage* was created, 1919, *Just Neighbors* was produced. This work clearly reveals a transition to a new comic character taking place. Lloyd's comic character is shown in a quiet suburban setting; he is a young, eager, white-collar worker wearing a neat suit, a straw hat, and a disarming, infectious smile. Interestingly enough, his neighbor, played by Harry "Snub" Pollard, still wears the habit of the traditional clown and has a large walrus mustache. Only when an altercation with his neighbor leads to a comic fistfight does Lloyd return to the gross slapstick like that employed in the earlier work, *Back Stage*.

The slapstick, farcical situations which still permeated Lloyd's work in 1918 and 1919 reveal the comedian's link with his predecessors. His 1915-1919 output still incorporated the characters and situations from an older tradition. With the older tradition he blended a newer, more genteel comedy of the stage and popular literature. Among his contemporaries were several young comedians who gained success in the film world by adopting a genteel comedy that did not draw on the slapstick tradition.

Harold Lloyd and the "Polite" Comedians

> Burlesque and farce are becoming less and less popular, and there is no real demand for stories of this type. The comedy producers are desirous of polite, plausible situation comedies, preferably founded upon an amusing situation that might very naturally occur in the life of almost any spectator.[20]

Frederick Palmer expressed this view in 1922 as he criticized a two-reel Christie comedy called *Her Bridal Night-Mare* in a book which was intended to be a guide for scenario writers. Looking at this statement with the historical perspective of today, it is obvious that Palmer overstated the situation. Many slapstick-filled bur-

20. Frederick Palmer, *Photoplay Plot Encyclopedia* (Hollywood, Calif., 1922), p. 92.

lesques and farces were ground out by the Mack Sennett and Hal Roach comedy mills even in the late twenties. There was a trend, however, which formed a basis for this overstatement.

When Lloyd created the young, shy character whose most distinguishing feature was large, horn-rimmed glasses, he wrote:

> A picture actor named Mortenson, who lived in the same apartment house on Fourth Street just off the Hill, and I talked over its [the comic character's] possibilities night after night. The glasses would serve as my trademark and at the same time suggest the character —quiet, normal, boyish, clean, sympathetic, not impossible to romance. I would need no eccentric make-up, "mo" or funny clothes. I would be an average recognizable American youth and let the situation take care of the comedy. The comedy should be better for not depending upon a putty nose or its equivalent and the situations should be better for not being tied to low-comedy coattails; funnier things happen in life to an ordinary boy than to a Lonesome Luke. Exaggeration is the breath of picture comedies, and obviously they cannot be true to life, but they can be recognizably related to life.[21]

The transition from the old to the new tradition from 1917 to 1922 was not so clear-cut as Lloyd's reminiscences would seem to indicate in his 1928 autobiography. The older tradition was still apparent in his works. In the early portion of *High and Dizzy* (1920)[22] the comic character which Lloyd had established in 1917 is strong; it is a portrait of a youthful, overeager doctor who falls in love with a beautiful girl who enters his office. When this character gets drunk, however, a large portion of the films returns to a more genteel version of the older slapstick comedies. As a drunk, the young man becomes brazen and mischievous. He engages in many altercations with people on the street and in a hotel. When he sobers up again and meets the young girl, he reverts to the pleasant young man. Only to a degree does Lloyd use the light, realistic comedy with sentimental overtones.

Get Out and Get Under, a two-reel work created for release in the fall of 1920, shows Lloyd's character evolving into its final form. As an owner of a new car Harold beams with pride. He is an optimistic soul with a wide smile for all who see him driving his automobile. The smile becomes increasingly hard to maintain as he meets many obstacles with his car. Most of the comedy in the early portion comes from his attempt to fix his highly prized and

---

21. Lloyd, *An American Comedy*, p. 102.

22. This work, an important progenitor of *Safety Last*, has been viewed, and a shot-by-shot scenario has been created for this study.

In **Get Out and Get Under** (1920) Harold has troubles with his automobile and a curious boy.

smart, wholesome comedy that will be an inspiration to the youth of the land."[25]

Douglas MacLean, another popular comedian during the late 1910's and early twenties, seemed to have employed a character similar to Hines's. Again, turning to the reviews of Bernard Sobel in the *Dramatic Mirror,* MacLean can be seen following the pattern of the magazine short story. MacLean created a young promoter in *One a Minute* who is efficient and hard-working; he discovers a panacea drug that cures everyone and makes him financially successful.[26] John Mongtomery classifies MacLean's output as "polite farces."[27]

Although Wallace Reid was not considered a high-ranking comedian in the late 1910's and the early twenties, he was a popular star who was versatile enough to play in both serious and comic works. In 1920 he applied his talents to a comic film with all the ingredients of the Hines and MacLean features. From the popular literature of the time, Reid's enactment of a rural comic type, ed Sylvester Tibble, provided another portrait of a young man ing for success. In this film, *The Dancin' Fool,* the young man the country looks for his fortune in the big city. With the ion characteristic of the Horatio Alger hero,[28] he sets his business on a profitable basis by putting his ingenuity to ver his uncle's resistance to a country lad who, the uncle not a responsible addition to his factory[29]

more closely linked with Harold Lloyd's comic works of ies is the work of Charles Ray. In 1919, comedian Ray in a feature-length film, *The Sheriff's Son,* a work which any similarities to Lloyd's *Grandma's Boy.* In theme, the are strikingly similar. In *The Sheriff's Son,* Ray played a meek, cowardly boy who overcomes a gang of out- his reputation for cowardliness.[30] A year later Ray a feature-length comedy called *Homer Comes Home,* a young man going to the big city to gain employment ecomes successful enough to be given a managerial

berg, ed., *The Film Year Book 1925* (New York, 1925), p. 192.
Review of *One a Minute, Dramatic Mirror and Theatrical World* 83 (June

47.

an American writer of popular fiction in the late nineteenth cen-
erson most responsible for promoting the rags-to-riches theme in
heme was often used in the magazine short story and the light
s.

tative Photoplays Analyzed (Hollywood, 1924), pp. 380-81.
Son, The Dramatic Mirror 80 (April 8, 1919): 30.

praised vehicle which chokes to a stop as he rushes to an amateur theatrical performance in which he is to play the swashbuckling role of a masked prince.

By far the most interesting portion of the film develops whe Harold commits a number of traffic violations and is pursued the police. He uses many ingenious ways of eluding two p men on motorcycles, revealing the devil-may-care flair of sessed young man that was to be the strong part of his tot portrait.

Using material which featured him on a high buil 1921 *Never Weaken* (others were *Look Out Below* in 19 *and Dizzy* in 1920), the comedian illustrated that suspense with comedy. His comic young man craw to girder on a building being constructed. In thi vealed a more genteel comedy with the young Mildred Davis). Yet, he always retained his —he would do almost anything to obtain quality seldom used by the genteel comedi of his contemporaries, however, were "polite" comedy features.

Johnny Hines, for example, created the late 1910's in which light come the trials of the "average Americar ties, Hines acted in many featur *Burn 'Em Up Barnes, Luck, The F* which, as the titles indicate, di trying to make good. Berna *Up Barnes* reveals the nat Evidently the film used s devil-may-care protagor town in a race car.[24]

Some of the char may be linked wit Lloyd's ambitious hero. An adver of this quality character. H tisement r

23. Mon
24. Ber
(Septembe.

post in his home town and wins the girl friend who has waited for him back home.[31] This plot development follows a theme which is similar to Lloyd's theme in *Safety Last.*

It becomes evident from the theme and plot material used by Charles Ray (and will become increasingly more evident in the next chapter) that Ray and Lloyd used similar basic material for their feature works. The reviewer of *Homer Comes Home,* furthermore, points out features of Ray's comic character which parallel the comic features of Harold Lloyd's character. Homer, the reviewer points out, was "another addition to Charles Ray's long string of country lads who make good in spite of tremendous odds."[32]

While Lloyd uses some of the same type of story material employed by Charles Ray, Douglas MacLean, and Johnny Hines, he treated his material differently. As he notes in his writings, he did not directly adapt material from the literature of the day, nor did he employ a scenario as did these other comedians. Lloyd's working method remained more flexible by the retention of the off-the-cuff story plotting and shooting methods of the one- and two-reel comedies of the 1910's. On the other hand, Ray, Mac-Lean, and Hines were often bound to the incidents of the magazine short story or the comic stage play. Such works as Hines's *The Live Wire,* MacLean's *One a Minute,* and Ray's *The Sheriff's Son* and *Homer Comes Home* are adaptations.

John Montgomery draws an interesting parallel between the comic characters developed by Lloyd and Ray:

> Ray had made his name in country comedies, and, like Harold Lloyd, he had been typed as a simple, slightly gawky, easily embarrassed youth. He was to be seen standing around looking bashful, shifting uneasily from one foot to the other.[33]

It should be noted, however, that a detailed analysis of the films of Lloyd will reveal a more complex use of comic character than Montgomery indicates in this comparison. Lloyd blended many facets into his screen character. There is a facet of will or determination present in the shy, young man that takes on some of the characteristics which Douglas MacLean and Johnny Hines employed in their comic characters. Lloyd, it will be shown, was eclec-

31. Review of *Homer Comes Home, The Dramatic Mirror* 82 (July 3, 1920): p. 24.
32. *Ibid.*
33. Montgomery, p. 143.

tic in the development of his comic character. This added dimension and flexibility of comic character may account in part for his eclipsing of the "country boys" and "go-getters" in popularity. In the early twenties, when he had turned to feature-length works, Harold Lloyd became the only comedian seriously to rival the king of the silent comedians, Charles Chaplin.

Lloyd's Working Method—A Blend of the Old and the New

While Keaton's and Chaplin's turn to the feature-length work was clearly by design, Lloyd's move toward features was evolutionary and unannounced. He expanded his material as he obtained a firmer grasp on character and plot in his many one- and two-reel works. According to Lloyd, both *A Sailor Made Man* in 1921 and *Grandma's Boy* in 1922, his first four- and five-reel comedies, were produced under a two-reel contract.[34] His departure from a two-reel contract in order to develop his comic material was, according to John Kennedy's report in *Collier's,* "against all traditions of the industry."[35] Since the distributor of his films, Pathé, had balked in 1917 when Lloyd wanted to change from the Lonesome Luke series to a series featuring a new comic character, Lloyd could not announce his intentions to develop a feature length comedy. His explanation of his dealings with the conservative Pathé organization when he created *A Sailor Made Man* and *Grandma's Boy* reveals Lloyd's shrewd actions:

> Each was begun with two reels in mind, but, the footage running long and the action and comedy justifying the extra footage, we threw in a reel or more to boot. Pathé was under no contractual obligation to pay us anything additional for this heaping measure. They did so voluntarily. It was not so much, perhaps, as we were entitled to in strict equity—certainly not so much as we could have forced from them by balking—but we preferred to keep faith and to build for future rather than immediate profits.[36]

The financial success of these longer works evidently convinced Pathé that Lloyd should devote his efforts to feature-length films:

> Two such longer and better pictures, coming together, gave us a mighty thrust forward that carried us out of the middle ground into

34. Lloyd, *An American Comedy*, p. 143.
35. Kennedy, p. 12.
36. Lloyd, *An American Comedy*, p. 143.

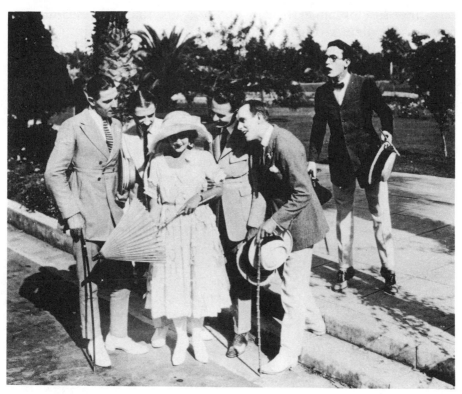

Moving toward feature films with the four-reeler **A Sailor Made Man** (1921). Mildred Davis is the object of everyone's attention.

the foreground of picture business. They demonstrated, too, that the public wanted what we know as feature-length comedies. *Grandma's Boy* was the last of the revised Pathé contract and, when we signed a new one in January, 1922, it called for six pictures of five reels or more.[37]

During the transition from one- and two-reel works to feature-length films, Lloyd's working methods contributed significantly to his growth as a major comedian of the twenties. Realizing the necessity of effective plotting and the advisability of employing a type of comedy that was in keeping with his age, he became a highly skilled craftsman. *A Sailor Made Man* indicated that he

37. *Ibid.*, pp. 144-45.

had handled his material with greater skill than in previous pictures. When he wrote in retrospect about his creation of this four-reel work, Lloyd realized the merit of a strong central idea to unify the story line:

> I played a rich young fellow who thought he could have and could do anything he wanted. Through a sequence of incidents he enlists in the navy and, much against his will, goes to sea. They take all the nonsense out of him there. His shipmates make a man of him, before they get through. So you see that the central idea was a real one; that hard knocks will bring out a man's mettle, if he has any.[38]

Lloyd also realized that his work was better because of the pains that he took to build up each comic incident. A comic fight in which his comic character, without engaging in combat himself, cleverly got his best friend to fight eight men was elaborately planned and executed in *A Sailor Made Man*.[39] Lloyd became, therefore, a creator who was aware of the fine points of comedy and story development. At the turning point of his career, it is little wonder that he later revealed his satisfaction with *A Sailor Made Man*: "I felt that I had at last arrived somewhere."[40]

An awareness of the need for fresh comic material and for effective plotting was fully realized by both Keaton and Lloyd in the twenties. Keaton expressed the view that "explosives, cops, stock situations, flivvers, pie throwing and bathing girls" were passé.[41] "A comedian today," Keaton continued, "no longer finds his dressing room filled with slapstick, property bricks, stuffed clubs and exploding cigars. Comic situations have taken the place of these veteran laugh getters."[42] In the same book, *The Truth About the Movies,* a compilation of many producers', directors', writers', and stars' views on the practices of the motion-picture industry, Lloyd expressed a conclusion similar to Keaton's:

> There must be suspense, or perhaps anticipation is a better expression, in comedy as well as in drama. We have noted, however, that audiences are drawing closer to an appreciation of comedy wherein the gags are mingled with story than in just straight gag comedies —pictures built entirely for laughs.[43]

38. Mary B. Mullett, "A Movie Star Who Knows What Makes You Laugh," *American Magazine* 104 (July 1922): 110.
39. *Ibid.*, pp. 110-11.
40. *Ibid.*, p. 113.
41. Buster Keaton, "What Are the Six Ages of Comedy [?]", *The Truth About the Movies,* ed. by Lawrence Hughes (Hollywood, Calif., 1924), p. 438.
42. *Ibid.*, p. 441.
43. Harold Lloyd, "Comedy Development," *The Truth About the Movies,* p. 411.

Lloyd's revelation of his concern for the audience's reaction to his work was more explicit than Keaton's. He also showed an awareness of a new taste which affected his working methods. He maintained that the audience of his age appreciated "more than ever comedy which has a fairly well-defined plot, with action that is not as rough as the old slapstick and still not too genteel, which is about the best way I know to express it."[44]

This quotation is a key to understanding the mixture of the old and new traditions which Lloyd used in developing his comic films. While humbly acknowledging his inability to verbalize his ideas effectively on his blend of slapstick and genteel comedy, he is conscious of his treatment of basic material.

One of the working methods used in the early one- and two-reel works continued into the twenties relatively unchanged. Even as they launched into feature-length works, Chaplin, Lloyd, and Keaton did not use scenarios. In 1928, Lloyd expressed his dislike for scenarios even though he realized that the increasing complexity of his productions seemed to call for such master plans.[45] Finding a scenario cumbersome when it was forced on him by a producer, Keaton voiced his objections emphatically, according to his reflection on the incident in *My Wonderful World of Slapstick*. During the shooting of *The Cameraman* (1928), he recalls the following statement: " 'Like Chaplin and Lloyd, I never worked before with a script written on paper,' I said, 'and I don't have to now. All I ask is that you let me throw away this script and the shooting schedule and permit Sedgwick and myself to decide what to shoot here.' "[46]

While it would seem that this off-the-cuff method of shooting a film would result in a formless work, there is much evidence to the contrary. Story conferences with writers were often held; the main plotting ideas influenced the comedians throughout the improvisational shooting of a comic film. Furthermore, as Lloyd points out, it was possible to shoot many more comic incidents than were needed; then, it was possible to cull out the unneeded material, to reshoot scenes, and to add new incidents which would give unity to the film.[47] By shooting without a scenario, the comedians gave themselves the flexibility that they needed. They were

44. *Ibid.*
45. Lloyd, *An American Comedy*, p. 95.
46. Buster Keaton, *My Wonderful World of Slapstick* (Garden City, New York, 1960), pp. 209-10. Keaton is referring to his director, Edward Sedgwick, in this quotation.
47. Lloyd, *An American Comedy*, p. 171.

schooled in the art of ad-lib comedy; many of their early one- and two-reel comedies were born of an impromptu sense of comedy that seemed to parallel the working methods of the strolling players in the heyday of the *commedia dell' arte*. The inspiration of the moment and even accidents assisted the silent-screen comedian in his efforts to create a comic film. Interviewed by John B. Kennedy in 1927, Lloyd indicated that some of the best moments of his films were products of impromptu actions.[48] In an early Lonesome Luke film, he was pursued by a trolley motorman who had answereed the call of "Stop! Thief!" Lloyd had to dash frantitically away from the trolley when it accidentally jumped the tracks as it pursued him. Preserved on film, the accident was comic and was retained as one of the high points of the picture.[49] Lloyd also found that some accidents in his feature-length pictures produced comedy. In *The Freshman,* his comic character was to reach for a fork from a dining table to pin up his pants—trousers which were without suspenders. Lloyd accidentally caught the tablecloth with the fork and pinned it to his trousers. This accident was retained, and elaboration was made on it.[50] It gave freshness to the final gag in this sequence.[51]

By far the most important type of impromptu action, however, came from the comedian himself. Inspiration often caught hold of the comedian as he acted out some planned action. He would embellish the action with a gesture or grimace that would change its whole nature. This working method, a practice of the major comedians, Chaplin, Lloyd, Keaton, and Langdon, continued in the creation of feature-length works of the twenties. Both Lloyd and Keaton frequently refer to this practice in their autobiographies.

One other, very important practice continued on into the twenties. The overall control of all areas of production remained in the hands of the leading comedian when his stature and power to resist the encroachment of the producer were great enough. Keaton, reflecting on the importance of this type of control, states the nature of this practice aptly:

We worked hard. We stayed with the story all of the way. In the old

48. Kennedy, pp. 12, 28.
49. *Ibid.,* p. 12.
50. *Ibid.,* p. 28.
51. This incident is described and analyzed in chapter 6.

days all of us—Chaplin, Lloyd, Harry Langdon, and myself—worked with our writers from the day they started on the story. We checked on the scenery, the cast, the locations—often going on trips with the unit managers to pick these out ourselves and make sure they were suitable. We directed our own pictures, making up our own gags as we went along, saw rushes, supervised the cutting, went to the sneak previews. . . . We were the ones who decided what should go into a script to make an audience laugh.[52]

Harold Lloyd's Success in the Feature-Length Comedy

One of the great achievements in feature-length comedy which paved the way for Lloyd's feature work was Chaplin's *The Kid,* a six-reel comedy created in 1920 and released in February 1921. This work was a tremendous success and provided a stepping-stone for other Chaplin works, and for Lloyd, Keaton, and Langdon. To sustain a longer work, Chaplin introduced the sentimental and the serious in *The Kid* as a basis for many plot complications. However, Chaplin's use of sentiment did not follow that employed by such genteel comedians as Charles Ray and Douglas MacLean; he used different characters and situations which seem more closely allied with the literature of the nineteenth century—especially the characters and situations which were employed by Charles Dickens. And, it is important to note, Chaplin retained much of the slapstick comedy and the well-executed pantomime that were typical of his one- and two-reel works.

In order to create an effective, full-length work, Lloyd retained many of the features of his one- and two-reel comedies and added sentimental plot complications in his first feature length comedy, *Grandma's Boy.* It was released a year after *The Kid.* In this work, Lloyd followed a different path from Chaplin's by combining slapstick with genteel humor. This use of genteel humor employed some of the same characteristic plot complications used by Ray, Hines, and MacLean. The combination gave Lloyd distinction and made him a popular success.

In the years 1922-1925, Lloyd became one of the most prominent comedians of the motion picture. His works of this period were *Grandma's Boy* in 1922; *Doctor Jack, Safety Last,* and *Why Worry?* in 1923; *Girl Shy* and *Hot Water* in 1924; and *The Freshman* in

---

52. Keaton, *My Wonderful World . . .* , p. 112. Keaton uses the word "script" loosely; he does not mean this literally. He means "story," "show," or "production."

1925. On the other hand, Chaplin created only two feature-length works during this same period: *A Woman of Paris* (1923), a sophisticated, serious work; and his famous nine-reel comedy, *The Gold Rush* (1925).

Only Chaplin was Lloyd's rival in popularity. In 1922 Keaton was still working with two-reel comedies, producing such works as *The Paleface*, *Cops*, and *Day Dreams*. In 1923 he launched his feature-length works. In the period covered by this study, he produced six feature-length films. The quality of his 1924 productions, *The Navigator* and *Sherlock, Jr.,* placed him in the front ranks of the film comedians of his day.

Without a strong popular rival competing on the movie market, Lloyd achieved outstanding financial success. From 1922 on, his films grossed from one to three million dollars each[53] at a time when production costs and taxes were low. Lloyd's popularity grew until his films soon earned more money than Chaplin's.[54]

Although Lloyd's audiences in motion-picture theaters were enthusiastic in their attendance and praise of Lloyd's films, magazine and newspaper critics sometimes found such works as *Hot Water* and *Girl Shy* inferior comedies. There was some disenchantment among the critics who expected Lloyd to exceed his early promise of great accomplishments. Nevertheless, the critics were impressed with his work in *Grandma's Boy, Safety Last,* and *The Freshman.*

In 1922, *Grandma's Boy* was the only comedy placed by the forty-eight critics in the *Film Year Book* in the list of top ten motion pictures.[55] The national Board of Review gave honors to both *Grandma's Boy* and *A Sailor Made Man* in the same publication without listing one top comedian such as Charles Ray or Charles Chaplin.[56] Lloyd obviously out-distanced his contemporaries in 1922.

Safety Last received high critical acclaim in 1923. Robert Sherwood in *Life,* Theodore B. Hickley in *The Drama,* and the reviewers in *Variety* and the *New York Times* all gave favorable reviews. In 1925, *The Freshman* was forced to share critical honors with *The Gold Rush.* Nevertheless, both films were listed among the top ten motion pictures in a poll of 114 critics of trade and newspaper

53. Benjamin B. Hampton, *A History of the Movies* (New York, 1931), p. 240.
54. Abel Green and Joe Laurie, Jr., *Show Biz: From Vaude to Video* (New York, 1951), p. 269.
55. Dannenberg, *Film Year Book* 1922-23, p. 349.
56. *Ibid.,* p. 350.

publications.[57] Of these 114 critics, 54 put *The Freshman* and 58 put *The Gold Rush* in their list of the ten best pictures of the year.[58]

Obviously, Harold Lloyd attained his popular and critical success through his skills as a comedian, but this brief history of his development of these talents also has pointed to another facet of his skill as an entertainer—his awareness of changing tastes—an awareness which seems to be the keystone of his popularity. Lloyd reached his peak as postwar changes in the social climate of this country took effect. Lewis Jacobs credits this change in the audience's tastes as instrumental in the creation of "a new sophistication" of screen humor. This change, he claims, was fermenting during the war years. "Gradually burlesques, chases, and slapstick," he writes, "were replaced by polite comedy, satires and farces. Raw, rough-and-tumble clowning was less popular with many audiences than satire, pantomime and gentle wit."[59] Lloyd was quick to realize this change and worked to develop comedies that suited the fancy of the audiences of his age. A perfectionist in his comic art, he worked long and hard to complete his films; studied previews of his works; and analyzed their effect on audiences. He gave the audiences what they wanted—a fast-moving, well-constructed, comic story with many gags. In return for the entertainment he gave the motion-picture audiences of the twenties, his public gave him the success he deserved.

By exploring Harold Lloyd's development as a comedian from his debut in 1915 to the period of his greatest success, the mid-twenties, we have established basic background material which will be incorporated in this study. We have observed Lloyd's link with his predecessors. His one- and two-reel works show many characteristics of Mack Sennett's and Charles Chaplin's work. His move in the direction of a more realistic comedy by abandoning the Lonesome Luke character for a newer, a horn-rimmed, spectacled youth, but with the retention of many characteristics of the older comedy, has been traced.

Lloyd's work has been observed in relationship to that of his contemporaries. In Lloyd's evolution toward a milder clown, an eager, go-getting young man, his work parallels the works of the "polite" comedians in the use of character and story material. Be-

57. Dannenberg, *Film Year Book 1925*, p. 31.
58. *Ibid.*, pp. 417-24.
59. Jacobs, pp. 267-68.

cause of his handling of the story material, however, Lloyd is different from these comedians.

An analysis of the content of the comedian's three feature films being used for this investigation will reveal basic comic patterns. A synopsis of each work will also serve to orient the reader to an in-depth examination of these comedy motion-picture classics.

2

The Story: An Overall View of the Material and Plot Development

Some of the broad characteristics of Lloyd's three films may be investigated through a summary of the story material and the plot line of *Grandma's Boy, Safety Last,* and *The Freshman.* While many of the overall characteristics will not be established until a full, detailed investigation of these films has been made, a synopsis of each work will give enough basic information for a preliminary analysis. From these synopses, the comic idea,[1] the motivation for plot action, the main crisis,[2] and the climax of the films may be at least tentatively examined.

A Synopsis of Grandma's Boy

(Released September 3, 1922. Directed by Fred Newmeyer. Story by Hal Roach, Sam Taylor and Jean Havez.[3] Edited by T. J. Crize. Titles by H. M. Walker.)

1. George Meredith, in *An Essay on Comedy* (see Wylie Sypher's *Comedy,* pp. 23-24, 56), maintains that the essential element in a comedy is the comic idea. John Howard Lawson's view on the use of the idea in drama may also be linked with this concept. To Lawson (*Theory and Technique of Playwriting and Screenwriting,* p. 76), the "unifying force" of the dramatic work is the idea.
2. The term "crisis" may be described as "the point of no return" from which the climax and resolution are inevitable consequences. The protagonist at this point of the drama is usually forced to take a particular action which determines his destiny.
3. Robert Sherwood credits Harold Lloyd with authorship in *The Best Moving Pictures of 1922-23,* p. 9. Throughout Lloyd's *An American Comedy* and his other writings, Lloyd reveals his degree of involvement in the plotting of his films. Screen credits, however, do not credit him with authorship. In this study, Lloyd will be designated as the person responsible for the final results of a film.

Cast of Characters:[4]

Grandma's Boy	Harold Lloyd
His Girl	Mildred Davis
His Grandma	Anna Townsend
His Rival	Charles Stevenson
The Rolling Stone	Dick Sutherland
Sheriff of Dabney County	Noah Young

Since infancy the Boy has shown extreme cowardice. Always the victim of a certain bully in the community, the young man encounters strong opposition from this bully when the bully becomes the Boy's rival in the courtship of the Girl.

Acquiring a mail-order suit to impress his Girl, the Boy meets the Rival, is bested by the bully and dumped into a well. Humiliated by this encounter, he meekly goes home to his grandmother and shows her his ridiculously shrunken suit. When a brutal-looking tramp enters the yard, Grandma asks the Boy to chase him away. The tramp ("The Rolling Stone") meets the Boy with a menacing glare that sends the Boy running. Grandma takes over the duty of the Boy and chases the tramp from the yard with her broom.

Determined to see the Girl again, the Boy is outfitted with an ancient suit of his grandfather's. It is attire of Civil War vintage. At his Girl's house, he suffers further humiliation from the glances of the Girl's parents. His girl is disturbed by the moth-ball odor of his clothes. His desire to make an impression is also stifled when cats lick the goose grease from his shoes. The goose grease has been used accidentally by Grandma in her attempt to shine his shoes.

The Sheriff of Dabney County arrives to recruit deputies at the Girl's house in order to find the tramp. The tramp has killed a merchant in town and the Sheriff desires an army of men to capture him. The Boy is sworn in, his face frozen with terror and his hands trembling as he awkwardly holds the rifle that has been given him. He reluctantly follows the posse into the dark night. He soon becomes separated from the group and is terrified by the sounds of the night. He throws down his rifle and runs home,

---

4. From the screen credits of the motion picture. The terms Boy, Girl, Grandma, etc., are used in this synopsis in the same way they are used in the film titles.

locks his door, and jumps into bed quaking with fear, the covers over his head.

Next morning, Grandma hears of his cowardice as the Boy tells of his difficulties of the previous night. To assist him in overcoming his crushing defeat, Grandma makes up a story about the Boy's Grandpa.[5] She tells of Grandpa's cowardice when he was a spy in the Civil War and of a talisman from an old voodoo woman that promoted great feats of courage from Grandpa. According to Grandma's well-intentioned fib, the Boy's grandfather conquered a group of officers at the Union general headquarters single-handedly.

When the Boy has the talisman purported to be the one used by Grandpa, he gets a great psychological lift. Clutching the talisman, which is thought to keep him free from harm, he takes over the duties of a posse that has surrounded the tramp in an abandoned cabin. Single-handedly he flushes the tramp out, chases him, and finally captures him.

Although the Boy is cheered by everyone in town, his rival still believes the Boy a coward. With his newly found bravery and strength, the Boy fights the Rival in a grueling hand-to-hand combat that exhausts both men. The Boy's pluck and unusual method of fighting win the victory. The Rival is finally subdued, tripped up and sent crashing into the well that had previously been used to humiliate the Boy.

Congratulated by Grandma and the Girl, he finally learns the truth. Grandma has told a white lie about the powers of the talisman—it is merely an ornately carved umbrella handle. The Boy realizes that courage is a state of mind and goes off happily with the Girl.

Analysis

From this synopsis the comic theme of *Grandma's Boy* may be seen to revolve around the theme of regeneration. Lloyd felt that he was an innovator when he developed a comic theme on a serious psychological problem. In 1928 he wrote:

5. Grandma's story is related in a dramatized flashback. This flashback will be examined in detail in chapter 5, "Midpoint of the Development."

Grandma's Boy had told much more of a story than we ever had put in a picture before. It was a psychological study of a boy, cowardly both physically and morally, transformed by a fable invented on the spur of the moment by his despairing grandmother. . . . Before the end the boy discovers, of course, that he triumphed only because he believed in himself.[6]

While this theme of regeneration would seem to assume a comic tone only by a particular treatment of character and incident, the synopsis does indicate an overall pattern that is comic. Grandma's fib takes on some of the quality of a colossal practical joke. The root of the comic idea is in the transformation that this fib creates in an incompetent, cowardly person. The Boy reverses his whole psychological bent and becomes an extremely brave man—much braver than the average man.

The synopsis indicates by the early revelation of extensive cowardice that the reversal of the comic character's psychological bent is extreme. The story line also indicates that both the former mode of behavior, cowardice, and the latter, artificially gained bravery, depend on comic overstatement to create comedy. Extreme cowardice on a comic level is culminated in the scene indicated in the synopsis that shows Grandma able to chase the brutal-looking tramp away with a broom after the Boy was frightened away by the tramp's menacing look. Extreme bravery is exhibited, as the synopsis indicates, when the Boy routs and captures the tramp even though a whole posse is afraid to take action.

Also important to the understanding of the overall plot development is the dramatic conflict in this film. An inner, emotional conflict is evident in the handling of the story line. The Boy is shown suffering humiliation after humiliation because of his cowardice. There are also two strong lines of physical conflict —the conflict between the Boy and the Rival and the conflict between the Boy and the tramp.

It might be concluded that the overall action of the plot is motivated by the Boy's desire to conquer his cowardice. However, at the beginning of the story he is powerless to act. There can be no doubt that he desires the Girl. If he were a man of action, he would take steps to get her. At the beginning of the story, therefore, the Boy is the receiver of the action—he is abused. The bul-

6. Lloyd, *An American Comedy*, p. 157.

lying Rival is motivated to abuse the Boy because of his desire for the Girl. The constant encouragement of the Boy's grandmother helps the boy solve his problem. Later on in the plot development, he takes direct action because of her assistance. The white lie provides the prime assistance. Grandma's counsel and action are, therefore, a strongly motivating force. The Boy cannot have the Girl until he overcomes the Rival. The pursuit and capture of the tramp therefore become a test of his courage, and the fight with the Rival becomes the method of overcoming the major obstacle to his successful love life.

Both the main crisis and the climax of *Grandma's Boy* are revealed in the synopsis. The crisis occurs when the Boy is forced to fight his rival. There is no turning back at this point. He must prove his mettle. The preceding action in which the Boy captures the tramp may be mistaken for the crisis, but this action is a test of the Boy's courage. Scott O'Dell, realizing that students of playwriting might make an error in evaluation, wrote: "This crisis has been confused with the climax by many students, but the capture of the tramp is incidental and the highest point of interest comes later."[7] Since the initial action of the Rival creates a basic conflict, the point at which this conflict is resolved is the climax. The climax is the Boy's conquest of the Rival. This point, the point of victory, harks back to a similar action early in the story, the initial action of the Rival. But at the climax the Rival ends up in the well. In this climax there is a complete reversal of the fortunes of the Boy and the Rival.

It is obvious from the preceding synopsis and the analysis of the synopsis that Harold Lloyd was dealing with material that is similar to that used by the genteel comedians Johnny Hines, Douglas MacLean, and Charles Ray. Except for the psychological treatment of the leading comic character, little originality is revealed in this particular synopsis. This is, however, an important emphasis which demands a detailed examination of Lloyd's execution of the comic incidents. The chapters that follow will attempt to analyze this emphasis and treatment of material.

Turning now to *Safety Last,* the reader will soon discover material that was widely used in this period (as indicated in Chapter 1)—it is the humorous treatment of the much used rags-to-riches theme exploited by Horatio Alger.

7. O'Dell, p. 348.

Synopsis of Safety Last

(Released April 8, 1923. Directed by Fred Newmeyer and Sam Taylor. Story by Hal Roach, Sam Taylor, and Tim Whelan. Edited by T. J. Crizer. Titles by H. M. Walker.)

Cast of Characters:[8]

The Boy	Harold Lloyd
The Girl	Mildred Davis
The Pal	Bill Strothers
The Law	Noah Young
The Floorwalker	Westcott B. Clarke

After tearfully saying good-bye to his sweetheart and mother, Harold goes to seek his fortune in the big city. City life, however, is not so rosy as Harold had thought it would be when he was in his little town of Great Bend. Living with a friend named Bill, a steeplejack, he finds that he and his roommate cannot make enough money to meet the rent each week. Nevertheless, Harold keeps up the pretense of success with his girl back home. To his sweetheart, Mildred, he writes, "My position with De Vore Department Store grows in responsibility every day. My progress has been simply marvelous. Be patient a little while longer. I hope to send for you just as soon as I can clear up four or five big business deals."

Harold's pretense is, of course, great. He is merely a common clerk in the dry goods section of a huge department store with a status just above that of a stock boy and a janitor. Even so, Harold is a good worker, and is very conscientious about getting to work on time. In fact, his overeagerness to please often gets him into trouble.

After a hard day's work struggling with an army of women at a bargain counter, Harold encounters a policeman who has also come from Great Bend to the big city. Leaving his friend from his home town, Harold meets his pal Bill and bets him that he, Bill, can strike a policeman and get away with it. He, Harold, will come to his aid and square the assault. Unknown to Harold, his

8. From the screen credits of the motion picture. While this introduction of the cast uses the terms Boy, Girl, etc., the titles employed in developing the story line of this film use the first name of the star as the name of the character he or she was playing—"Harold," "Mildred," etc.

friend from Great Bend has been replaced by another policeman who has come to use the corner police phone. Bill takes the bet and pushes the policeman over. Realizing the error when he sees the face of the policeman, Harold crawls into a nearby box to hide as the policeman jumps up and pursues Bill. Harold watches Bill escape the policeman by climbing straight up the side of a building.

When Harold receives his weekly pay check for his work as a department-store clerk, he spends the entire week's wages of $15.50 on a lavaliere for his girl friend. When Mildred receives this gift in the mail back in Great Bend, her mother urges her to go to the big city to help Harold. The mother thinks that her daughter could keep Harold away from the dangers of the big city by her good influence on him.

Entering the department store to surprise her sweetheart, Mildred greets the dumfounded Harold. He puts on an act in front of his fellow clerks to make his girl friend think he is a boss. He even takes over the department store manager's office in order to carry out this deception.

Harold develops a publicity scheme that he hopes will put him in good with his boss and give him some ready cash. Harold arranges with Bill to have him climb the twelve stories of the Bolton Building, a building that houses the De Vore Department Store. Harold convinces the boss of the merits of this "human fly" show and is assured of $1,000 if the scheme is successful. His pal, Bill, who has demonstrated his ability as a "human fly" by escaping from a policeman, is eager to climb the building. Harold feels that his future with Mildred will be secure and that his scheme will prove his merit in the business world.

The next day Harold's promotional scheme goes awry when the policeman whom Bill has assaulted sees Bill coming up to the Bolton Building. Forced to flee, Bill asks Harold to take over his role as the human fly until he can escape from the policeman's sight. Bill runs up the stairs inside the building in order to exchange places with Harold on the second-floor ledge. Harold reluctantly accepts the role of the human fly.

Since Bill cannot shake the policeman from pursuing him, Harold is forced up one floor after another. Very inept in the art of climbing a building, Harold nearly falls many times. Obstacles get in his way to complicate further his frightfully dangerous ascent. He is bothered by pigeons, gets tangled up in a tennis net, is hit by a painter's board, chased by a dog, and has a mouse run up his leg while on a narrow ledge. By miraculous luck he is able to transcend these obstacles. When he finally arrives at the top of the building, Harold sees his pal Bill still being chased by the policeman. Although greatly shaken by his dreadful experience, Harold is soothed by the presence of his girl friend who has come up to the top of the building to urge him upward. They leave the top of the building arm in arm, confident of a brighter future.

Analysis

Since the writers of *Safety Last* did not attempt what Harold Lloyd would call a "psychological" approach to their material, the comic idea in this work is more direct than it is in *Grandma's Boy*. The synopsis clearly indicates a comic idea based on the leading character's driving desire for success. This driving desire makes him concoct ways of either appearing successful or becoming successful. Frequently his schemes backfire. Each reversal of fortune is an end product of his own invention. To appear successful before his girl friend, he must feign the role of a department store manager; and to carry out a publicity scheme, he must take over his friend Bill's role of a human fly. To put it simply, *Safety Last* presents the comic idea of the pretender to success who is forced to endure dangers that might cost him his job or even his life—a man who gets caught in the web of his own manipulations. Only his pluck, unusual ingenuity, and better than average luck save him. As in *Grandma's Boy,* the synopsis reveals that an overstatement of situation assists in achieving this comic idea.

No strong conflict between Harold and an adversary exists in *Safety Last.* This synopsis does not include a minor conflict between Harold and the Floorwalker because this development is not a major obstacle to Harold's success. Other obstacles are more important. Harold's tendency to brag to his pal Bill gets them both in trouble with a policeman, and this tendency causes him to lie to his girl friend. Harold is, therefore, the creator of his own obstacles in many cases. Obviously from the manipulations of the "Harold" of this film, there is a much different comic character being used from the one in *Grandma's Boy.* This is not the shy young man from the country—this is the breezy, brash young fellow, the go-getter type that Johnny Hines and Douglas MacLean employed in their films.

Frederick Palmer held the view that conflict exists between Harold "and the difficulty of climbing up the outside of a building" and "between his pal and the policeman who chases him through the building."[9] While these conflicts exist in the latter portion of the film, they are merely two of a series of obstacles that provide Harold with one great hurdle in his drive toward success. The difficulty with the policeman is not just his pal's concern; Harold is placed in a difficult position as a result of this feud with the policeman. There is, therefore, a series of obstacles throughout the film drama that may be said to promote the dramatic conflict in this work. Any strong deterrent to Harold's success might be said to promote the necessary conflict in this story. While it may appear that a series of situations with many different types of conflict would lead to disunity, Harold's tussle with these various difficulties still seems to maintain a clear focus and create a strong unity in the story. This is, however, a tentative conclusion. A detailed examination of the incidents may or may not uphold the view that unity seems to exist in the story.

Harold's desire for success provides the motivation for the major part of the plot development. In *Grandma's Boy*, Grandma provides the all important action to set the Boy on a course of self improvement. No secondary "plot mover" is provided in *Safety Last* and no antagonist forces Harold into action. The leading comic character is on his own. Each action Harold takes in this latter film is motivated by a powerful drive either to appear successful or to be successful.

The crisis develops when Harold's publicity scheme is almost ended by an intervening policeman. Harold takes over Bill's position as a human fly in order to carry through with the scheme. It is the point of no return for Harold. He must climb the building or he falls. The climax of the whole feat (and of the drama) comes when Harold overcomes the last obstacle and reaches the top of the building. Harold therefore succeeds in the enterprise that will bring about a turn of fortune for him. This "turning point" is the climax.

The material used in *Safety Last* is standard story material for the comedies of the early twenties. Theodore B. Hinckley in 1923 recognized this familiar material as a reworking of the "poor country boy trying to make good" theme.[10] The reviewer for the

9. Frederick Palmer, *Technique of the Photoplay* (Hollywood, Calif., 1924), p. 75.
10. Theodore B. Hinckley, "Movies of the Month," *The Drama* 13 (August-September 1923): 361.

New York Times also noted the use of this stock material in the Lloyd comedy.[11] While *Grandma's Boy* derived freshness from an unusual psychological emphasis in its use of familiar material, *Safety Last* used the building climbing sequence as fresh material for the feature-length comedy.[12]

In *The Freshman* Lloyd used a different type of material that was also employed by other films in the twenties.

Synopsis of The Freshman

(Released July 12, 1925. Directed by Sam Taylor and Fred New-meyer. Story by Sam Taylor, Ted Wilde, John Grey, and Tim Whelan. Edited by Allen McNeil.)

Cast of Characters:[13]

The Freshman	Harold Lloyd
Peggy	Jobyna Ralston
The College Cad	Brooks Benedict
The College Hero	James Anderson
The College Belle	Hazel Keener
The College Tailor	Joseph Harrington
The Football Coach	Pat Harmon

At home Harold Lamb dreams of college. He is obsessed with the idea of becoming a popular man on the campus when he goes to Tate College as a freshman. He imagines that he might become a campus hero like the one in a movie he has just seen called *The College Hero*. From the movie he has picked up a little jig and a handshake with an accompanying exclamation, "I'm just a regular fellow—step right up and call me 'Speedy.' "

Traveling by train to Tate College, Harold meets a girl named Peggy. When he finally arrives at the station in the town in which Tate College is located, several upperclassmen play a practical joke on him by telling him he is assigned to a car with a chauffeur. Unknowingly Harold takes the car belonging to the Dean of the college and is driven to Tate Auditorium where the Dean was

11. Review of *Safety Last, New York Times,* April 2, 1923, p. 22.
12. Further examination of the use of this material will be taken up in chapter 7, "The Climactic Sequence." Lloyd was an innovator in the use of what he called "thrill comedy."
13. In the titles of this film that follow these opening credits, "The Freshman" is given the specific name of "Harold Lamb" and "The College Hero" is called "Chet Trask." These names will be used in the synopsis.

to give a welcoming speech to the student body. Harold is shoved on the stage in the place of the Dean by the upperclass pranksters. He gives a fumbled speech of greeting to the student body, ending with the exclamation, "I'm just a regular fellow—step right up and call me 'Speedy!'" Harold thinks he is a hit with the student body, not realizing that he is the object of their laughter. He treats a great portion of this group to ice cream at the corner soda fountain.

After this extravagance, Harold is forced to move into less suit-able living quarters. There he meets the landlady's daughter—a girl who turns out to be Peggy, the girl he met on the train. They once more strike up a friendly relationship.[14]

Harold's extravagance has gained him recognition on the campus. The campus newspaper published Harold's picture with the caption: "Speedy the Spender—This Freshy Freshman is Just a Regular Fellow, who is Leaving a Trail of Empty Ice Cream Cones on his Dizzy Dash to Popularity." Harold is too naive to detect the ridicule in this caption, but he does realize that he is far from being a rival to the campus hero, Chet Trask. According to "The College Cad," Chet has achieved fame by playing football. Hearing this, Harold goes out for football. He proves to be highly incompetent in football practice and is ridiculed by Tate's blustering coach. Harold is humiliated by being given the duty of substituting for the tackle dummy. After practice he arrives home racked with pain.

Determined to be the most popular man on campus, Harold tries to buy his way into the college crowd by being host at the Fall Frolic. At this party, Harold is humiliated once more when a suit he is wearing falls to pieces. His tailor had only enough time to baste the suit.

At this dance the College Cad tells Harold what the college crowd really thinks of him. He declares, "You think you're a regular fellow—why, you're nothing but the college boob!" Crushed by this revelation, Harold is confronted by his girl friend, Peggy. She urges him on: "Stop pretending, Harold! Get out and make them like you for what you really are and what you can do!" Harold pulls himself together and declares, "There's just one chance left—if I ever get in that big game against Union State, I'll show them!"

14. Lloyd does not use the hackneyed "love at first sight" incident in this work as in the early two-reeler, *High and Dizzy* (1920). It is avoided in all three of the works being examined in this study.

At the big game, Harold is finally put into the game because the coach has no more substitutes left. In his attempt to battle against Union State, Harold displays a pathetically inadequate knowledge and skill in playing the game of football. With only seconds left in the game, however, Harold gets the ball and runs with grim determination toward the goal line. His unorthodox way of playing the game pays off in these last seconds of play. He runs across the goal line for a touchdown and a victory for Tate.

From this feat Harold becomes a campus hero. The crowd that once ridiculed him carries him to the dressing room on their shoulders. Outside the dressing room, Harold sees not only the student body but the coach himself trying to imitate the little jig and handshake that was once a source of amusement to the college wags. Now that he is accepted, Harold's thoughts turn toward his girl friend, Peggy. His success is one that can be shared with Peggy—and this is the important thing in Harold's mind.

Analysis

In theme and comic idea *The Freshman* and *Grandma's Boy* share similar characteristics. Both deal with a young man's desire for social acceptance. The earlier work, *Grandma's Boy*, depends on a comic idea which shows a sharp inversion of a man's behavior from cowardly to heroic. *The Freshman* demands an inversion also, but the shift in behavior or attitude comes from a social group and not from the leading comedian. In this work Harold succeeds (despite an outrageous display of incompetence as a football player) and is acclaimed a hero by his peers. He has saved the day and is accepted. As in *Grandma's Boy*, this work plays with the idea of the hero on a comic level. It is not outstanding skill that makes either the character of the Boy or Harold Lamb heroes; it is an almost manic drive for success coupled with luck that pushes both characters from a low state in their societies' eyes to a high level of social acceptance.

The comic idea of *The Freshman* is vague when it is compared to the clear cut concept of *Safety Last*. It seems to be centered on the achievement of success through an unusual way (which is thus comic in nature)—through luck and determination and not through any particular skill. The comic idea would therefore come into existence in the latter part of the story and would not be an integral part of the total story. This possibility will be investigated in detail later.

The conflict in this particular work is both internal and external. As in *Grandma's Boy,* the leading character has a great psychological problem. In *The Freshman* the social level of conflict is accentuated. The College Cad is the embodiment of the social forces that keep Harold Lamb an outcast. As an antagonist the College Cad reveals the true attitude of the college students toward Harold at the college dance. Prior to this we see Harold's struggle for acceptance before a crowd that laughs behind his back. Harold is assisted by an ally—his girl friend Peggy. A parallel might be drawn here between the encouragement that Peggy gives Harold and the encouragement the Boy is given by the Grandma in *Grandma's Boy.* In this earlier work, however, the grandmother takes positive action while Peggy in *The Freshman* serves a function not much stronger than that of a cheerleader at a football game.

The motivation for the development of the action in this story comes from Harold's desire to succeed as a college leader. Only in the latter part of the story does increased motivation spring up as a result of his interest in Peggy. She serves as a confidante—an inspiration in Harold's struggle toward his goal.

The crisis in this work is reached when the College Cad reveals the true attitude of the college crowd toward Harold. It is a moment in which Harold can either wilt in defeat or resolve to make a final effort to achieve his dream. He declares his intention to "show them"; his determination at this revelation has been strengthened. From this main crisis Harold goes into the football game and with a great deal of luck and fortitude wins the game. The moment of victory is the climax since it brings the turn of fortune or social acceptance that Harold Lamb desires.

From this synopsis, it can be seen that Lloyd followed traditional material in *The Freshman* with a little stronger emphasis on the psychological problem of the comic character. This story outline, however, reveals this aspect only to a limited degree. While Lloyd claims that the success of *The Freshman* touched off a flood of football pictures,[15] he does not claim any innovations in the handling of the story as he does in *Grandma's Boy* and *Safety Last.* Earlier works, Charles Ray's *Two Minutes to Go* (1921) and Ernest

---

15. Lloyd, *An American Comedy,* p. 160.

Truex's *Little, But Oh My!* (1921) handled the same material. According to reviewer John Geoffrey, writing of Truex's work, the attempts of the comic character, "Shrimp" Briggs, to be a football hero were motivated by his desire to win the girl and to best the rival as a football hero.[16] Lloyd avoided the much used triangle situation of the light, comic, magazine short story in *The Freshman,* even though he retained the standard boy-meets-girl situation. In *Grandma's Boy,* however, the triangle is employed.

From the synopses of the three films, therefore, some broad characteristics of Lloyd's works are discernible. Each of the works handles a success story in a comic way. *Grandma's Boy* focuses on the problem of cowardice in the leading figure and illustrates the way this personality problem is solved. To make this problem concrete and overt, the film employs a triangle situation, with the leading character strongly opposed by a rival. *Safety Last's* plot development seems more direct in synopsis form even though there is no rival or comic villain to oppose the leading figure of the story. The young man has a series of obstacles to overcome before he is a business success. A comic villain who is the embodiment of a social group's opposition to Harold Lamb is evident in *The Freshman* in the character, The College Cad. As in *Grandma's Boy,* a personal problem of the leading comic character, social acceptance, is the focal point of the plot development.

The type of material used in a dramatic story and the plotting of this story, however, account for only part of the effectiveness of the work. Charles Chaplin's famous works, *The Kid* (1921), *The Gold Rush* (1925), and *City Lights* (1931), for example, seem like stock dramatic works if only the story material in synopsis form is examined. Many of the merits and defects of a dramatic work may be found in the specific handling of its material.

Now that an overall view and appraisal of the plot lines of *Grandma's Boy, Safety Last,* and *The Freshman* have been presented, attention should now be focused on the specific development, crisis, climax, and resolution of these works.

16. John Geoffrey, Review of *Little, But Oh My!, Dramatic Mirror and Theatrical World* 84 (December 17, 1921): 890.

3
Exposition

In order to begin a dramatic story, certain basic information must be set forth. The exposition of a dramatic work generally reveals (1) the characters in the story; (2) the location of the story; (3) the time of the story; and (4) the situation, the past and present relationships of the characters, which causes the story to develop. While exposition is necessary to set up new sequences at any point in a film drama, concentration will now focus on the material that is presented within the introductory part of the drama.

Certain conditions, character relationships, situations, and potentialities for a dramatic action are established at the beginning of a dramatic work, regardless of the medium that uses the dramatic story. According to John Howard Lawson, film exposition is "more dynamic and more complex in organization"[1] than exposition for a theatrical play. The motion picture, he claims, generally deals with a more elaborate body of material and often visualizes material which can only be narrated by a character or characters on the stage.[2] The "point of attack" of the playwright in handling material for the cinema often is earlier. That is, the story may pick up threads of the basic story situation at an earlier point in the life of the characters; a late "point of attack" is closer to the high point or climax of the drama. As the following discussion of the three films will show, Lawson's view has some bearing on Lloyd's works.

In order to organize an examination of the exposition as it is used in Lloyd's films, the opening shots and titles of a work will

1. John Howard Lawson, *Theory and Technique of Playwriting and Screenwriting* (New York, 1949), p. 409.
2. *Ibid.*, p. 410.

be examined first; then, the use of exposition as it exists in the first sequence; and last, the latter part of the exposition.

An early "point of attack" is used in *Grandma's Boy*. A direct presentation of the required information in the opening titles and shots explains the early life of the Boy. Verbal and visual elements go hand in hand to develop the "who, where, and when" of this opening portion of the drama. The scenario reveals these characteristics:

TITLE 1 The Place—Blossom Bend: One of those slow towns where the Tuesday morning express arrives Wednesday afternoon—if Monday's train gets out of the way.
TITLE 2 The Boy—At the age of eleven months and four teeth—afraid to call his cradle his own.
1 CU A baby with large, black, horn-rimmed glasses holds a sugar cookie in its hand.
2 MS Another baby takes the cookie from the bespectacled baby. The first baby exhibits no resistance to this action.[3]

From this brief opening, it is obvious that the exposition reveals the central problem which plagues the Boy in this story—lack of courage. Both the "where" and "who" are presented directly, with the second title humorously pointing out the Boy's problem. The phrase, "afraid to call his cradle his own," receives visual reinforcement by a simple action which illustrates the problem. From birth, this brief portion of the film relates, the Boy was a coward. This basic character trait, therefore, is directly explained by both verbal and visual means.

The significance of the bespectacled baby in the first close-up depends a great deal on a previously established character that Harold Lloyd developed in his one- and two-reel comedies. The glasses are a label that immediately suggests the comic. Just as the comic character of Charles, the little tramp, was identified by a derby hat and a cane, Harold Lloyd's comic character had become famous enough by this time to be identified with black horn-rimmed glasses.[4] The visual presentation of the baby's lack of

3. The symbols CU and MS mean "close-up" and "medium shot," respectively. A description of the action of each shot follows these symbols. As indicated in the preface, scenarios have been created from the three features.
4. Certain bodily and facial characteristics and eccentricities of dress have been used from the dawn of the comic drama which immediately indicate that the player is a comedian. Every major comedian of the silent movies developed distinctive features of dress and manner to assist him in establishing a comic character. These features work as labels which immediately bring a response from an audience who have seen the character in previous comedies.

courage therefore becomes humorous. Without this identification, the incident would not be comic even though the titles have set the material in a humorous framework.

It should also be noted that the title which gives the location of the drama, a small town named Blossom Bend, is humorous. The directness of the expository device is softened by humor; the audience is also informed that the material which follows is humorous.

A strong emphasis on the psychological problem of the leading character is reinforced in the opening sequence after the first shots of the Boy as a baby. Title 3 declares, "At School he rubbed great holes in his stockings—where his knees shook together." The scene that follows shows the Boy as a child refusing to fight after he has been insulted by another little boy. This incident ends the first sequence which I have called "The Early Life of the Boy." It scores a single point without establishing character relationships which create the conflict and develop the story. Thus, at the end of less than two minutes of the film, the Boy's lack of bravery has been firmly established, and a mild humorous treatment of this material indicates the comic tone of the film drama.

Having established the Boy's meekness, the second sequence presents a triangular love relationship between the Boy, the Girl, and the Rival. The introduction of the Boy and the Girl is handled through a gag that is created by editing and the camera:

TITLE 5 Nineteen—meek, modest and retiring. The boldest thing he ever did was sing out loud in church.
14 MS (an iris-shot) The Boy as a young man is revealed cranking laboriously on a handle that looks like a crank for starting an early model car. No car is visible in this tight iris-shot. The Boy stops cranking and breathes heavily.
15 CU The Girl looks down at him as if to inquire about his difficulties.
16 MS to MLS (The iris opens and the camera dollies back with a slight pan of the camera to show the whole scene.) The Boy shakes his head and cranks again. It is revealed that the Boy is really cranking an ice-cream freezer. Both the Girl and the Boy are now visible. He stops his labor and puts salt on the ice in the bucket.[5]

Lloyd uses deception and a sharp reversal of meaning by reve-

5. MLS is a shot halfway between a medium shot (MS) and a long shot (LS).

lation in order to create this gag. It is an artfully handled revelation gag that is especially effective because it comments on the Boy's character. It shows a physical weakness that is linked with his psychological problem in a humorous way. Editing, highly important in the opening gag of *Safety Last*,[6] is not a strong factor in creating this gag; the camera is the main tool.

The Rival is introduced immediately after this gag in Title 7: "The Rival—He bullied his way through school—and licked the teacher as a graduation exercise." H. M. Walker's consciously clever title is followed by a series of shots which show in pantomime the undesirable character of the Rival. The Rival is shown maliciously throwing a stick at a cat and laughing uproariously as the frightened animal runs away. The nature of this act, while it illustrates an undesirable trait in the Rival, is hardly villainous. Since the action reveals childish maliciousness, the Rival becomes a comic villain.

When the Rival meets the Girl and the Boy, the triangle is soon established. This relationship is developed when the Rival extends a friendly gesture to the Girl and a hostile gesture to the Boy. He gives a bouquet of flowers to the Girl and sticks the Boy with a pin. The Boy smiles faintly and tries to cover up his anguish as he sees the Rival taking the Girl's attention away from him. Through pantomime, comedian Lloyd shows the Boy trying to take gracefully the practical joke that has been played on him. The reactions of the comedian in this incident are the focus of attention. Lloyd gains this focus by playing his reactions to the camera—close-ups are not used to reinforce his comic frustration.

Another strong gag, developed from the triangle situation, is almost as strong as the revelation gag which opened this sequence. From a shot of the three principal characters sitting on a bench (shot 27), a reverse angle of this shot in a close-up view reveals the following detailed movements:

28 CU The hands of the girl and the Rival rest on the back of the bench. The Boy moves his hands to the back of the bench and accidentally brushes against the Girl's hand as she adjusts the belt of her dress.

The gag is developed by an effective combination of good acting in six shots:

6. This revelation gag will soon be discussed.

29 MS A front view again shows the three principals of the triangle smiling. The Girl is between the two young men.

30 CU The hands are shown on the back of the bench again. The Boy moves his hand to where he thinks the Girl's hand is. His hand moves toward the Rival's hand instead.

31 MS The three young people are shown again. Both men show embarrassment. They express shy delight in their nervous smiles.

32 CU A shot of the Boy's and the Rival's hands is presented. They are holding hands with each other.

33 MS The Boy and the Rival (in the front view once more) are showing increasing delight as each thinks special affection is being shown him by the Girl.

34 MLS The Girl is holding the bouquet of flowers with both hands. The two men look down with a puzzled expression as they both notice the position of her hands. She gets up and the two men look down and back to see that they are holding hands with each other. They release hands with disgust.

As these shots indicate, the gag is fully exploited by the use of the medium to reinforce, clarify, and magnify the joke. Close-ups of the men's hands taken in a reverse angle from the medium-shots of the three people on the bench provide the necessary emphasis to make the most of the gag. A much earlier version of this gag in *A Night in the Show* (1915), a two-reel work produced by and starring Charles Chaplin, did not take full advantage of the medium. The art of editing to emphasize a gag had not been perfected in the silent screen comedy of this period. The comedian Chaplin, playing Mr. Pest in this early work, flirts with a young woman seated next to him as he watches a vaudeville show. Mr. Pest accidentally grabs her husband's hand instead of hers in what Theodore Huff calls a "substitution" gag.[7] As in *Grandma's Boy*, the conflict is firmly established when the Boy is defeated by the Rival as the two men vie for the affections of the Girl.[8] An important fourth character, Grandma, is introduced in sequence IV, "The Boy Fails Against Another Foe—the Tramp." She becomes a

7. Theodore Huff, *Charlie Chaplin* (New York, 1951), p. 52. This term has some merit in describing this method of achieving comedy. A comic substitution generally shows the replacement of an object or person to be quite different from the object or person that is being supplanted.

8. This portion of the film will be analyzed in detail in the following chapter. It is part of the development.

"Mrs. Fixit" in the plot development by assisting the Boy in over-coming his cowardice. A fifth character is also introduced in this sequence—the tramp—a derelict who provides a test of the young man's bravery.[9]

By the time these five principal characters are introduced, a fifth of the total length of the motion picture has been used to establish the character relationships, and the Boy's personal prob-lem has been clearly illustrated. Exposition blends with plot de-velopment by this time, and all the conditions prerequisite to the development of the story line have been established. Most of the humor in this portion of the movie is mild, but indications are present which show its growth toward stronger comic incidents.

Safety Last

The first title and the opening shots of *Safety Last* show even greater ingenuity that was displayed in *Grandma's Boy*. Exposition is developed unobtrusively—through the use of an elaborate gag. While it is difficult to verbalize a visual gag of this kind, some of the characteristics of this spectacular joke can be seen in the fol-lowing portion of the scenario:

TITLE 1 The Boy—He has seen the sun rise for the last time in Great Bend—before taking the long, long journey.
1 MCU to MS (an iris-shot) Harold, his face sad and pensive, is re-vealed behind bars (this iris frame opens). Something which looks like a scaffold with a dangling rope moving in the wind is revealed behind Harold (the camera dollies back to LS). A girl and an older woman are shown outside the bars bidding Harold farewell. A man in uniform enters behind the bars and taps Harold on the shoulder. Harold looks sadly toward the "rope." A minister enters now and shakes Harold's hand in a farewell gesture. The girl and the older woman leave (off frame right) and reappear inside the bars with Harold. Harold kisses the girl. The whole group moves toward the "rope."
2 LS A train station with a large sign "Great Bend" above the train platform is revealed. Harold and a group of people

9. Once more, plot development is blended with exposition. Details of this incident will be examined in the next chapter.

The first shot of **Safety Last,** one of the comedian's most elaborate revelation gags.

enter. In the foreground the "rope" is obviously a wooden message catch used by railway station attendants to convey information to incoming trains. The group come through an opening labeled "To Trains." People on the platform of the station hail Harold as he enters.

3 MS A railroad clerk puts a message on the "message catch."

4 LS A train moves into the station, and a message is taken from the "catch" by an engineer as the train passes by. The railroad clerk watches this action.

This opening gag caught the attention of Scott O'Dell who described it thus:

The set is so arranged as to make it appear that Harold is going to his

execution. . . . Then the scene is turned to surprise as the gate is
opened and the mother and sweetheart hurry through; the priest
(only a traveler) picks up his bag and departs.[10]

While O'Dell makes some minor errors and additions in his description of this comic incident, he has detected the essential material that was used in the execution of the scene. The concept of
"suprise," which he notes as the essential comic device, indicates
the reaction that a sharp reversal of meaning will have on the audience. This gag may be described as a comic reversal. This is a
more complicated version of the revelation gag which has been
described in examining the use of exposition gags in *Grandma's
Boy.*

The use of the medium to achieve this comic reversal should be
pointed out. Because of the limited view of the camera lens (assisted by an iris opening), this scene develops the deception immediately and then adds further details to build up this deception. With the aid of staging (the train "message catch" in the
background), the viewer of this scene is led to believe that Harold
is in the death house because the first title has implanted the misconception in the minds of the audience. A double-meaning
statement has been purposely presented. The "long, long journey" becomes, of course, not the journey into an afterlife, but a
literal train journey to the big city. The "rope" turns into a "message catch." This fact is established visually by the action in shots
3 and 4.

In the films used for this study, this is Lloyd's most elaborately
developed gag which uses revelation. According to Rudolf Arnheim in *Film As Art,* some of the most effective uses of the
medium are the withholding of information by the use of the limited view of the camera's lens, the proper camera angle, and/or
editing.[11] Lloyd has incorporated all of these aspects in the creation of this comic incident. The opening title also assists this gag.
Editing of the first four shots creates the gag; the last two, 3 and
4, have been included to show the deception clearly corrected.
Close examination of a still picture of the opening shot reveals all
the qualities of a studio shot.[12] Both "on location" shots in a real
depot (e.g., shot 2) and shots in a studio setting were undoubtedly

10. O'Dell, p. 77.
11. Rudolf Arnheim, *Film as Art* (Berkeley and Los Angeles, 1957), pp. 76-78.
12. This illustration also appears in Lloyd's *An American Comedy* opposite page
177 with the caption: "What appears to be the Death House is disclosed a moment later as a railway station."

used. Careful editing, therefore, was needed to establish the relationship between shot 1 and shot 2 in order to execute the comic reversal.

This elaborate revelation gag is particularly effective at the beginning of *Safety Last* because it sets a humorous tone immediately and launches gracefully into the exposition. As Robert Sherwood wrote in his review in *Life, Safety Last* uses a "fast opening."[13] This opening incident assists in moving the drama quickly and effortlessly into the complications and conflict that create the story line.

Digging into its material more quickly than *Grandma's Boy, Safety Last* establishes important character relationships which infuse in Harold a strong motive for success. The mother and the girl friend of Harold are shown at the train station saying their good-byes and covering Harold with affection. When Harold declares, "Mother, Mildred has promised to come to the city and marry me—just as soon as I've made good," in Title 2, a key motivation for all future action by the leading character is established. Further support for this motivation is created in Title 3 by the mother's statement: "Oh, Harold, it would break my heart if you failed," and in Title 4 by the sweetheart's reassuring remark: "I know I'll get nothing but good news from you."

Visually these attitudes are, of course, strongly reinforced, but it is interesting to notice that a great deal of weight is given to the verbal in order to present the influences on Harold as he leaves for the big city. These statements by the girl friend and the mother do not mean, however, that this incident is without comedy. Harold's reactions to Mildred, his sweetheart, are comic. He embraces her and looks at her with soulful eyes. As he dotes on her, he nearly misses his train.

After presenting important expository material, this opening sequence ends with two effective gags which help establish Harold's character. In his rush to the train, Harold excitedly picks up the wrong suitcase, a traveling bag with a Negro baby strapped to a small seat on top of it. Harold runs halfway to the train before a very distressed mother catches up with him and rescues her baby. Flustered considerably by this mistake and preoccupied with his adieus, Harold grabs what he thinks is the hand rail on the back of the train. Unfortunately, the platform on which he finds himself standing is the back entrance to a horse-driven ice wagon that happened to be crossing the train track as Harold made his

13. Robert Sherwood, "The Silent Drama," *Life* 81 (April 26, 1923): 24.

Waving goodbye to his mother and sweetheart, Harold thinks he has caught the train—from **Safety Last.**

mad dash. Discovering his second mistake as the ice wagon rolls down the road, Harold is forced to scurry frantically after the train as it starts to pick up speed leaving the station. His mistakes are made comic by overstatement[14] of the situation and colorful substitutions that plague the comedian's efforts to get on a train.

Three effective gags, therefore, have been incorporated into the introductory sequence of *Safety Last,* and important motives, character relationships and character facets have been established.

14. Overstatement in comedy is the practice of magnifying a situation, a character, an emotion, or action beyond the normal. In this case, Harold's wild dash to the train and his frustration when he discovers his mistakes are exaggerated in a comic manner.

The later exposition of *Safety Last* is accomplished in a fashion similar to the setting up of basic potentials in *Grandma's Boy*. The method of introducing important characters, however, is not always so direct. Bill, Harold's friend in the big city, is introduced in Title 5: "After a few months—'Limpy Bill,' the boy's pal—one pocketbook between them—usually empty."

This title is followed by a scene which shows Bill trying to darn his sock. Harold enters the room, and he and Bill discuss their financial problems. Even the introductory title, it should be noted, stresses situation rather than character, and the scene which follows stresses the financial plight of the two friends. A clever piece of pantomime is introduced which is reminiscent of the type of routines used in vaudeville and the music halls. When the landlady knocks on Bill's and Harold's door, the two young men put on their coats and hang the tops of the coats over hooks on the wall. With their legs doubled up under the coats, the two men are completely concealed from the landlady as she enters to look for them. This unusual way of hiding permits them to avoid any argument with the landlady over the payment of the rent. Lloyd then uses a variation on this old comic routine which gives it freshness. Harold tries to write a letter to his girl friend, but is constantly annoyed by Bill's presence. Desiring to write his letter in private, Harold sneaks up to the door and knocks without being seen by Bill. Thinking that the landlady has returned, Bill climbs into his coat once more and hangs on the wall. With a contented smile, Harold sits down to finish his letter undisturbed. Both uses of this routine show comic ingenuity at work. It is a comic device that is introduced in this work for the first time. In order to solve a problem, the comedian executes an unusual action.

No elaborate analysis of the necessary exposition that shows Harold working as a clerk in a big city department store need be undertaken here. A blend of expository material and plot development is skillfully handled. Only H. M. Walker's consciously clever title for the introduction of Harold's boss follows an earlier, more direct method of exposition used in *Grandma's Boy*. Title 11 reads: "Mr. Stubbs—Head Floorwalker—musclebound—from patting himself on the back." Stubbs serves as a minor threat to Harold's future success and is an important character in several gags that will be discussed in later chapters in the analysis of *Safety Last's* plot development.

As in the construction of *Grandma's Boy,* a great deal of expository material in *Safety Last* stretches far into the work. These two films illustrate and seem to support John Howard Lawson's generalization on the complexity of motion picture exposition.

The Freshman

In contrast with *Safety Last's* effective beginning, a more stock, mundane opening is used in the first few titles and shots of *The Freshman:*

TITLE 1 Do you remember those boyhood days when going to college was greater than going to Congress—and you'd rather be Right Tackle than President? (fade out and into)

TITLE 2 The home of Harold Lamb. His father was the best bookkeeper in the country and the worst radio liar in the State.
(fade out and into)

1 MLS The mother and father of Harold Lamb are seated in their living room. The father smokes a pipe contentedly as the mother looks at a small account book.

TITLE 3 "Look, Pa, how much Harold has saved to take to college for spending money—just selling washing machines."

2 MLS The father looks at the book.

3 BCU The account book is shown with the account number 1675. The final balance is $485.

4 MLS The father looks at the mother approvingly.

TITLE 4 "He's been upstairs in his room all evening dreaming about going to college—he simply can't think of anything else."

5 MLS The father hands back the book. Mother leaves the room (off frame right). The father puts on earphones to the radio which is next to his chair. (a fade out)

Visually, this opening scene contains no humor. It is an example of straight exposition of the most elementary nature. The only humor is in Title 2. The term "radio liar" is a gentle poke at the early radio enthusiasts who bragged about the remote stations that they picked up on their radios. This gentle humor is also a plant for a joke that soon develops when Harold's activity in a room above makes the father think he has received a Chinese broadcast. This opening, while it is unimaginative, clearly establishes Harold Lamb's eagerness to attend college. This information is not conveyed visually, however. Exposition by titles is used in a manner similar to that of the nineteenth-century living room or "teacup" drama. Two characters reveal the basic desire of the leading figure before he arrives on the scene. It is not until the next scene in the expository portion of *The Freshman* that the resources of the medium come strongly into play.

The three films, therefore, have contrasting approaches to the story material. Only *Safety Last* digs quickly into comic material in its opening title and shots. All three, however, establish the comic nature of the treatment early and introduce more comedy later in the first sequence.

After a slow, relatively humorless beginning, *The Freshman* picks up its use of comedy as soon as the leading comic character, Harold Lamb, is introduced. As in *Safety Last* and *Grandma's Boy*,

The leading cheers revelation gag in **The Freshman.**

there is a revelation used to create a comic reversal. Arthur Knight finds the use of the camera "superbly functional"[15] in the introduction of Harold Lamb: "The film begins with an iris-shot of Harold in collegiate sweater and cap leading a rousing football cheer, then opens out to reveal that he is leading the cheers in front of his bedroom mirror."[16]

With the introduction of Harold and the first visual gag of the film, *The Freshman* begins to recover from the pedestrian opening. The revelation technique, however, is not so effective as the use of revelation in *Grandma's Boy* and *Safety Last*. The iris-shot is not held closed long enough to set up a deception that is effective.

In the scene that develops after this opening shot, Harold cheers with the typical nonsense language of many college cheers and thereby creates noises which his father believes to be coming from a Chinese radio station over his receiving set. After this mild bit of humor, the medium assists in reinforcing the impression of Harold's strong desire to go to college and helps reveal his glamorized view of college life. Harold's view of college life is basic to the whole comic development of the film. It is an important concept to stress at this time since he later becomes a boob because he uses the fictionalized conception of college as presented by motion pictures as a basis for all his actions.

Harold is shown admiring a movie poster on his bedroom wall which reads, "Glorious Art Films Co. Presents Lester Laurel in *The College Hero*." He looks at the *Tate College Year Book 1924* and sees a picture of Chester A. Trask, a football hero who has been voted "the most popular man in college." Harold dreams that he takes over his position. By a simple technique of the dissolve, Harold's picture is substituted for Chester Trask's to show the nature of Harold's dream. Harold's dreams of glory become firmly established without verbal support. This is, of course, one of the most important points of the opening sequence of the film. As in *Grandma's Boy,* the psychological traits of the comic character are essential to the development of the action.

As the first expository sequence comes to a close, Harold shows his father a little jig he has copied from the motion picture, *The College Hero*. Harold supposes that this little jig, accompanied by a greeting, is typical of a college campus greeting. A forewarning of

15. Knight, *The Liveliest Art* (New York, 1957), p. 122.
16. *Ibid.* Knight is mistaken in one detail: a short scene preceding this shot starts the film. Knight, however, indicates in his description of the incident that he understands the device for achieving humor.

'I'm just a regular fellow - step right up and call me Speedy'

GLORIOUS ART FILM CO.
Presents
LESTER LAUREL
IN
THE COLLEGE HERO

The source of Harold Lamb's glamorous view of how to be popular in **The Freshman.**

the trouble that will plague Harold is firmly and bluntly established when Harold's father says to the mother in Title 17, "I'm afraid, Ma, if Harold imitates that movie actor at college, they'll break either his heart or his neck!"

The concept of the social pressures which may make trouble for the comic hero is, therefore, presented at the end of the first sequence in *The Freshman*. Five minutes of the film have been used to establish this dramatic potential.

The later part of the exposition concentrates on the facets of college life and the people who affect Harold Lamb's destiny on the college campus. The scene shifts directly to Tate College in sequence II, "The College: Activities at the Train Station"[17] before Harold arrives. A parallel type of exposition is developed to show what is in store for Harold. Sequence II starts with one of the best titles of the film: "The opening of the fall term at Tate University—a large football stadium with a college attached." This title (Title 18) sets a strong tone of burlesque which continues throughout the film. Since the college motion picture was part of the lighter movie fare of this period, the material being used was familiar to the audience of the time. As it has already been pointed out, Harold patterned a little jig and handshake after the actions of the leading character in the movie *The College Hero*. A burlesque of this type of movie, therefore, pervades all the comic material that follows. Many of the clichés and distortions of college life which were used by the motion pictures of that time are employed.[18]

In the second sequence of *The Freshman*, the "College Cad," a surly, sneering young man, is introduced. He is the embodiment of the social opposition which the aspiring Harold Lamb encounters. Accompanied by his friends, the College Cad is shown hazing students who are arriving by train at the Tate station. This visual plant of what Harold has in store for him is an anticipation of the conflict which soon develops.

The girl, Peggy, an attractive young lady who becomes a confidante and morale builder for Harold Lamb, is introduced in the third sequence as Harold rides on the train to Tate College. Some

17. Descriptive sequence titles have been established by the author in order to label each unit of the film.

18. Even in the forties and fifties, academic institutions were often depicted with some of these clichés and distortions. There is no room for libraries and serious study in the light-headed Hollywood versions of the social-centered campus (e.g., *Mother Is a Freshman*, 1949, and *She's Working Her Way Through College*, 1952).

of the characteristics of *Grandma's Boy*, therefore, can be seen in this method of building the plot potentialities. There is a direct introduction of the character and an indication of the relationship which the character will have with Harold Lamb.

The fourth sequence shows Harold arriving at the train station. As he arrives, Harold catches a glimpse of the college hero, Chet Trask. The recognition given to this hero is in sharp contrast to Harold Lamb's self-conscious arrival. Harold is shown as a pathetic, lone figure on the edge of the crowd that worships this campus idol. Harold's position as a nonentity is effectively handled by the correct angle of the camera. No titles are used to reinforce this point—they would be superfluous. Harold stands alone, looking admiringly at the man he desires to emulate.

The potentialities of the main story line are therefore established at the end of the fourth sequence. These four sequences in *The Freshman* are more solidly packed with exposition than are similar portions of the other two works, and expository material is not as extensively blended with plot development in Lloyd's comedy on college life.

Several general conclusions may be reached after examining the sequences of exposition of the three Lloyd films. All three works depend heavily on titles to advance such fundamental information as time and place of the drama. Humor is displayed in the titles to set the comic tone of the treatment of the story material. Because *Grandma's Boy* and *The Freshman* use a psychological problem of the leading character as a basis for the comedy, the opening humor is mild. The exposition concentrates on the character of the leading figure with special attention being devoted to his desires. *Safety Last,* on the other hand, starts out with strong, humorous incidents which present some of the facets of the character, leaving the full development of the comic character until later in the drama. Also, this film does not concentrate on Harold's drive to be successful until much later in the story. Filled with action in its opening sequence, *Safety Last* presents motivation for Harold's drive but does not dwell upon his desires.

All three films employ the medium to create a comic reversal in their early portions—the first sequence in *Safety Last* and *The Freshman* and the second sequence in *Grandma's Boy*. *Safety Last* employs the most elaborate and most successful revelation gag; *The Freshman* employs the least successful because of the short period of time taken to set up the deception that is necessary to bring about a comic reversal. The use of the medium in the expository part of each film can also be seen in the use of titles. Titles are used more extensively and are more important in this part of the films than in any other part.

It should also be noted that the leading comedian's role is generally characterized more strongly than those of other characters in the opening action. The lion's share of pantomime is given to the leading character. Minor characters are stereotyped and require little pantomiming of their traits. The title which introduces a minor character may reveal that trait which makes him comic. For example, Title 50 in *The Freshman* introduces Tate's tough football coach: "The head coach—so tough he shaves with a blowtorch." This treatment seems typical of Lloyd's method of introducing minor comic characters.

Character development of the leading figure in these films is advanced considerably in the exposition. Both *Grandma's Boy* and *The Freshman* present the most important facets of the comic character Harold Lloyd portrays within the early part (or expository part) of the film drama. *Safety Last,* with its faster plot development, presents the qualities of overeagerness and naiveté in the comic character of Harold. An almost simpering devotion to his girl friend, Mildred, is presented in pantomime. These character facets, however, are only touched upon in a light manner; they are reinforced and enlarged later in the film. *Grandma's Boy,* on the other hand, presents a direct, strong portrait of the shy, naive young man, through titles and pantomime in the expository part of the film. *The Freshman* spends a great deal of time revealing the impractical, naïve attitudes which Harold Lamb holds on college life. These attitudes reveal a basic innocence which borders on "boobery." The overeager qualities of the young man are also stressed.

In the exposition, three distinct comic characters are established. "The Boy," "Harold," and "Harold Lamb" are individual portraits. While each of these characters possesses some traits which are common to all of Harold Lloyd's comic characters, there is enough individualization of character facets to provide three distinct portraits. Lloyd realized that sameness in characterization would lead to stagnation in his work. He was afraid of being typed when he started work on *The Freshman* and expressed concern that he might be playing "a freshman for life."[19] He also pointed out in his autobiography that he was careful in the development of his comic character in order that a different character would evolve in each of his feature-length films.[20]

From the emphasis placed on the leading comic character in the expository portion of the films, Lloyd evidently desired a character-based comedy. That is, he evidently wanted the situations to spring logically from the character's reactions to certain problems that he encounters in his life.

19. Lloyd, *An American Comedy*, p. 159.
20. *Ibid.*, p. 149.

4
Preliminary Development

While development of a dramatic story is a continuous, cumulative process, it is advantageous to break down the development of each Lloyd film in order to handle the material for analysis. Since the progressive characteristics of certain portions of a drama show increasing complication and stronger, more direct action with each successive unit of the story as it unfolds, it is possible to separate the development of Lloyd's works into steps. Development, therefore, will be described and analyzed in four steps: (1) a preliminary step, (2) a middle step, (3) a step which leads to a crisis, and (4) a final step which leads to the climax of the drama.

This portion of the development, the preliminary step, is marked by an inceptive action which starts the dramatic movement. Exposition does not concentrate on this type of "movement," but is concerned with the establishment of character relationships, the present and past situations, and the potentialities of the character relationships and situations. In short, the preliminary step starts the story toward an inevitable goal or end.

Grandma's Boy

The inceptive action of Lloyd's first feature work takes place when the Boy is pushed into the well by his Rival. As the bully grabs the lapels of the Boy's coat just before the Boy is pushed into the well, a very important close-up is used by the editor. A

78

price tag on the Boy's coat is shown with the inscription "$10.00 Never Shrink Brand." In this way, information which is used soon after this incident is planted.

After the Boy is pushed into the well without a struggle, Harold Lloyd as the Boy executes effective bodily and facial pantomime. The Boy, thoroughly soaked, climbs out of the well. At first only a mop of wet, stringy hair and two sad eyes appear over the edge of the well. The shot that follows (shot 47) shows the Rival and the Girl going down the road together away from the Boy. Then the shy lad's head and eyes are once more revealed as he looks sorrowfully after them. In a longshot that follows, Lloyd shows the plight of the comic character by exhibiting a long face and hanging head as he climbs out of the well. The gesture is a comic overstatement of the Boy's predicament. While it achieves the comic effect intended, it also provides a degree of sympathy for this meek young man. The execution of this simple gesture is noteworthy; it demonstrates Lloyd's ability to gain sympathy in a comic situation.[1]

After this inceptive action, a short sequence shows the Boy going home. Hardly more than a transitional sequence, the journey homeward reinforces the first defeat of the Boy. A minor humiliation develops which is a direct result of the inceptive action. The Boy's suit shrinks in the sun; the bottoms of his trousers are only a few inches below the knees, and the sleeves are just a few inches below the elbows. This minor humiliation provides a link with a long chain of major defeats and minor humiliations.

Shot 54 in this sequence, sequence III, "The Boy Goes Home Defeated," is important in the way that it helps develop the comic character of the Boy. The shyness of the Boy is exhibited in front of the four girls who watch him walk past them in his shrunken suit:

54 ls The four girls line the walk to a gate, looking at the Boy as he comes up to the gate. He stops, steps back, and then nods in a friendly but shy way to them as he walks slowly past them. They can no longer hold back a laugh as he passes by them. He turns around, visibly hurt by their laughter, but he immediately smiles bravely and walks by them backwards. His

1. Film critics are almost unanimous in their praise for the skill Charles Chaplin displayed in his blend of comic and serious material. As this study will show, Lloyd also blends these ingredients in his work.

smile becomes almost coy; his walk, a backward shuffle. Suddenly he falls over a rope that has been stretched across his path. The girls roar with laughter. He jumps up and dashes wildly toward the house which is visible in the background.

Clothes "unmake the man" in shot 54 of **Grandma's Boy.**

Lloyd uses the Boy's suit as an instrument of comedy in this incident. Though Lloyd abandoned the comic habit of the clown in 1917, he used odd attire when it was directly related to the plot development.[2] This incident is, however, more important as an illustration of Lloyd's skill as a pantominist. He smiles in the face of adversity in an effort to cover up his inner feeling of embarrassment. The smile is started bravely and broadly, but it falls in

2. Lloyd uses clothes for comic effect later in *Grandma's Boy. The Freshman* creates an elaborate sequence of gags from the comedian's difficulties with a basted suit. See chapter. 6.

spirit because the painful humiliation of the moment cannot be disguised. This sharp juxtaposition of two emotions provides the mirth.

The Boy soon meets another obstacle which leads to another major defeat and more humiliation. When he arrives home, Grandma asks him to chase a tramp from the back yard. Grabbing a broom and swinging it several times to test it as a weapon, the Boy advances toward the tramp. As soon as he catches sight

Asked to chase the tramp in **Grandma's Boy**—with Dick Sutherland and Anna Townsend.

of the grotesque, menacing face of the intruder, he quickly changes his intended action to the innocent action of sweeping the walk. This short incident is cleverly executed in shot 65 and displays good timing on the part of the leading comedian. The cowardice of the Boy motivates this comic reversal of intent.

The extent of the Boy's plight is humorously revealed when the frail little grandmother takes the broom and chases the tramp away. Scott O'Dell calls this incident the first crisis of the drama.[3] It is a test of the Boy's courage. Coupled with another test, it motivates Grandma to help the Boy solve his problem.

After she has chased the tramp away, Grandma says in Title 14, "We made him scoot, didn't we?" In Title 15 the Boy replies, "There's only one we, Granny—that's you." These two titles are verbal reinforcements of the Boy's problem which is the basis for this film comedy. Evidently Lloyd is following in the footsteps of Charles Chaplin's *The Kid* (1921) by establishing a serious situation as the basis of his comedy. By so doing he has given his clown figure added depth. As this incident reveals, a new dimension is introduced in Lloyd's work. This dimension is more often noted by the critics when they write about Charles Chaplin's comedy. In 1924 Frederick Palmer wrote of Chaplin's work:

> One feels—though perhaps not entirely realizing it—that he has the power which, if he wished to use it, would bring the tear with the smile. In fact, he does do this in "Shoulder Arms," in "A Dog's Life," in "Easy Street" and "The Kid." One sees what he hides. And the thing one feels is the racial heart inheritances which make the whole world kin. His comedy is tensely human. Being human, it is universal. The intensely human comedy is the effective, the really great comedy everyone understands.[4]

Lloyd, in *Grandma's Boy,* evidently is headed in this same direction—toward a warm, human comedy. He blends serious material with comic material and he attempts to provoke sympathy for his comic character.

A complication which has developed from the inceptive action is introduced soon after the verbal emphasis on the Boy's problem is set forth. Since the Boy's suit has been ruined by the Rival's malicious act of pushing the Boy into the well, he has no suit to wear to a party at the Girl's house. Innocently unaware of the hoary style of a suit once worn by his grandfather, the Boy accepts this attire from the grandmother. The wearing of this suit provides a link with the next sequence, sequence VI, "The Party at the Girl's House."

At the Girl's house, the Boy experiences a series of humiliating situations which are essentially minor. Nevertheless, these humilia-

3. O'Dell, p. 347.
4. Palmer, *Technique of the Photoplay,* p. 132.

tions provide a sequence that is filled with comedy. The Boy is embarrassed when he sees everyone's reaction to his ancient suit; he gets his finger stuck in a vase, has cats licking his goose-greased shoes, and accidentally swallows a moth ball. Each of these embarrassments or humiliations is increasingly trying for the Boy, and each progressively provides stronger comedy situations.

Of these experiences, the reaction to the Boy's suit is probably the least important. The suit of vintage 1862 happens to look just like a suit worn by the Negro servant who greets the Boy at the door. The reactions of the Girl and her parents when they see the Boy in the odd attire wilt the initial enthusiasm which the lad had on entering the Girl's home. After this incident, the sequence builds to increasingly funny situations.

The next incident reveals the Boy listening to the Girl play a small foot-pedaled organ and sing "You Are the Ideal of My Dreams." Lloyd's execution of the comic business in this incident is worth quoting in detail:

125 LMS He moves his hand up a small table next to his chair as she sings to him. He nervously moves his fingers and smiles. Then he absentmindedly "walks" his fingers up a vase on the table and sticks one of his fingers in the vase. He suddenly realizes that his pointing finger is stuck, and his smile fades. He tries to shake the vase off and once more displays a smile (this time, a forced smile) to the Girl as she sings. He alternates concern for his finger with a forced smile in her direction. He shakes harder and tries to pull the vase off with his other hand. He finally pulls it off as she looks the other way. Hurriedly he hides the vase between his legs as she turns back. Finally he sets the vase back on the small table as the Girl looks away from him again.

Without the aid of special reaction shots or different angles of shots, the incident provides an opportunity for a solo performance for the leading comedian. The attempt of the Boy to get the vase off his finger without revealing his plight is made comic by the comedian's juxtaposition of two pantomimic expressions. He alternates between a frantic effort to get the vase off his finger and a forced, insipid smile at his girl friend. The comedian advances the comedy of the incident with each change of expres-

Refurbishing a gag similar to the one used in **Grandma's Boy** for **Feet First**
(1930) with Barbara Kent. This time Harold has his whole hand caught in a
vase.

sion. The method of building up this pantomimic joke parallels
the building up of a verbal gag. Pantomime is accelerated and exaggerated. The business with the vase and the smile to cover up
the embarrassing situation becomes more elaborate and frantic
until the vase is removed.

The third minor embarrassment to the Boy while he is a guest
in the Girl's house is created quite differently from the two preceding ones. The medium is instrumental in creating the incident.
Cats gravitate to the odor of the Boy's goose-greased shoes. Only
by the use of set up shots can these animals be made to act in this
manner. Training a large group of animals to execute such an action is obviously difficult even in the motion picture. Off-camera

An embarrassment gag in **Grandma's Boy** develops when kittens lick the goose-greased shoes of the Boy.

enticement of food can be used to control such a group. Close-up reaction shots of the Boy's distress when he is surrounded by cats that are licking his shoes also show a strong dependency on the medium to create the full impact of the situation on the embarrassed young man.

The fourth and final embarrassment in this sequence occurs when the Boy tries to get rid of some moth balls which have been accidentally left in the ancient suit which his grandmother gave him to wear to the Girl's party. Noticing the girl friend sniffing the air at the odor of the moth balls, the Boy takes them from his coat pocket and drops them on a table. Unfortunately, he accidentally drops the moth balls into a candy box. As the Girl plays a little game with the Boy by asking him to shut his eyes and open his mouth, she mistakes the moth balls for candy and pops one in his mouth. Too shy and embarrassed to spit up the moth ball, the young man listens bravely to the Girl's conversation. When she turns her head away from him as she talks, his forced smile dissolves into the expression of a tragic mask. Once more two emotions are placed in juxtaposition—this time a wide, false smile is alternated with a drawn, dispirited look of intense agony. The incident is built up by the comedian, who shows increasing discomfiture, and by the Rival's entrance on the scene. Unwittingly, the Rival pops two moth balls into his mouth. Both men are then shown simultaneously smiling when the Girl talks to them and privately choking in agony when she does not look directly at them in her conversation with them.

When the two men manage to get away from the Girl to wash out their mouths, the Boy gets blamed for the incident by the Rival and receives a fist to the chin from the bully. The series of comic embarrassments ends with an emphasis once more on the Boy's cowardice and the triangle situation which exists between the Boy, the Girl, and the Rival.

This series of four incidents makes sequence VI, "The Party at the Girl's House," one of the major comic sequences of the film. Much of the comedy is centered on what James Agee calls "the comedy of embarrassment,"[5] a type of humor that is not in the slapstick tradition, but may be associated with a more genteel tradition. Comedy using material of this nature depends on the protagonist's desire to avoid detection in the embarrassment that plagues him. Jacques Tati, a French comedian of today, in such films as *The Big Day* (1951), *Mr. Hulot's Holiday* (1952), and *My Uncle* (1958) employs material of this type for his comic character. As Mr. Hulot, for example, Tati achieves his best comic moments when he shows his character going to great lengths to avoid detection in a socially embarrassing situation.

One final complication brings the preliminary development of *Grandma's Boy* to a close. The Boy's cowardly behavior defeats him once more. The Sheriff of Dabney County arrives at the Girl's party to recruit a posse in order to capture a tramp who has killed a store owner in the community. Trying to hide his fear, the Boy is sworn in as a deputy, gets lost from the posse in the dark,

5. James Agee, *Agee on Film* (New York, 1968), p. 11.

The Rival, Charles Stevenson, blames and attacks the Boy in **Grandma's Boy.**

and runs home in mortal terror when he steps on a rake, the handle of which flips up and hits him on the back of the head. As the Boy dashes madly home, accelerated motion is used to assist in making his flight humorous. The effect is such a drastic departure from the normal action of a person that this overstatement of the Boy's fright becomes comic. It is the first time in *Grandma's Boy* that this old comic device, a hand-down from the one- and two-reel comedies, is used.

With the close of the preliminary development in *Grandma's Boy*, there is the crisis which is the culmination of three failures —the first with the Rival, the second with the tramp, and finally a third with the Sherriff's posse. These three failures prompt Grandma to action—a response to the Boy's difficulties which will be analyzed in the next chapter.

Reluctantly the Boy prepares for the manhunt in **Grandma's Boy**.

Safety Last

As in *Grandma's Boy*, the initial action in *Safety Last* that sets the plot into motion blends with the exposition. This inceptive complication develops in the second sequence of the work when Harold and his friend Bill are shown struggling to exist in the big city. This is, however, only a root situation which promotes the initial action. Harold feigns success when he writes a letter home to his girl friend: "My position with the De Vore Department Store grows in responsibility every day. My progress has been simply marvelous. Be patient a little longer. I hope to send for you just as soon as I can clear up four or five big business deals."

This letter provides an initial action for many complications that follow. Success is, of course, far up the ladder for Harold. The letter is also symptomatic of the lengths to which the young man will go to achieve success. Harold, consequently, gets caught up in his own manipulation.

A sequence which I have named "Trouble Getting to Work" (sequence IV) is the first elaborate sequence which shows Harold meeting one of the many obstacles that hinders the young man in his climb to a high position in the business world.

The sequence starts with Harold sitting on the back of a laundry truck that is parked by the employee entrance of the De Vore Department Store. He is writing a letter while waiting to get into the store. His "early-bird-gets-the-worm" code of success suffers a setback when he is accidentlly locked up in the laundry truck by an old driver who is hard of hearing. Harold is driven to the other side of the city by the driver who cannot detect his frantic banging on the window of the truck. When he finally gets out, he is forced to find a way back to work once more. He tries all available means of transportation.

Harold's first frantic attempt to return to work is by means of a streetcar. Each attempt to board a streetcar brings a new frustration which results in broader comedy. Failing to find a place on a crowded streetcar, Harold gets on an empty car in front of the full one. Harold's streetcar starts and turns in the wrong direction. Disgustedly, Harold jumps off and heads for the crowded car once more. He tries to get on the front platform but is pushed off by its occupants. Frantically, he climbs on the "cow catcher" and is pushed off by the conductor.

The climax of this comic study in frustration is finally reached:

78 ls Running to the rear of the car, he tries to push his way
onto the rear platform once more, but he gets pushed down
by the people on the platform. Desperately, he jumps onto
the back of a man who seems to be clinging to the rear of the
platform. The streetcar moves off and Harold is left hanging
on the back of the surprised, annoyed bystander. Harold
jumps off, runs after the streetcar, and finally gets on it.

With some exaggeration to gain comedy, the material used is
common to the big city dweller. The frustration of people who
are dependent on public transportation is fully exploited. An en-
largement or overstatement of the situation makes it comic rather
than merely frustrating.

Lloyd continues to exploit his material as the comic character,
Harold, is shown clinging to the side of a streetcar. Harold hails a
passing motorist and gets the gullible driver to pull his car over to
the side of the streetcar. As the desperate young man starts to
transfer from the moving streetcar onto the automobile, the
streetcar turns a corner. Hapless Harold falls to the street. This
fall is an elaborate, clearly motivated pratfall (i.e., comic fall), a
comic device inherited from the one- and two-reel works of the
1910s.

Harold tries to get a ride in an automobile two more times. He
makes a hasty exit from the first car when the driver is stopped
by a policeman and given a ticket. Harold then sees a man cranking his car in an attempt to start it. Harold offers to help him in
order to get a ride. He cranks the car, gets it started, and jumps
in the vehicle only to find the driver making a U turn to go in the
opposite direction.

One more desperate effort is made by the leading comedian,
and he achieves his goal. It is achieved by one of the many examples of comic ingenuity which the young man uses to overcome an
obstacle. The Boy in *Grandma's Boy* and Harold Lamb in *The
Freshman* are not highly gifted in this respect. The many obstacles
in *Safety Last* are usually surmounted by the unusual logic of the
aspiring young man. It is the logic of a comic character and not
the type of logic possessed by the "normal" non-comic characters
in the film.

The leading comic character's execution of comic ingenuity
starts in this incident when Harold observes an accident in which
a man who has been injured has recovered sufficiently to refuse

the service of an ambulance. While the man is protesting to the ambulance attendant that he does not need treatment for his minor injury, Harold takes off his hat and lies down next to the stretcher that was to carry the man who was presumed to be seriously injured. The prostrate Harold appears to have fainted when the attendants discover him. They examine him and put him in the litter. Harold is conveyed from the scene in a speeding ambulance. As the ambulance winds its way through the thick downtown traffic, Harold periodically peeks at his wrist watch and looks out the curtained window of the ambulance to see if he is coming near the De Vore Department Store. The attendant who is taking notes on Harold's condition does not detect these movements because Harold cleverly "plays dead" as the attendant looks up from his notes. When Harold sees that he has almost arrived at his destination, he calls over a phone to the cab of the ambulance. He instructs the driver to stop at the next corner. To the amazement of the attendant, Harold nonchalantly gets up, dusts himself off, puts on his straw hat and leaves the ambulance.

Comic ingenuity reigns in this incident. The audience viewing this film finds the clever trick enjoyable; the gall of the comedian delights them. He labors mightily to achieve a simple goal—to get to work on time. The comedian's labors in this incident show a strong spirit of play at work. Max Eastman holds the view that a play spirit must function in all material which is to be taken as funny.[6] In this situation, however, the "play spirit" is seen in even a more specific sense. The comedian is engaged in a ruse which he finds delightful; he indicates his enjoyment by his execution of the actions—as if he were a child playing a game. The comedian's nonchalance when he has arrived at the De Vore Department Store tops the comic incidents in this portion of the sequence. His obsession to get to work makes him blind to the trouble he has caused others.

There is one more incident in this sequence which provides the highest point and conclusion of the sequence. Once more the leading comic character employs comic ingenuity. When Harold arrives at the employees' entrance of the De Vore Department Store, he realizes that he is late for work despite all his frantic efforts to avoid it. In order to enter the store undetected, he kneels on a short stand after dressing himself as a woman mannequin. A

---

6. Max Eastman, *Enjoyment of Laughter* (New York, 1936), p. 21.

Negro porter, thinking Harold's disguise is merely another display for the store, carries the young man past a time clock. Harold quickly punches the time clock after setting the hands of the clock back to make sure he is not marked late to work. As Harold is being carried down the aisle of the department store in his mannequin disguise, he sneezes. The horrified Negro porter drops what he believes to be a mannequin that has suddenly and mysteriously come to life. The porter runs away, climbs a ladder, and remains clinging there even though he is urged to come down by several girl sales clerks.

This fantastic ruse employs material that is hoary with age and places it in a new setting. Comic drama from the time of Aristophanes to the present has developed intrigue from such disguise material. Because it creates a ludicrous substitution for comic effect, a man is often disguised as a woman. This type of material was used frequently in the one- and two-reel forces of the 1910's Chaplin, for example, developed a two-reel work, *A Woman* (1915), which depends on a disguise for its intrigue. The little tramp puts on his girl friend's clothes in order to see her. While the father objects to Charlie's presence, he is captivated by the "womanly" charm of the disguised Charlie. The little tramp is thereby forced to flirt with the father. The comedy which develops from this intrigue is similar to that achieved by the *commedia dell' arte* sketch of the past. The sexually based humor of Charlie's use of disguise in this early film is certainly more Plautine than Lloyd's relatively mild use of disguise in *Safety Last*.

Lloyd places this ancient comic device in such a position in the sequence "Trouble Getting to Work," that many of the improbable characteristics of the action are made believable. That the comic character would not be detected because of his weight while playing the mannequin is a defiance of logic. That the porter would pause long enough for Harold to punch the time clock is another improbability. However, this incident comes at the end of a series of more logical comic incidents. By this time, the audience will suspend belief if the execution of the improbable incident is effective. The leading comedian shows the dash—the flair—in his execution of the material to make this incident using disguise believable.

Two short sequences which are necessary to plot development but do not contain strong comic incidents are used to conclude the part of the film which I have labeled preliminary development. Harold is shown slaving away as a clerk in the dry goods department of the De Vore store. In this fifth sequence, "At Work in the Department Store," Harold is shown to be a hard worker who is frustrated by the whims of the customers who are "just looking around." His eagerness to make a sale makes his actions comic. The sixth sequence, "Trouble With the Law Begins," functions as a plant for later development. Harold's friend, Bill, gets in trouble with a policeman when Harold bets him that he, Harold, can soothe the temper of a policeman who has been physically menaced. The policeman, who Harold believes to be a friend from his home town, turns out to be another man, and Bill is forced to flee by climbing straight up the side of a building. This special feat by Bill is later used by Harold as a promotional stunt, and the antagonism of the policeman who has been eluded helps develop *Safety Last's* climactic sequence. Sequences V and VI are, therefore, important to show Harold striving for success and to show a minor altercation with the law which later becomes a major threat to Harold's success. At this point of the development, however, sequence VI appears to be a side track from the main plot. It is not until the climatic sequence of *Safety Last* that this episode fits clearly into the structure of the total plot.

The Freshman

After certain conditions, characters, and potentialities are established in the exposition of *The Freshman*, the inceptive action occurs with the first practical joke played on Harold Lamb when he arrives at Tate College. The College Cad tells Harold that he has been assigned a car with a chauffeur. Harold unwittingly takes a car intended for the Dean of the College. This joke by the upperclassmen precipitates Harold's struggle with the campus wags. From this point on, Harold is the butt of many jokes until he finally proves his merit to the college crowd.

This inceptive action leads Harold to a fumbling impromptu speech before the whole student body. Driven by the Dean's chauffeur to Tate Auditorium, Harold takes all his luggage through a side door of the auditorium and deposits it behind a curtained stage. Puzzled by this "room," Harold has his attention diverted by a kitten walking on top of a light border above the stage. Harold mounts a speaker's stand in order to rescue the kitten. Just as he grabs the kitten, the College Cad arrives and pulls the curtain, revealing Harold in an unusual pose before the entire student body who have gathered to hear the Dean of the College's welcoming address for the new school year. Not knowing what to do with the kitten, Harold hides it by stuffing it under his collegiate sweater.

The embarrassment of Harold in this incident, as revealed in shot 135, is an effective display of the comedian's ability to execute carefully timed pantomime. As in *Grandma's Boy*, the comedian uses the tight, embarrassed smile of a young man who is trying to make the best of a bad situation—as if a smile would erase the awkward situation and let his onlookers know that all is well with him.

When Harold tries to get down, the stand beneath him begins to teeter back and forth. The medium assists in making the most of this predicament:

137 MS Harold sways on the pedestal. He tips backwards and then from side to side.

In this shot, a closer view is given to emphasize Harold's plight. The long shot which follows catches the broad action of the fall:

138 LS He falls (toward frame left) and twists backward as he crashes to the floor.

And then, a quick cut to another closer view shows the results:

139 MS Harold sprawls back over his luggage. He pulls out his ukulele from behind him—it is shattered.

The stock pratfall which has been handed down to Lloyd from the past is refurbished with the assistance of the medium. The fall, like all pratfalls, is an elaborate, sprawling one with suitable overstatement to make it funny. This pratfall, in execution, is closer to the standard comic fall than Harold's fall from the streetcar in *Safety Last*. The medium, however, assists the comedian in comic emphasis by building up the gag in *The Freshman*. Shot 137 is especially effective since it helps delay the comedian's eventual fall.

After this fall, Harold tries to make a hasty exit off stage, but as he gathers his belongings in his arms, he finds that he cannot hold everything. Golf clubs, a tennis racket, and suitcases are too much for him. After spilling these articles and stumbling many times, he exits with most of his luggage. The College Cad stops him in the off-stage area and talks Harold into going back on the stage to make a speech. In Title 37 he says, "Why, every new student must make a speech—if you don't you'll be the most unpopular man on campus." After reluctantly considering the College Cad's words, Harold looks painfully at the audience. His fear of speaking is punctuated by an example of a "subjective" special effect by the camera. A long shot from Harold's view point of the audience as he peeks around a curtain shows his dizziness at the thought of talking to the student body. In this special effect, the camera assumes the identity (and vision) of the leading comedian. It is necessary to throw the photographed view out of focus in order to show his dizziness from stage fright.

Harold finally moves onto the stage with a meek, side-shuffle step. He realizes that he has his fencing foil in one hand and a notebook in the other. He puts the notebook in the fold around the waist of his sweater and hides the foil behind him. Title 38 effectively supports the nervous behavior of the young man as he attempts to speak before the student body. "My friends," the title reads, "I am here—yes, there is no doubt but that I am here. . ." After Harold drops his foil and displays a forced smile, Title 39 reaffirms the torment and confusion that stage fright creates in the young man: "Yes, I repeat that I am here—er—you are here—in fact, we are all here."

As the comedian fumbles with his speech to the student body, he makes effective use of the foil which he has absent-mindedly brought on stage with him. He nervously moves the tip of the foil along the edge of the footlights. The medium comes into play with a close-up that shows clearly the results of Harold's nervous moments:

159 CU The tip of the foil goes into an empty light socket of the footlights. Sparks fly.
160 MS Harold reacts to the shock by shaking his hand in pain as if he were stung. Then he recovers and smiles weakly. The pained expresssion returns for an instant, but another smile is attempted to cover up his pain.

Harold Lloyd can once more be seen using the comic material which is highly important to the development of his comic character. The leading figures in *The Freshman* and *Grandma's Boy* attempt to cover up any public embarrassment. The key to the comedy presented by the Boy and Harold Lamb in such a situation lies in this obsession.

The comedian, a great imitator in the silent-screen comedy, often assumes the role of another person to get out of some difficulty. The imitation is frequently a burlesque of the type of person being copied. Harold decides to use his foil to advantage; he flourishes the foil up toward the heavens and down toward hell in an imitation of the great orator. The tip of the foil is shown entering another empty light socket in the footlights. The next shot (162) shows Harold's violent recoil as he receives another shock. The foil flies back stage and out of sight. The following shot displays the audience roaring with laughter.

Editing continues to assist in creating the comedy of Harold's address to the audience. Just before his fall from the speaker's stand Harold has placed the kitten he rescued under his sweater. The mother cat comes to claim her offspring. A close-up reveals the cat looking up at Harold and putting her paws upon Harold's legs as if she wants her kitten. A very close shot reveals the kitten's tail sticking out from under Harold's sweater. The kitten begins to wiggle under Harold's sweater. Harold registers extreme discomfiture as the kitten squirms frantically to get out. A cutaway shot shows the crowd laughing hysterically at Harold's predicament. When the kitten finally wiggles out the top of Harold's turtleneck sweater, Harold sets the animal down.

Again, the comedy of embarrassment is exploited. With his famous tight-lipped smile, the comedian tries to cover up this adverse situation. The medium obviously assists the comedian by emphasizing all the details of the situation.

Copying a phrase used by his movie idol, Harold recovers from his ordeal with the kitten sufficiently to end his speech with the flourish of an old-style orator. "I'm just a regular fellow," he declares as he taps his chest, ". . . and I want you to step right up and call me 'Speedy!' " To end this exclamation he waves his arms to the stars and then brings a hand back to his chest. The student body cheers mockingly. Unaware of the laughter behind their cheers, Harold invites a small group of upperclassmen to the corner drug store for ice cream. The College Cad invites others to join the group as they walk along the campus. At first Harold is delighted, but as the groups of students who join become larger and larger with each turn in the sidewalk, he realizes how much his treat will cost him. Arthur Knight notes that the camera work in this scene is "superbly functional" as "a moving camera keeps pulling farther and farther back as more and more undergraduates join the merry throng en route to the ice cream parlor."[7]

Only two more sequences are necessary to complete the preliminary development of *The Freshman*. They are important to the plot development but are not essentially comic in tone. No special techniques of the film medium are employed.

Harold meets Peggy once more in an inexpensive boarding-house. He sees his picture in the paper with the caption, "Speedy the Spender—This Frisky Freshman is Just a Regular Fellow Who Is Leaving a Trail of Empty Ice Cream Cones on His Dizzy Dash to Popularity." Harold is shown in this last episode admiring what he thinks is fame; he does not realize that the caption ridicules him. Peggy, on the other hand, is shown cutting out his picture in order to have it near her, but she cuts off and crumples the caption disgustedly. At this point, the end of the preliminary development, the audience viewing the motion picture knows that while Harold is obsessed with a naive view of college life that makes him blind to the ridicule directed at him, his friend Peggy understands the true nature of Harold's social position with the college crowd.

The preliminary development of Harold Lloyd's three films uses one elaborate sequence in each of the films which contains the meat of this portion of the films. In *Grandma's Boy,* the sixth sequence, "The Party at Mildred's House"; in *Safety Last,* the fourth sequence, "Trouble Getting to Work"; and in *The Freshman,* the fifth sequence, "Before the Student Body"; highly effective comic episodes are presented which are like one-reel comedies. They are almost independent units in the films. These sequences, each running between nine and ten minutes, do not contain strong plot developments. They are, however, important to the character development of the leading comedian. They also afford the leading comedian an opportunity to display his skill as a pantomimist. Each of these sequences shows a series of occurrences which build up with each comic incident until a high point or climax of the comic sequence is reached.

7. Knight, p. 122.

Since the greater portion of the comedy is achieved by the leading comedian in these sequences, camera shots are not highly important in the creation of the comedy. *The Freshman* has more variety in the use of close-ups, medium and long shots, especially in the portion of the sequence that shows Harold addressing the student body. Reaction shots are also used more frequently in this work than in the other two films. *Grandma's Boy* uses some reaction shots effectively when the Boy is besieged by cats, but most of the shots in this sequence are long shots or medium shots which show broad actions. Since the action is very broad in the sequence which shows Harold trying to get to work, *Safety Last* uses very few close-ups in this portion of the film.

Each successive film shows greater sophistication in the editing of the material being used to create the comic situation in this portion of the film story. The main comic sequence which contains the bulk of the humor in this portion of each film shows this trend. *Grandma's Boy* has seventy-two shots; *Safety Last,* eighty-four; and *The Freshman,* eighty-five. The last two films employ more shots to emphasize the comic situations in their main comic sequences. *Safety Last* may be thought by the casual observer to have considerably more shots in its main sequence than *The Freshman.* The great amount of physical action in *Safety Last* seems to leave this impression. The content of the shot that involves a great deal of action often holds the attention without a great deal of cutting. The many reaction shots and special set-up shots of animals in this part of *The Freshman* account for the large amount of shots in a situation which is comparatively static.

Fewer titles are used in the preliminary development of all three films than were used in the exposition of the works. *The Freshman,* dealing with the Boy's speech to the student body, must use more titles than the other two films; nevertheless, titles are held to a minimum. Visual humor receives the greatest emphasis.

While the comedy in this portion of the film clearly springs from the character of the leading comedian, some interesting stock comedy devices are used by Lloyd. To achieve comedy in *Grandma's Boy,* he employs ill-fitting clothes. The Boy, after being pushed into a well by the Rival, finds his allegedly unshrinkable suit improperly labeled. His suit shrinks drastically in the sun. *Safety Last* uses ancient material when Lloyd is disguised as a mannequin to get into the De Vore Department Store. Lloyd, however, achieves genteel humor with his use of women's clothes.

While the intrigue contains as many improbabilities as disguise-promoted intrigues in comedies of the past, Lloyd does not use his appearance in women's clothing for risqué humor. The standard pratfall is refurbished in both *The Freshman* and *Safety Last*. This device is carefully motivated and worked into the intrigue, with the medium assisting in building up the incident that employs it.

Much of the comedy in the films, however, does not fall into the spirit of the slapstick tradition of the past. Many of the embarrassments which the Boy in *Grandma's Boy* and Harold Lamb in *The Freshman* experiences are in the spirit of a more genteel comedy. In each of these works, the comedian is placed in a frustrating situation which is made comic by the leading character's obsessions. This type of comedy was seldom used by the one- and two-reel slapstick films in the 1910's; merely embarrassing a person was not enough—the older school of comedy had to debase an individual with a fall on a banana peel or a well-placed custard pie. *Safety Last* does not use the comedy of embarrassment in this portion of the film as the other two works do. It deals in the comedy of frustration. With a great deal of sophistication, *Safety Last* retains some of the spirit of the early one- and two-reel comedies in its use of broad, action-filled intrigue.

The comic character of the leading comedian is advanced by the preliminary development in each film. In fact, this seems to be a major function of this portion of the film. The attempts to cover up embarrassments by the Boy in *Grandma's Boy* and Harold Lamb in *The Freshman* reveal the leading characters' obsession with social acceptance. The over-eagerness of Harold to get to work in *Safety Last* illustrates the lengths the young man will go to be successful.

5
Midpoint of the Development

While the midpoint in the development of a film drama may be fluid and, at times, difficult to pin down, certain manifestations of this portion of the drama may be described in order to analyze Lloyd's three films. Preliminary development in Lloyd's works is much concerned with character. The complications have not reached a point at which a great deal of direct action evolves. That is, the plot development is not revealed in direct, clear-cut action. That the midpoint of the development of a drama is a point of greater complication is obvious. It is also a part of the drama will tend, in each film, to crystallize the question and present complications that will make the goal more difficult or offer sions. In *Grandma's Boy* the dramatic question is evolving by this time: "Will the Boy's cowardice be conquered?" By this time *Safety Last* presents the dramatic question: "Will Harold be a success in the business world?" In *The Freshman* the question is: "Will Harold Lamb be accepted by the campus set?" The midpoint of the drama will tend, in each film, to crystallize the question and present complications that will make the goal more difficult or offer some possibilities by which it may be attained, or both.

Grandma's Boy

As we approach the midpoint of the development in *Grandma's Boy*, the Boy is found in deep despair. He has failed many times. To his grandmother he declares in Title 36, "It's no use,

Granny—I'm a coward—I'm a coward—I'm a coward." At this point the Boy breaks down and cries on the shoulder of his grandmother.[1] Lloyd attempts to promote sympathy for the Boy by this action. It is, however, difficult to sympathize with the comic figure in this work to the degree that Lloyd desired. The comedian plays this scene realistically; there is no attempt to make the material comic. There is, therefore, a strong shift from the half-serious and half-comic treatment of many of the Boy's previous reactions to failure. The emotional breakdown in *Grandma's Boy*, however, is more subdued than the breakdown in *The Freshman*. In contrast to Harold Lamb's goal in *The Freshman*, the goal of the Boy is worthwhile, and some sympathy is established by this incident. The goal of social acceptance by a snobbish college crowd does not seem as worthy as the vital, sincere attempt on the part of the Boy to conquer his cowardice.

The incident calculated to promote sympathy is brief, and the film story line moves into the comic realm with a tale told by Grandma. She points to a picture of Harold's grandfather, a portrait which shows the Boy as almost a carbon copy of his grandfather. A close-up shot (247) of the grandfather's picture is comic because of his stiff pose in a soldier's uniform, the startled, meek expression on his face, the sideburns, and (best of all) glasses that have square horn-rimmed lenses.

Grandma begins her story of Grandpa's adventures as a Confederate spy. Her story is an elaborate ruse to get the Boy to overcome his cowardice. Related in a flashback,[2] Grandma's tale is a short drama in itself.

Grandpa is shown in the first incident of this flashback running fearfully through the woods with shells bursting all around him. He is dressed in a Confederate uniform. When he approaches Union headquarters, he is confronted by a hideous old hag who has been maltreated by Union soldiers. From a place out of sight of the headquarter guards, the old hag declares in Title 41, "I hates 'em all—go an' get 'em!" Grandpa cringes and says, "I can't! They sent me to steal General Bell's Code, but I can't go through with it—I'm a coward—I'm a coward." The final exclamation of

---

1. A similar breakdown occurs at the crisis of *The Freshman*. There were critical objections to this scene in Harold Lloyd's comedy on college life. See chapter 6.

2. A technique of narrating a story in both the novel and the cinema. The narrator frequently frames the story by introducing, sustaining, and concluding it. This technique may be used to introduce material that is necessary for developing the plot or understanding the character.

Lloyd dressed for the role of Grandpa in **Grandma's Boy.** On the set with him are his father and mother in this special publicity still.

Grandpa in Title 42 is a repetition of the Boy's words during his breakdown in his grandmother's arms. This is a hint that reveals the fabricated nature of Grandma's story.

To assist the would-be spy in his endeavors, the old woman hands him a charm which she declares will give him the ability to conquer anyone without personal injury to himself. At first he drops the charm fearfully as the hag puts it into his hands. As he bends over to pick it up, one of the first chance accidents prevents the comic hero from being hurt. A Union sentry has spotted Grandpa and charged him with lowered bayonet as he bends down to pick up the charm. The bayonet misses him and becomes lodged in the side of the house which the Union officers are using for their headquarters. At this moment, the old hag hits the soldier on the head with a piece of wood. Grandpa straightens up, amazed to see that he has not been hurt by the thrust of the soldier's bayonet. As soon as this soldier is dispatched, another sentry rushes at the ineffectual Confederate spy with lowered bayonet. Grandpa backs over a porch step that has a loose board. When he steps on one end of the board, the other end flies up and hits the soldier squarely on the chin, knocking him out. Sprawled on the ground, Grandpa, who has been upended by the board, believes the magical power of the charm has knocked out the second sentry.

This second incident of the elaborate flashback sequence displays a type of comic substitution which is the core of the humor. Two levels of thought are in operation. While Grandpa believes that the fate of the two soldiers has been swayed by the power of the magic charm, it is obvious to the viewer of *Grandma's Boy* that each sentry is dispatched by a lucky accident, although the first soldier's fall receives some assistance from the old voodoo woman. As Siegfried Kracauer points out, chance is more readily accepted in the development of a comic story.[3]

Grandma's Boy capitalizes on chance in this incident, especially in the action of the soldier who gets his bayonet stuck and the sentry who gets hit by the loose step. In both cases, however, this chance accident is carefully handled. Each action in the incident is motivated and executed to make the action plausible.

When the old voodoo woman dispatches the first soldier, her action becomes comic because of the mechanical smoothness of

3. Siegfried Kracauer, *Theory of Film* (New York, 1960), p. 272.

the knockout blow and the ease with which the action is performed. A normal knockout blow demands herculean efforts, but
the voodoo woman substitutes an easy swing to accomplish the
same result. When Grandpa, with his newly found power, leaves
the voodoo woman, he employs the same action to fell a servant
who is preparing punch for the officers of the Union army. Using
a handy piece of wood, he knocks out the servant with great ease
and puts on the servant's clothes.

As Harold's grandfather continues the preparation of the
punch, he creates a powerful drink by pouring three bottles of liquor into the punch bowl. Assistance of the medium is brought
into play in order to create a gag. A high angle, close-up shot
(292) of the punch bowl fades in and out of the image of a kicking mule. This superimposition creates a comic comment on the
nature of Grandpa's potent cocktail.

Disguised as the servant, Grandpa serves the drink to the officers as they discuss their plans for the next battle. He tries his
hand at some crude spying as the officers drink and talk over war
strategy:

301 LS Grandpa moves around the table and looks at one of the
officers. He sees that the officer is looking at the General
who is standing by a wall map. Harold's grandfather looks at
some papers on the table; he peers at them as if he were
myopic. His spying becomes obvious to the officer, and the
officer glares at the intruder. Grandpa straightens up and affects innocence.
302 CU The officer pulls up the servant's apron and sees
Grandpa's Confederate trousers.
303 MS The officer grabs his sword hilt; immediately, Grandpa
grabs the officer's pistol and effortlessly knocks him out with
the butt of the weapon.

Grandpa then arranges the unconscious form of the officer as
if he had merely passed out from too much liquor. The other officers, who have been too intent on the lecture to notice the violence, see the prostrate form of the officer and laugh at his inability to consume liquor without passing out.

As the incidents show, the level of probability is again stretched
by the comic drama. The deftness with which Grandpa wields the
gun, however, not only assists in creating the comedy; it also

makes the incident probable. Thus, the comedian's execution of the pantomime supports the use of material which might otherwise seem improbable.

Important to the comedy of this incident, as in the previous incidents, is the ease with which physical violence is employed to fell a man. Obviously, all forms of violence employed for comic effect must deviate greatly from the normal act in order to place violence on a comic level. While a comic fall (a pratfall) will often deal in overstatement of the act, the knockout in this case is an understatement of the normal act.

The would-be spy tries again to look at plans lying before another officer. The officer becomes suspicious and raises his gun to hit Grandpa. However, Grandpa counters the threat by quickly stepping on the officer's foot, grabbing his gun, and hitting him with the pistol which was intended to stop Grandpa. A comic reaction which differs from the reaction to the preceding knockout follows:

312 MS The officer then stands up from his chair with a blank expression on his face. His eyes roll. Grandpa pushes him on the head until he sinks down in the chair. The officer then faints; his head falls on the table. To avoid detection, Harold's grandfather fans the unconscious officer with his hat and affects an innocent smile.

Again, the nonchalant attitude of the leading comedian as he deals out physical violence which will, step by step, conquer the officers, provides the proper climate to achieve the comic. Once more the knockout blow is achieved with a finesse and ease that place the action on a comic level. The reaction of the recipient of the blow, however, is different. An unusual reaction to being knocked out is shown. Instead of falling, the officer stands up in a dazed condition and takes a normal unconscious position only when the comedian pushes him back into his chair. The officer's rolling eyes are comically exaggerated.

In the next variation of this same type of action, Lloyd builds up the comic incidents toward the peak for this portion of the film. The conquering of a third officer in shot 316 shows the following action:

Grandpa moves to another officer who is sitting at the table. The officer indicates that he wants another drink. He playfully punches the bogus servant in a friendly gesture of appreciation. He enjoys the potency of the drink Grandpa has mixed. Grandpa, with a broad smile, returns the friendly action with a pistol butt to the officer's head. When the officer passes out, Grandpa puts a lily from a flower vase in the officer's hand.

This third incident which involves the last officer who is seated at the table employs strong contrast and a sharp reversal of action in order to achieve comedy. For a friendly gesture, the comedian substitutes an act of aggression *as if he were being friendly.* The smile of the comedian as he deftly hits the officer provides the contrast which helps create comedy. The comedian's final touch as he places the lily in the limp hand of the officer illustrates the nonchalance of the young man who fights his opponent in a perverse way. The serious profession of spying becomes a game. The comedian, in an almost childlike way, takes innocent delight in his newfound ability to deal in violence.

Chaplin often employed a similar childlike behavior when he fought an opponent. He used this attitude extensively when, as a policeman in *Easy Street* (1917), he battled against a bully; and in *The Adventurer* (1917) when, as an escaped convict, he fought the police. In *Easy Street,* Charlie nonchalantly dropped an iron stove from a window on the head of a bully who stood on the street below. Pursued by policeman in the opening sequence of *The Adventurer,* Charlie feigned injury, then jumped up to kick a policeman over a cliff. Invective actions of this nature were strong in such early works of Chaplin. Charlie's actions were like those of a wicked child who is engaged in a fight for pure enjoyment. A Lloyd two-reel work, *High and Dizzy* (1920), used invective humor also. The mischievous behavior of the leading comedian accounts for a great deal of the humor. Lloyd's Grandpa in *Grandma's Boy,* on the other hand, participates in violent action with an air of innocence. His smile does not reflect the impish glee of the little tramp in Chaplin's early works or Lloyd's comic character in *High and Dizzy.*

One final encounter with an officer, the General, provides the peak of the action in the midpoint of *Grandma's Boy's* development. Grandpa turns around to finish his one-man assault on the officer's headquarters of the Union army. He finds himself face to face with the General as he holds a gun ready to hit the stern-faced officer. Hesitating only for a moment, Grandpa turns the direction of his intended swing toward the wall in order to hang up the gun. He gives the gun a final touch to straighten it and smiles innocently (but weakly) at the General. Again, a reversal comes into play to achieve the comic. In this case, the intended violence is rapidly switched to feigned innocence. It is a change from the previous encounter with the third officer when playful innocence was switched to violent, aggressive action.

Lloyd then develops an elaborate comic fight between Grandpa and the General. This action provides the climax for the flashback sequence in *Grandma's Boy*. The fight develops into a duel with swords. Grandpa, obviously no swordsman, holds a sword he has grabbed from the belt of one of the unconscious officers with both hands and whacks back at the General's sword. Grandpa throws an apple at the General which luckily lands on the tip of the officer's sword. Finally Grandpa hits the General in the jaw with his fist and gives him a kick that sends the officer sprawling on top of the table. The table collapses under the General's weight. The room ends up in a shambles; broken chairs and the table with officers lying among the debris form a mountain of disorder which is proof of Grandpa's victory.

Immediately following this fight, a Confederate General and his men arrive to observe the wreckage. The General puts his hand on Grandpa's shoulder and declares, in Title 46, "You're no soldier—you're a regiment!"

Grandpa's fight with the Union General is comic because of the unusual fighting methods employed by the leading comedian. While the General fights in a traditional manner, Grandpa employs unorthodox tricks which spring from his lack of knowledge of swordsmanship. A strong inversion of logic creates the comedy; the unskilled person wins *because* he is untrained.[4] The unorthodox way of fighting wins Grandpa the victory. Prompted by the alleged attributes of the magic charm, the Confederate spy fights with everything at his command. He stamps on toes and kicks with finesse. He uses his fists in a sword fight. As the result of this one-man attack, the Union headquarters are pictured lying in shambles. Grandpa has attacked with the force of a Hercules or a whirlwind.

At the end of Grandma's story, the main action of *Grandma's Boy* is resumed. The flashback story has had its effect on the young man. He is completely transformed when Grandma gives

4. Comedy is achieved by this type of material in the climactic sequences of *Grandma's Boy* and *The Freshman*. See chapter 7.

In the elaborate story about Grandpa's victory in **Grandma's Boy**, the Confederate troops discover "the one man army."

him the alleged charm which, she reports, gave Grandpa the courage of a lion. The Boy is stimulated with great confidence and goes off to battle the tramp who has been molesting people in the village. This action is prompted by the elaborate tale told by Grandma. It becomes an action that is an important turning point in the development of the story.

Safety Last

Lloyd's film on the strivings of a young man to become a success in the business world employs an elaborate series of incidents in the middle portion of its development. Parallel action is used to portray Mildred, back in Harold's home town, making a decision to come to the big city to see Harold, while Harold is shown at work in the department store.

When Mildred receives a lavaliere from Harold, a gift which has cost Harold a week's salary, Title 27 reveals the advice Mildred's mother gives to Mildred: "Don't you think it's dangerous for a young man to be alone in the city with so much money?" In Title 28 she adds, "If I were you, I wouldn't wait. I'd go to him right away." This short sequence ends with a clear indication that Mildred will visit Harold in the big city. It is primarily a sequence of exposition to plant and motivate Mildred's visit to Harold's place of work in a later sequence, sequence X.

The following sequence launches into a series of rapidly developing gags. In a series of madcap incidents, Harold is caught in the middle of the frenzy of a bargain-day sale. Title 30 begins this sequence by a comment on the situation that soon develops: "Mother instinct was right. The Boy IS in great danger." The opening shot of sequence IX, which I have named "Bargain Day Troubles," employs the medium for a revelation gag. The first shot of *Safety Last,* it will be recalled, was deceptive in content in order to set up a comic reversal. This incident is more simply executed. A dolly shot pulls back to reveal the true nature of the comedian's following reactions: Harold, a look of mortal terror on his face, is shown backed against a wall, his clothes in disarray, apparently pleading with someone who is threatening him off camera. At this point the camera dollies back for a longer shot of the scene: It reveals a more innocent situation than previously indicated. A group of women are shown rummaging furiously through some clothes on a bargain counter in the department store. It is not so effective as an earlier revelation device used in this film. The scene is brief and there is a lack of clarity in visual detail. In short, this incident does not communicate the contrasting ideas with the sharpness of the first shot in *Safety Last* or the use of revelation in an early scene of *Grandma's Boy.*

The series of rapidly developing comic incidents which follows this opening shot of the sequence, on the other hand, communicates effectively. Comic ingenuity is the main ingredient of the sequence. As Harold is pulled vigorously back and forth between two middle-aged Amazons who desire to be waited on first, he slips out of his coat to escape them. When two women desire one piece of material, he employs the wisdom of Solomon and cuts the material in two—much to the dismay of the women. As a woman is knocked down by a brawny, matronly woman in a fight over dress material, Harold holds up the victor's hand and counts the prostrate loser out. This comic incident employs what may be called a reversal of roles. The comedian assumes playfully the role of a referee in a boxing match when he sees a situation which he believes to be analogous to this sport. Strongly injected with the spirit of play, this type of humor was frequently used by Chaplin in his two-reel comedies.

One more bit of comic ingenuity is incorporated by the leading comedian when he attempts to get a package of material to a little old lady who has been pushed back by the more aggressive women at Harold's counter. Harold shouts, "Who dropped that fifty dollar bill?" (Title 33). As everyone in the crowd drops quickly on hands and knees to look for the money, Harold reaches over the prostrate forms of the well-fed women and hands the package to the little old lady.

The concluding incident of the bargain-day counter episode employs a pantomime which also illustrates a reversal of roles on the part of the leading character. A woman jabs him in the ribs with her umbrella to get his attention. Two long-shots to show the broad action show Harold's solution to this annoyance:

306 LS Harold grabs a yardstick and deftly fences the woman's umbrella thrusts. With his free hand, Harold grabs some material and passes it to the wrapping clerk. He finally knocks the lady's umbrella from her hand.

307 LS Stubbs, the floorwalker, comes up behind Harold and jabs him to get his attention. Without looking around, Harold returns Stubbs's jab with a thrust of his yardstick to the floorwalker's stomach. In a sweeping motion, Harold catches a piece of material on the end of the yardstick and passes it up to the wrapping clerk to cover up his error. By this motion he hopes to cover up the mistake of jabbing Stubbs in the stomach.

The use of a yardstick for a foil in this brief incident illustrates the inventiveness of the comedian. His pantomime is highly effective as he thrusts with the aplomb of a master fencer. As in Chaplin's 1916 tour de force, *One A.M.*, the camera merely photographs the pantomime of the leading comedian from a long shot position. The skill of the comedian is all that is needed to create humor in this incident.

A transitional sequence which follows functions in the same manner as other transitions in Lloyd's works. Comic incidents are not stressed. Mr. Stubbs informs Harold that his unkempt appearance should be corrected; the inflexible floorwalker cannot grasp the cause of the clerk's untidy appearance. The comic tone of this part of the film, as in all Lloyd's transitional sequences, is mild. In sequence X, "Harold's Dual Life," a new set of comic incidents evolves.

The key or central sequence in the mid-portion of the development of *Safety Last* shows Harold being forced into a position of living his lie about his successful position with the De Vore Department Store. When Mildred comes to the city to visit him, Harold must feign success by pretending to be important in the management of the department store. Lloyd places the leading character in a series of situations in which he must feign a position of leadership so that Mildred will not discover his lowly position as a clerk.

When Mildred surprises Harold at work, she greets him with the exclamation: "We're SO proud of you, Harold, and your W-O-N-D-E-R-F-U-L position!" The emphasis by capitalization and dashes as displayed in Title 38 shows title writer H. M. Walker's attempt to capture Mildred's bubbling enthusiasm as she admires Harold. It helps characterize this innocent young girl. Harold's thoughts following this greeting are mirrored by a pained expression in a reaction shot. Harold is obviously in position in which his deception can be unmasked. A fellow clerk hands him a caricature of Mr. Stubbs which has been sketched by one of Harold's co-workers on a small sheet of paper. Harold looks at it, affects a dignified air and puts an "O.K." on the piece of paper. The clerk leaves with the paper, greatly puzzled by Harold's superior air. Again, comic ingenuity can be seen operating to achieve the humor in the film.

Harold presents what his fellow clerks believe is strange behavior when he verbally chastises a wrapping girl for throwing him a customer's packaged goods to deliver. Title 39 supports the incident which shows Harold still trying to maintain a false front: "Must I personally supervise every sale in this department?" After this incident, Harold tries to get Mildred to stay in the department store's soda fountain. But Mildred cannot stay away from her boy friend. She comes back to find Harold waiting on a customer. When he sees Mildred looking at him with a puzzled expression, Harold immediately shifts into the role of supervisor once more. "Now observe me closely," Title 40 reads as Harold taps a clerk beside him on the shoulder, "I will illustrate the correct form of salesmanship."

Comedy is achieved in these incidents and in the many incidents to follow by Harold's sharp reversal of roles. Harold alternates his role of a meek clerk with that of a domineering boss. He must maintain his position as clerk in order to avoid being caught by Mr. Stubbs, but he must also convince Mildred that he is a supervisor in the store. The contrast of roles between the boss and the lowly clerk becomes increasingly sharp and therefore more comic as each new complication arises.

Forced to visit the manager of the De Vore Department Store because of a report Mr. Stubbs submitted regarding his untidy dress while waiting on customers at the bargain counter, Harold is unable to avoid having his lowly position magnified by his nervous behavior before his boss. The pantomime executed by Lloyd as he stands before his boss is worthy of direct quotation from the prepared scenario:

376 MS Harold enters the office and walks slowly up to the General Manager's desk. He tries to present the note that Stubbs has given him regarding his unkempt appearance. The General Manager is too busy to notice Harold. Harold tries to hand the note to him again but without success. Nervously, Harold puts the note between his teeth and unconsciously bites the center out of it. The General Manager finishes the business in front of him and accepts Harold's mutilated note. The boss frowns and asks him for the rest of the note. Harold looks around, not realizing that it is between his teeth. The boss motions to Harold's face. Harold finds the piece of the note and hands it over. Nervously and unconsciously, Harold takes the phone on the manager's desk off its hook as the boss pieces the note together. The General Manager notices that Harold is holding the phone in his hand and gestures curtly at the nervous employee to put it back. Harold absent-mindedly puts the phone in his pocket, then realizes his error and puts it back on its hook.

Before the boss of the department store, Harold is painfully meek and rattled. The extent of his nervousness creates the comedy of the incident. His actions are the overstated actions of many of the jittery, absent-minded movements which many people perform when under stress. These little gestures of frustration are made comic by the effective execution of a skilled pantomimist. The other major comedians of the twenties, Chaplin, Keaton, and Langdon, were also masters at handling such simple material as this.

After Harold receives a threat of dismissal unless he displays the proper attire of a clerk at all times, he comes from the office crushed by the authority that thwarts his success. Mildred sees him standing outside the General Manager's office and assumes that Harold has just come from his own office. Harold is forced to go along with this faulty assumption; he becomes more entangled in his lie of success. Misunderstandings and assumptions of this nature are often the root of many comic situations. Harold is the victim of not only his big lie, but also a victim of Mildred's naiveté. The role that Harold must now assume becomes more dangerous to his present position. Impersonation of the General Manager may result in dismissal. This complication allows emotional stress to advance the comic nature of the scenes that follow. A strong emotional basis for the growth of the comedy has therefore been added.

When the General Manager leaves his office temporarily, Harold takes his girl friend into the office to show her around. Inside the room, Harold's fear of the boss's return produces great nervousness. As he stands beside the General Manager's desk with his girl friend, he runs his finger nervously along the desk and accidentally pushes an intercommunication call button. An office boy comes in, answering the buzzer. The comedian's ingenuity gets him out of the situation. Winking at the boy and throwing a dollar bill into the waste basket, he orders the boy to empty the basket. When the boy takes the basket to the door, Harold calls him back to pick up another piece of paper (one which Harold has wadded up and thrown on the floor). By this means, Harold plucks the dollar bill from the basket as the boy leans over to pick up the wad of paper.

Greater emotional tension plagues Harold when Mildred decides to push a button to see whom it will bring. He tries to stop her, but she insists and gets her way. Frantically, Harold sits down at the desk and hides behind a newspaper. He peeks over the edge of the paper and registers a look of horror when he sees Mr. Stubbs enter. Behind the paper, as Title 49 indicates in large type, Harold evidently disguises his voice to impersonate the gruff, loud voice of the General Manager. Not only does the comedian avoid detection by his ingenuity; he also injects a comment that helps secure his position. In Title 50 he says, "I don't wish to be annoyed by any more of your petty complaints about personal appearance," and boldly adds in Title 51, "You know, you're no collar ad yourself."

Once more a complication nearly exposes Harold. He accidentally presses a whole row of call buttons as he holds Mildred's hands and unthinkingly sits on the General Manager's desk. Many doors leading into the office fly open, and the office boy, secretary, Mr. Stubbs, and other members of the office force enter. Quick-wittedly, Harold jumps into line with the office personnel. The line of people look at each other questioningly, and with a puzzled shrug each one goes out his separate door. Harold looks at Mildred and declares in Title 53, "Fire Drill. I try them out every day."

The comedy of the above incident is not achieved by full employment of the medium. Most of the action is photographed in long shots without special effects or reaction shots. The wooden, mechanical action of the regimented office staff as they pop in from their many doors shows, however, an emphasis on staging to assist the comic situation. Bergson's theory of rigidity or mechanism in a comic depiction of human behavior may be applied here as a concept to describe the character of this particular incident. We laugh at this scene because of the overstatement of regimentation demanded by authority. The actors are like so many puppets which follow a command as if they had strings attached to them and were being operated by a puppet master. Such a strong deviation from the normal action arouses laughter.

One of the interesting features of this incident is the use of verbal humor in a title to cap the humor of the situation. At this point, the title writer assists the comedian in his use of ingenuity. In playing his double role and switching from his status as clerk to that of bogus leader of the department store, Harold's action of jumping into line with his co-workers is explained by this simple yet ingenious statement. As in previous incidents when Harold worms his way out of a situation that might expose him, the use of verbal humor tops the comic incident. Harold must not only pantomime his bogus role, he must also explain his actions to convince Mildred. Verbal humor is, therefore, more important in this portion of *Safety Last* than in any other part of the film.

When Harold finally gets his girl friend outside his boss's office, he finds that he has impressed her greatly. In Title 56 Mildred says, "And just think—you've made money enough already for our little home." A reaction shot, shot 451, reveals Harold's distress coupled with the famous weak smile which attempts to cover up his discomfiture. Therefore, at this point of the plot development, the pressure to succeed is increased. Harold has overplayed his hand in his attempt to impress his girl friend and avoid exposure. Harold is not a prime mover at this point in his struggle to succeed. He is a victim of chance and his own designs. Here lies the core of the comedy in this part of the film. Harold is caught in a chain reaction. Each new complication brings on a more trying obstacle. The humor gains momentum in a way that might be called a "snowball effect," a term which Henri Bergson uses to indicate the linking of one comic incident with another and the growth of humor from this chain.[5]

The Freshman

In the mid-way development of *The Freshman,* the central figure, Harold Lamb, attempts to become a popular man on the college campus. An incident which motivates the action in this part of the film shows the campus idol, Chet Trask, driving a car overflowing with beautiful girls. To the amazed, envious Harold, the College Cad declares in Title 48, "You see, you can never be as popular as Chet Trask unless you play on the football team." This incident, showing the College Cad's successful baiting of Harold Lamb, plants the motivation for Harold to go out for football. An elaborate sequence follows in which Lloyd exploits the game of football for comedy.

The development of the football practice sequence receives an overall comic mood from an introductory title. An overstatement of the nature of the game is made, and the psychological characteristics of the men involved in the sport receive comment when the comic aside by the title writer observes: "Football Practice

5. Henri Bergson, *Laughter, Comedy,* ed. Wylie Sypher (Garden City, N.Y., 1956), pp. 112-14.

—where men are men and necks are nothing." This title, Title 49, is an obvious take-off on the saying, "Where men are men and women know it." Then a beefy coach with the face of a bulldog is introduced in Title 50. "The head coach," the title reads, "—so tough he shaves with a blow torch."[6]

Harold Lamb comes upon this seminar in group violence as the coach is urging his men into action. The coach praises Chet Trask as a superior player who serves as a model for all the team. Harold steps through the gate of the practice field and takes his place between the coach and Chet Trask. Too intent in his pep talk to notice this substitution, the coach continues his tribute to the best player. The contrast between Trask and Lamb develops clearly when the two men are observed together. Trask has all the features of the all-American football player; Harold is physically weak in appearance, and his football garb is ludicrous. Instead of the plain colored jersey of the team, Harold wears a striped one. He wears glasses and a huge nose guard.

Once more, as in *Grandma's Boy,* Lloyd returns to the use of ludicrous clothing to achieve comedy. However, there is no return to the older comic tradition of standard clown or tramp clothes to assist in building a comic characterization. In this incident, the leading comic character dons the uniform which he thinks will assist him in football practice. His choice of uniform is, of course, naive. Its strong deviation from the attire of the young men around him places his habit on the comic level.

As Harold Lamb is being mistakenly praised as "a regular go-getter—a red-blooded fighter," in Title 54, he naively responds to this praise with a coy smile. The coach does not discover his error of pointing to the wrong man until he urges the men on by saying, "You're all afraid of getting hurt! I'd like someone to show me a real ROUGH tackle!" (Title 55). The camera then switches to a functionally more effective high-angle shot to show the comic business which follows this remark:

282　LS An assistant to the coach pulls a blanket out from under Harold as he stands next to the coach. Harold is thrown off balance and sprawls forward, hitting the coach. Both men tumble to the ground. Harold jumps to his feet and tries to help the coach up.

6. The reviewer of this work for the *New York Times,* September 21, 1925 (p. 12), finds both of the above titles effective examples of humor. These titles are more strained in their humor than most of the titles in the three films being analyzed. They function as "comic asides" since they are not directly related to the story line.

A victim of an ill-timed move by one of the coach's assistants, Harold immediately receives the coach's rebuke because he thinks that Harold took his words literally. As the investigation of this comic sequence will show, Harold is often the victim of the action of subordinates who move around in the background picking up gear and placing it in another location.

Harold does not let this accidental "tackle" of the coach hinder him in his desire to be a football hero. He immediately introduces himself by executing the little jig and handshake which he has witnessed in the movie *The College Hero.* By this time, the little jig has become what is commonly called a "running gag."[7] The action is accompanied by dialogue in Title 56: "I'd like to play on your football team if you don't mind." The appearance, actions, and words of Harold, therefore, establish him as a very unlikely candidate for the football team.

When Harold attempts to kick a football, he demonstrates his lack of ability. He kicks the football backwards; it flies over a fence behind him. Told to go after the football, Harold finds the ball by the doghouse of the team mascot, Mike. Chained to a metal post, the dog snaps viciously at him. In shots 299 through 302, Harold Lamb executes one of the film's few actions which demonstrates comic ingenuity. Extensive use of this type of comedy would run contrary to the comic character which has been established. However, *Safety Last,* it has been revealed, uses this type of humor frequently because it is an integral part of the comic character in this film. The incident in which comic ingenuity is used in *The Freshman* is therefore a simple, mild form of this type of comedy which is not out of character for Harold Lamb. In order to get the ball without being bitten, he gets the chained dog to chase him in circles. The chain is thereby wound around the metal post so that Harold can move safely in to pick up the football.

Harold is allowed to join the men in a lineup in which the team is engaged in tackling a dummy suspended by a rope and pulley. As Harold tries to tackle the dummy the first time, an assistant to the coach, who is holding the rope which suspends the dummy, moves over to the coach to receive instructions. As a result of the

7. Frequently employed in vaudeville as a short comic routine that appeared and was repeated periodically throughout the complete performance. It usually featured a final line or bit of business (a "topper") that gave the joke a clever twist. Repetition was a strong feature in this comedy routine. The device of substitution also comes into operation. The repeated action or exclamation is often inappropriate—it does not fit the situation in which the clown uses it.

Trouble retrieving a football in **The Freshman.**

assistant's action, the dummy is moved above Harold's wild tackling leap. Harold misses the dummy completely. As he gets up to figure what has gone wrong, he sees the dummy in its proper position. The assistant has moved back to his former spot. Harold shakes his head bewilderedly and moves back into the line to try once more.

The quality of this type of humor is like that of a practical joke. We laugh at the person who has been fooled. The added strength of this type of gag, however, lies in the promotion of the situation through an unconscious act. The assistant coach is not aware of the confusion he has caused in the victim. Theodore Huff calls this type of humor the uses of the "unconscious gag."[8] Chaplin, Huff points out, uses this type of gag in *The Bank* (1915) in the simple business of shouldering a mop which hits a man in the face. To be effective, this type of humor demands that the pro-

8. Huff, p. 52.

moter of the indignity be totally unaware of the results of his action.

This type of comedy is exploited even further in *The Freshman*. The assistant gives the coach the rope which holds the dummy so that he may look at a piece of football gear. Harold flies at the dummy with increased fury, hoping that his doubled efforts will produce a good tackle. Not expecting the tackle at this time, the coach is sent sprawling once more. With threatening gestures, the coach tells Harold to leave the playing field.

The humor of this incident is closely related to the comic quality of the pratfall. Much of the humor of the whole sequence, in fact, harks back to this primitive type of humor. The comic fall is a basic part of the action of the earlier comic film. This sequence presents a sophisticated version of this comic device. The falls are clearly motivated by the nature of the game of football. When the pratfall is produced by underling Harold Lamb, who trips up authority, the coach, the humor is given new strength.

The use of the pratfall and comic assault attain new heights in the sequence in which Harold Lamb is called back by the coach to replace the broken tackle dummy. The planting of the broken tackle dummy at this time is a set up for a later gag. Shot 333 shows the coach looking disgustedly at the tackle dummy which is minus one leg.

Six effective incidents are created when Harold replaces the tackle dummy. The first shows Harold pleased with the chance to get back into the practice session; he does not realize the lowly position he has been given—that of a tackle dummy. Harold takes his new role in great spirits and congratulates the first tackler who has bowled him over. His glorified concept of team spirit is comically exploited in this incident. Harold, clearly the butt of the aggression, substitutes a friendly smile and a handshake for the violent tackle he has received.

In the second incident of this part of the sequence, Harold once more congratulates a tackler for his efforts. Another tackler hits him as he makes a friendly gesture to the first. Unprepared for the jolt, Harold falls over into a somersault. A bit dazed, he struggles to his feet. The friendly smile of the comedian begins to fade. When the coach exclaims in Title 60, "This is no petting party! That's not half hard enough," a medium close-up of Harold discloses an amazed, pained, and puzzled expression on his face.

Harold is tackled with increasing violence. In the third incident,

Harold receives a high neck tackle. He goes spinning around and down. As in all comic falls, there is a broadness or overstatement of movement. Comedians in the 1910's and 1920's were adept in executing such falls. There is an almost ballet-like grace in the movement of the master pantomimist even when he executes a violent movement. No realistic fall is attempted; no pain in the fall can be noticed by the audience. The slapstick itself, for example, is an abstraction from reality. While it makes a great deal of noise, the audience never considers it a painful instrument that inflicts real injury on the comedian.

In the fourth incident, the coach demonstrates how *not* to tackle a man, by throwing a hammer lock on Harold's neck. The coach then throws Harold on the ground and jumps on him. "You see that didn't hurt me a bit!" declares the coach in Title 62 as Harold clutches his stomach in a comic show of pain. And in the following title the coach explains, "And besides, if you

The coach (played by Pat Harman) demonstrates, using hapless Harold, how not to tackle in **The Freshman**.

tackle high, they'll get you with the straight arm—now, watch me!"
The coach rolls up his sleeve, winds up his arm, and smashes
Harold in the face with his version of a straight arm. Harold flies
back and falls on his back on a slanting outside cellar door.

The above incident is one of the best examples of two contrasting attitudes being used to promote comedy. The physical
punishment dealt Harold nearly knocks him out. He is dazed and
horrified at each new blow to his frail body. The coach, on the
other hand, remains apathetic—oblivious to the strength of the
blows that he inflicts on Harold. The coach's cold-blooded de-
monstrations and his explanations best illustrate the supposition
that this whole sequence, in its calculated study of aggression and
violence, is poking fun at the sport of football. It cannot be said,
however, that the humor becomes satirical; there is light, burlesque treatment of this material.

In the coach's demonstration, the most elaborate of the six incidents of this film, Harold prepares for another illustration of
tackling techniques by placing a canvas on the slanting cellar door
to protect himself from another fall. Unfortunately, as he is tackled by the coach, one of the football assistants opens the cellar
door, and Harold rolls head over heels down the cellar steps into
the basement. The medium comes into play at this point and
shows the coach's tackle and Harold's roll in accelerated motion.
The action is thereby placed on the level of overstatement which
makes it comic.

In the fifth incident, Harold is once more tackled by members
of the team. A passage of time is indicated by a fade out of the
scene into:

379 MS Harold's shadow is shown on the sawdust. It indicates
that he is dazed and staggering after a long session of physical abuse. The shadow suddenly stiffens and readies for
another tackler. The camera pans slightly to catch a tackler
coming into view and hitting Harold, spilling him violently
into the sawdust. Harold struggles to get up.

This is an excellent example of an unusual shot employed in
this film. Since it conveys the information in a novel way, it en-
forces the point effectively. With this shot of Harold's shadow, the
audience realizes with greater impact the grueling punishment

Harold has undergone. It is a type of shot more often used in serious works.

The gag that follows this unusual shot provides one of the highest comic moments in the whole sequence:

380 LS Harold rises to his knees. He finally gets up, staggers, and reels like a drunken man. He falls flat on his back.
381 MS Harold starts to get up. He appears to have both legs extended as he rests on one knee. To the right and behind him

Shot 381 of **The Freshman** shows one of Lloyd's best gags used in the football practice sequence.

lies the dummy which has lost a leg. Harold's left leg seems to extend forward as if it were grotesquely twisted out of joint. Harold looks down at his leg, horrified at the sight. He grabs what he thinks is his leg and it is free, as if his leg has come off. Dazed, he sits back and pulls the left leg which is, in reality, safely bent under him. The loose leg before him is the dummy's leg which has previously been torn off in tackling practice. Relieved to find this out, Harold crawls off.

As Arthur Knight points out, the above incident illustrates the use of a particular angle whereby the shot may display the comedian's leg as if it were a "grotesquely broken leg."[9] This shot does even more than Knight indicates. The audience might share the comedian's interpretation if the camera angle did not also reveal the tackle dummy minus one leg in the background. This knowledge of the situation presents a much different type of humor from that presented by the use of the revealing technique which has been explained in chapter 3, "Exposition." The true nature of a situation is withheld in a revelation technique of achieving humor. The audience draws a false conclusion; a new shot or a pan to reveal the whole scene corrects this conclusion. This incident could be treated by the revelation of the tackle dummy in a follow-up shot or by a pan within shot 381. This method, however, was not employed in *The Freshman*. Part of the effectiveness and impact of the humor is achieved by the audience's knowledge of the situation and the comedian's incorrect assumption. The audience grasps the situation before the comedian does and laughs at his mistake.

The end of this series of six fast-moving incidents occurs when Harold crawls over to the coach, stands up, and then collapses in his arms, only to slide down the coach's body until he lies on the ground with his arms grasping the coach's ankles. The coach looks on apathetically. He calls an end to practice only because an assistant tells him it is time to quit.

This sixth and final incident uses humor and provokes sympathy at the same time. There is a comically grotesque stagger by the dazed comedian, but his childlike clutching of the coach, who has caused his misery, as he goes down to the ground, has an appeal to the sentiments of the audience. It is pantomime that could only be equaled by Charles Chaplin. It is one of the best touches of the sympathy-producing pantomime executed by Lloyd in the three films used in this study.

A short sequence following the football practice indicates that

9. Knight, p. 122.

the coach, under the urgings of Chet Trask, will allow Harold to be classified as water boy, but Harold will not know that he is not a member of the playing team. The aftereffects of the brutal mauling appear as Harold is shown being helped out of a cab by a cab driver. He is bent over and stiff from football practice. An upperclassman and his girl friend approach Harold and greet him. The upperclassman forces Harold to do his little jig and handshake. A comic variation on the jig results when the usually lively routine becomes a halting, staggering dance topped with Harold's weakly extended hand. As I have indicated, the jig and handshake have become a running gag by this time. This variation creates a fresh, humorous slant on the same material by interrupting a series of the same movements.

A final complication develops when Harold meets his girl friend, Peggy, and informs her that he has made the team. She has learned from the College Cad that Harold has not made the team. Harold Lamb, therefore, is placed in a more humiliating position than before. While he believes that he is on the first rung of the ladder to social success, he is actually lower than ever before, in the estimation of the forces that oppose him. In short, by the end of the mid-section of *The Freshman,* social acceptance is further from Harold's grasp than before.

A few generalizations can be drawn now in the treatment of the midpoint of the development of *Grandma's Boy, Safety Last,* and *The Freshman.* All three works show a marked increase in complication. The complication in *Grandma's Boy* is different from the complications in the other films because the turn of events at the end of this part of the story favors the Boy. He is given courage artificially and is on his way to prove himself a man. In both *Safety Last* and *The Freshman,* the comedian's bids for success have run up against strong opposition. At this point, in these two films, the future seems dim for the leading character.

Both *Grandma's Boy* and *The Freshman* incorporate one long sequence with a highly developed series of gag incidents in this portion of the story. *Safety Last* incorporates two sequences of major importance, one short and one long, with a series of rapid-fire gags. Structurally, *The Freshman* displays the strongest continuity at this point of the story. Each sequence combines effectively with the others. I find some fault in the extended treatment of the grandfather's struggle with the Union army in *Grandma's Boy.*

While a close examination of the scenario used in this study reveals that many of the attitudes and the exact words of the Boy are used by Grandma in her fabricated tale (thus tying the story with previous actions in the plot), the extent of the treatment may be questioned. Unity of an organic nature may also be pointed out as being developed when Grandpa employs some of the methods of combat that the Boy uses later in the plot. Nevertheless, Lloyd fully exploits the material in the flashback. It seems that he could not resist the temptation of extending his treatment. A degree of disproportion in relation to the main theme exists, therefore; the audience becomes absorbed in a seven-and-a-half-minute story concerning Grandpa.

This portion of the film clearly indicates a difference in the humor of the three works. This difference is closely tied to the characterization of the leading comic figure. *Grandma's Boy* displays a comic hero, Grandpa, engaged innocently in a war as if he were a child playing a game. This flashback sequence is permeated with the spirit of play rather than the spirit of invectiveness. On the other hand, the leading comedian in *The Freshman* is the butt of everyone's joke. He is the boob who is the object of laughter. The incompetence of Harold Lamb in *The Freshman* is also in sharp contrast with the comic ingenuity of Harold in *Safety Last*. This portion of *Safety Last* displays a greater use of comic ingenuity than has been witnessed in any part of Harold Lloyd's three works thus far analyzed.

Lloyd's use of two comic traditions shows an interesting switch in emphasis from the preliminary development of the films. The last chapter revealed that *Safety Last* incorporated broad visual comedy that was more inclined toward the spirit of the older slapstick tradition, but this portion of the film shows an about-face. Sequence X, "Harold's Dual Life," exhibits a genteel comedy which places more stress on verbal humor by incorporating a total of twenty-one titles, most of them humorous. There are few moments in this portion of the film that even suggest a use of the older tradition. *Grandma's Boy* and *The Freshman* also show a shift of emphasis following their prelimiary development. While the mild comedy of embarrassment was used formerly, broad, physical comedy is emphasized in the mid-portion of these films. The grandfather in *Grandma's Boy* engages in warfare against the Union army by hitting and kicking his enemy in a violent manner. In *The Freshman,* "Football Practice" (sequence VIII), the comic protagonist takes a deluge of physical punishment that outstrips the comic beatings of a Plautine farce or a *commedia dell' arte* sketch. In the mid-portion of the films, therefore, *Grandma's Boy* and *The Freshman* are more closely tied to the spirit of the one- and two-reel comedies of the 1910's, while *Safety Last* is more closely related to the genteel comedy of the early 1920's which featured Johnny Hines, Douglas MacLean, and Charles Ray. In each case, however, the emphasis is only temporary; a shift in emphasis will be detected throughout Lloyd's works.

Complications increase more rapidly from this point on as the difficulties and the trials of the leading comedian are woven more tightly into stronger actions in the plot line.

6

Development to the Crisis

In the latter part of the development of a dramatic work, there is generally stronger action and complication. There is a sharpness of conflict which leads to a crisis which requires the protagonist to take positive action. Such generalizations apply to the latter part of the development in Harold Lloyd's three comic films. The leading comic character in these works is forced into situations which make him take specific steps to solve the problem or problems confronting him.

Grandma's Boy

In the beginning of sequence XII of *Grandma's Boy,* a sequence which I have entitled "The New Man Goes to Battle," the leading character is shown transformed by his belief in the power of the talisman which Grandma gave him. He thinks that he will receive from the charm the necessary protection to accomplish heroic deeds. In pantomime, he practices his planned assault on the tramp. Before a wicker chair where he first saw the tramp, he tries out his new role:

340 LS The Boy comes out of the house and sees the wicker chair in which the tramp sat after he invaded Grandma's yard. The Boy picks up a cloth bag filled with hay and sets it on the wicker rocker. He retraces his steps and then approaches the chair boldly. He dramatically and sternly motions for the

127

"person" in the chair to leave. Then he hits the bag a heavy
blow with his fist, picks it up, and throws it away. With the
proud, strong strut of the victor, he walks off.

This pantomime is executed in the mood of play; it shows a
sharp reversal from the Boy's previous meekness to a boldness
that is similar to that of a child playing the role of an adult. Lloyd
executes this short pantomime and many of the later actions in
this sequence in a mock-heroic manner in order to achieve the
comedy.

After this trial display of courage, the Boy finds it necessary to
steal a plow horse from under the nose of an old farmer in
order to follow the posse in its pursuit of the tramp. Again a
mock-heroic pose is created as the Boy heads off an overloaded
car filled with members of the posse. Shots 350 through 352 are
photographed in accelerated motion to assist in making the spectacle of the Boy on the plow horse ludicrous. In an amazing feat
which harks back to the chase sequences in Mack Sennett's one-
reel films of the 1910's, the husky plow horse overtakes and passes
the automobile. Dressed in a suit and straw hat, the Boy presents a ludicrous figure as he rides ahead of the crowded car
brandishing a crooked stick as if he were a general leading an
army into battle.

Once the posse has arrived at its destination, the Boy tries to
lead the men in an attack on the cabin in which the tramp has
held off an earlier posse. While the men in the combined posses
are amazed at the Boy's behavior, they are not sufficiently stimulated by his newly found courage and gestures of leadership to
storm the cabin.

Realizing that he is alone in his venture, the Boy hesitates
briefly and then bravely heads for the cabin in a zigzag course
which he thinks will help him dodge the bullets from the tramp's
gun. He stops only momentarily when his hat is shot off. He picks
up his hat and proceeds once more toward the cabin. As this incident indicates, the hat of the comedian is his prize possession. He
will clutch it desperately in the face of hurricane, battle, and
flood. This is a standard comic gesture which was also used by
Charles Chaplin, Buster Keaton, and Harry Langdon. This action
results in incongruity. The comedian seems more concerned
about his hat than his life.

Lloyd's ingenuity in the use of humorous incident is evident in the handling of the Boy's approach to the cabin. A series of delaying actions by the comic hero produces new comic twists and increases the emotional tension of the incident. When the comic hero first steps toward the door behind which the tramp lurks with a log poised threateningly above his head, the Boy suddenly steps back to see if he still has his charm with him. This delays the outcome of the threatened action and promotes strong anticipation in the audience. The Boy's withdrawal proves a lucky move. He is out of range of the tramp for the moment.

Then the sheriff calls to the Boy, and the Boy takes a few more steps backward. When the Boy starts to tiptoe back to the door with more caution after a warning by the sheriff, a black cat crosses his path. Alarmed at seeing the cat, he takes a circular path around the front door to avoid the cat and thereby discovers a side door—a door which has a good-luck charm (a horse shoe) hanging over it. By entering through this door, the Boy has the advantage over the tramp who does not detect the Boy's change in approach.[1]

The Boy enters the cabin, slips handcuffs over the tramp's upraised arms, grabs the log from his hands, and hits him over the head, knocking him out. This sharp reversal of fortunes employs comic ingenuity by the leading comedian—that unusual way of accomplishing a feat which only the comic hero possesses. It is the first display of this type of behavior by the Boy in *Grandma's Boy*. Grandpa, in the flashback sequence, has, however, employed it extensively in his fight against the Union army.

The Boy calls to the posse, "Come on—nothing to fear—I GOT HIM!" in Title 51 of the film. But he does not realize that the brute has regained consciousness. The tramp breaks the handcuffs on his wrist as if they were made of string. His action is similar to that of the bully subdued by gas from a city street light in *Easy Street* (1917). This bully breaks his handcuffs when he regains consciousness as easily as the tramp in *Grandma's Boy*, but this Samson is an even more grotesque figure than the tramp.

As the Boy watches the tramp break the handcuffs, he is so amazed by the feat that he nearly forgets to escape. He moves, however, when the tramp lunges at him. He jumps up to a low-hanging beam on the ceiling of the cabin; the apelike rush of the tramp cannot be stopped; the brute hurls himself out the door in

---

1. The same type of intervening good luck, it will be remembered, assisted Grandpa in overcoming his enemies in the Civil War flashback sequence.

front of the posse. The tramp turns away from the posse as the whole group frantically scramble over each other to get into the automobile in order to chase him. At this point an elaborate chase sequence develops.

Robert Sherwood mentions the chase sequence as one of the most delightful portions of *Grandma's Boy*.[2] James Agee also mentions the chase sequence as one of his favorite episodes in the movie.[3] It is understandable that these two critics find the chase sequence more firmly impressed on their memory than the fight sequence in the climactic portion of the movie. While this fight is more important to the total design of the movie, it does not have the lively actions and the fresh twists of the chase material. Maurice Bardèche and Robert Brasillach, in their history of the movies, write of the comic chase in the twenties:

> The automobile chases especially, making use as they did of the rapid-motion photography, began to take on a grotesque quality which has delighted us since in many a Harold Lloyd and Buster Keaton picture. Part of the fun consisted in the fact that these films were a parody of the automobile chases—grimly serious, of course—in so many screen dramas of the day. Then fresh conceits were introduced every few minutes to tickle the audience and save the film from its own naiveté.[4]

Lloyd makes the most of the automobile chase material in *Grandma's Boy*. He does not make the mistake of incorporating the chase material without proper motivation. This mistake, as Béla Balázs points out, was made in the naive plotting of the early comedy films. "A human avalanche was let loose," he writes, "carrying everything before it in a senseless and purposeless rush."[5] Lloyd develops clear motivation for the chase after the tramp—a chase which may be divided into two parts or sequences according to content. One part features the Boy's attempt to join his fellow townsmen in an automobile during their frantic chase to catch the tramp; another part (or sequence) shows the Boy chasing the tramp in an automobile.

In an attempt to join the chase-bent crowd who have covered an open-top car like a swarm of bees, a spectacle reminiscent of the Keystone Cops' method of boarding a patrol wagon, the Boy

2. Sherwood, *The Best Motion Pictures of 1922-1923*, p. 11.
3. Agee, *Agee on Film*, p. 228.
4. Bardèche and Brasillach, *The History of the Motion Pictures* (New York, 1938), p. 83.
5. Balàzs, *Theory of the Film* (London, 1952), p. 26.

finds no place to stand on the car. With the same desperation that the comedian exhibits in his attempt to board a streetcar in an early sequence of *Safety Last,* the Boy grabs onto an old man standing on the runningboard of the automobile. As the car speeds away (in the much used accelerated motion of the chase sequence), the Boy is revealed clinging to the man's suspenders. While the suspenders stand the strain of his weight, the buttons which anchor the suspenders do not. Soon the front buttons give way from the pants, and the Boy is left hanging backwards until the back pair of buttons fly off. The old man is left with the dilemma of either saving his dignity or holding onto the car. It is a comic situation which is never resolved—the focus is shifted back to the Boy.

The Boy, unlike the Keystone Cop who has been thrown from an automobile only to dash back and jump in again, is unable to climb aboard. He grabs the rear of the car and runs with superhuman strides, only to be toppled and thrown into a violent roll which sends him crashing into the bushes where the tramp crouches in hiding.

This portion of the chase is developed in only eighteen shots and lasts only a few seconds over a minute (1:06). Accelerated motion, plus the action itself, gives it a lively pace. The treatment of the material is less broad than the early slapstick films. The tone and pace of the action change, however, as the Boy sadly watches the crowd of pursuers disappear in the dust, their car careening madly down the road. Not realizing that the Boy has joined him in the bushes, the tramp crawls out and shakes his fist at the car as it races out of sight. The young man clutches his good-luck charm fearfully. An idea strikes him. He presses the charm to the back of the tramp's neck as if it were a gun and forces him to march down the road to town.

Comic ingenuity, a type of humor which has been pointed out previously as highly important in Lloyd's works, comes fully into play when the Boy captures the tramp. The clever use of the charm works. However, when the young man decides that he has walked far enough and gets the tramp to pull him in a wheelbarrow, his cleverness backfires. The Boy tumbles out of the wheelbarrow when it hits a huge rut. The tramp takes advantage of this upset and runs off before the young man can get to his feet. This action is obviously a comic reversal. It prevents the use of comic ingenuity from becoming monotonous and gives the leading character more variety by showing that his cleverness is not infallible. The joke, this time, is at the Boy's expense.

Forced to pursue the tramp once more, the comedian runs up to a parked car and takes it without a word to the owner who has just gotten out of the automobile. This action is similar to the brash, brassy action the Boy takes in an earlier sequence when he commandeers a farmer's plow horse. It is the typical behavior of the man of action and contrasts sharply with the meek, mild character which has been established before the Boy's manliness is artificially stimulated.

Again the unusual cleverness of the comedian is shown when the Boy attempts to capture the tramp by driving after him in the car he has stolen. He attempts to lasso the tramp from the automobile. Steering with one hand and sitting on the top of the front seat of the car, the Boy twirls a rope above his head as a professional cowboy would do. But, once more his cleverness backfires. The rope misses the tramp and catches on a rural mailbox. Since the comedian has the rope tied about his waist, he is sent flying from the car with a violent jerk. Editing comes into operation in order to make this incident effective. With progressively shorter shots, from four seconds to one and a half seconds, the Boy is shown lassoing the mailbox instead of the tramp. This incident is accomplished in six shots which vary from long shots to medium shots to show the action and emphasize this comic reversal. The variety in the content of these shots, the movement, and the time of the shots assist in giving this incident vitality. It is one of the few moments in *Grandma's Boy* that show editing as a strong factor in achieving the comic.

One other moment in this part of the film depends greatly on editing to achieve comedy. After the foregoing incident, the Boy returns to the car from which he has been thrown and relentlessly pursues the running tramp. The tramp runs at a furious pace (through the use of accelerated motion); he finally tires and falls, thoroughly exhausted. The young man brings the tramp into town to show to everyone. The townspeople recoil in horror at the sight of the brute's snarl. Members of the crowd who first catch sight of the ugly tramp run around the corner of a building and peer around this corner fearfully a moment later. A duck is shown fleeing at the same time—and like the townspeople, it goes around the corner and peeks back at the tramp. The duck is presented in a direct relationship to the people by parallel actions and shots. The comedy of this "editor's joke"[6] is tinged with satire. The comment on the crowd is much stronger in this incident than in other scenes in *Safety Last* and *The Freshman* which also show the foolishness of mass reactions.[7] This incident depends on editing to create a comic comment on the reactions of man and duck.

At the end of the sequence, the Boy has tested himself and displayed courage. He now must prove himself by besting the Rival. The crisis develops when he finds it necessary to fight him. This complication shows a blending of the crisis and the climax. It will be described in chapter 7.

Safety Last

The sequences which precipitate the climactic sequence of *Safety Last* follow a different pattern from those of *Grandma's Boy* because of the marked different in plot and character development. The comic character in *Safety Last* does not need to test his courage like his counterpart in *Grandma's Boy,* nor does he need to "win friends and influence people" like the hero of *The Freshman* in order to be socially accepted. Harold in *Safety Last* must exercise his ingenuity to be a success in the business world. Preparation for a promotional stunt which will assist him in his goal is the main plot material employed by *Safety Last,* and complications of this part of the film lead to the crisis in the development because of his designs.

The sequences which lead to a crisis begin with Harold's tasks of recovering a purse which Mildred left in the General Manager's office. With comic anxiety, Harold stands before the boss's office door, afraid to enter. The scene is completely turned over to the actor. Lloyd executes a brilliant piece of pantomime out of simple material. The camera remains at a neutral, medium shot position as an interesting step-by-step study in comic anxiety is developed:

458 MS Harold starts to knock on the General Manager's door

6. Karel Reisz, *The Technique of Film Editing* (London, 1957), pp. 108-9. In this juxtaposition of two shots, which create the "editor's joke," the material in the shots need not be essentially comic.

7. Reactions of the crowd in the climactic sequence (see chapter 7) of both *Safety Last* and *The Freshman* have some satirical thrusts. The bargain-day sequence of *Safety Last* (see chapter 5) also contains this type of humor.

and, in a continuous motion of his hand, turns the direction of his knock into a grasp at his collar.

He returns to his task of entering once more. He moves his hand to the door but stops it short and hesitatingly touches the frame of the door rather than the door itself.

He screws up his courage and starts to knock. His hand swings in the air three times without hitting the door. He moves his hand up to the back of his head and down his face.

He steps back and gathers up his courage again with his fist poised in the air. His courage withers, and he puts his hands in his pockets and walks a few steps away from the door.

He hesitates; then he comes back to the door and strikes the determined pose of a fighter, with both hands extended. Both hands start to knock but end up only waving limply in the air. Harold nearly collapses from fright and leans against the door. The door opens from his weight. Horrified, he grabs it to keep it from opening any farther.

This incident is a brilliant tour de force. The pantomime is executed with a skill that shows why Harold Lloyd found a place in the sun beside the strong competition of the master pantomimist, Charles Chaplin. His routine is interestingly developed by a variation on one action which builds up to sharp reversals. Comedian Harold Lloyd shows his comic character exerting a great deal of effort which ends up in inactivity. It is a comic situation which Arthur Koestler describes as typical of the clown's accomplishments. "The mountain labored, the birth was a mouse," is the figurative saying which Koestler uses to explain the nature of this type of comedy. "The clown," Koestler continues, "is a man of gigantic effort and diminutive accomplishments."[8]

While the clown, Harold, in this situation does not achieve a simple goal of knocking on the door, he overhears his boss declare, "I'd give a thousand dollars to anyone for a New Idea—one that would attract an enormous crowd to our store" (Title 58). This statement from the General Manager prompts Harold to recall Bill's unusual feat of escaping a policeman by climbing up a building.[9] With only a moment's reflection, Harold barges into

8. Koestler, *Insight and Outlook* (New York, 1949), p. 87. It should also be pointed out that the opposite effect may also be produced by the clown. Laurel and Hardy often turned a minor altercation into mob warfare in such works as *Two Tars, You're Darn Tootin'*, and *Battle of the Century*, two-reel films produced by Hal Roach in 1928.

9. The medium assists at this point by dissolving into this former scene and back again to show Harold's thoughts.

the office and declares that he will draw a crowd to the store. The boss, started by his determination and honesty, gives Harold a chance to use his scheme without knowing clearly what it entails.

Harold leaves the office and makes arrangements with Bill to climb the Bolton Building, a building which houses the De Vore Department Store, for a promotional stunt. In title 65 Harold declares to Mildred, "Darling, dreams do come true. We'll be married tomorrow." This portion of the sequence may be termed transitional. Story material is placed directly before the audience without elaborate gag situations. Exposition sets up the situation for a new sequence.

The policeman, whom Bill has offended earlier in the film story, is once more introduced in sequence XII. A comic drunk is introduced at this point also, the only time a comic drunk is used in the three films being studied.[10] The drunk looks in a newspaper at a photograph of a "mystery man" with his face blanked out. The "mystery man," according to the paper, is to climb the Bolton Building. To Bill's antagonist, the policeman, the drunk laughs and points to the photograph and remarks, "Look! Thish guy ain't got any face. They mustta run outta ink."[11] By a superimposition which dissolves Bill's face in and out on the blank face of the newspaper's "mystery man" photograph, the medium indicates the policeman's mental attempts to link the "mystery man" with the man who escaped him by climbing a building.

In the opening of the sequence that follows, sequence XIII, "More Trouble with the Law," the policeman stands by a sign, waiting for Bill to arrive. The sign in shot 510 reads, "Watch the Mystery Man Climb This Building at 2 P.M. Today." In mock imitation of the policeman, the drunk stands next to the officer with folded arms and a determined countenance.

Exposition blends into the execution of some strong comic material. Harold and Bill see the policeman and realize that their plans may be thwarted. Harold tries a series of tricks to distract the policeman from his vigil. He first tries a simple, non-comic way of drawing the policeman around the corner. He merely speaks to the policeman pleasantly and motions to him to come

10. In 1920, in *High and Dizzy*, a two-reel progenitor of *Safety Last* that was directed by Hal Roach, comic drunkenness is fully exploited. Harold Lloyd as a character simply called "The Boy" and "His Friend" get drunk on homemade liquor early in the film and become involved in many altercations with people in the street and in a hotel. Consequently, Lloyd's comic character is quite different in this work from those presented in the three films of this study.

11. Title 70. The attempt to capture the faulty articulation of a drunk is employed throughout the following sequences and into the climactic sequence.

with him. The policeman remains riveted to the spot. Next, Harold tries a more complicated means of moving the policeman from his post. He feigns horror, grabs the policeman, and points to a shack used by a construction crew across the street. He hurries the policeman toward the shack. Here a clever comic reversal develops which is created partly by the medium and partly by the staging of the incident:

526   MLS   Harold and the policeman pause before the door of the shack. The policeman goes into the shed, and Harold hurriedly locks the door. (The camera pans to the other side of the shack which has not been revealed until this time, showing another door which is open.) The officer walks out this door with a puzzled expression on his face. Unaware that the policeman has walked out of the shack and is eyeing him with suspicion, Harold takes off his hat and mops his neck with a handkerchief. Much relieved, Harold moves off, not realizing that the policeman is right behind him.

Once more a revealing technique is employed to produce a sharp, humorous reversal of a situation. The medium continues to assist in creating comedy immediately after this incident. In shot 527, a travel shot with Harold walking toward the camera, the policeman is shown walking behind Harold, eyeing him suspiciously. Harold looks down as he walks. The camera shows what Harold sees as he looks down; it reveals the shadows of two men walking—one of them swinging a billy club in his hand. Shot 529 returns to the same angle and travel shot as shot 527. Without looking back, Harold twists his mouth into a nervous, worried grimace. This expression can easily be interpreted in this medium shot. It shows the way in which slight facial movements are captured in the motion picture medium. The execution of this grimace is comic because it is a sharp reversal from the self-satisfied smile which Harold had before. His trick has backfired and he is in greater trouble than previously.

Realizing he is in trouble, Harold manages an ingenious escape. Once more the position of the camera is functionally effective and assists in the comic situation. From the view of the policeman, Harold is seen crossing the street. A car passes between the policeman and Harold. The pursued man seems suddenly to disappear as if by magic. The following shot, shot 531, explains this illusion by a reverse angle of the previous shot. Harold is shown squatting and clinging to the runningboard of the car which passed between the policeman and himself.

Not satisfied with this display of comic ingenuity, Lloyd tops this gag when the car comes to a halt by a street construction project. In his squatting position on the runningboard, Harold gets burned by a blowtorch in the seat of the pants as the car comes to a stop. With pain and indignation, Harold gets off the running-board, turns the blowtorch around so that a construction worker, bent over his work, receives the same embarrassing injury as Harold. By the time the worker can look around, Harold is gone. The worker looks at the position of the blowtorch with a puzzled expression.

This type of humor—the assault on the human posterior and, consequently, human dignity—is as old as the comic drama itself. The satirical fantasies of Aristophanes, the farces of Plautus, and the improvised works of the *commedia dell' arte* used this type of impropriety extensively. The one- and two-reel comic films of the 1910's employed it often. Lloyd does not often use this type of humor in his feature-length works. This incident, however, is indicative of the fact that early comic devices continued to be used in the film comedies of the twenties.

Unfortunately, Lloyd continues along this same line after he has treated material of this nature effectively. Harold tries one more device, a practical joke, to get rid of the policeman. With chalk he writes "Kick Me" backwards on the side of the Bolton Building at a height which would transfer the inscription onto the back of someone who leans against the building. As the policeman tries to get the drunk to go home, he comes near the inscription. Harold pretends to lose his balance as he ties his shoelace and pushes the policeman against the wall. The inscription "Kick Me" is passed onto the policeman's back; the drunk sees the sign and kicks him. Angrily, the policeman leads the drunk away. Harold laughs heartily at his accomplishment and accidentally leans back against the building. Caught in his own practical joke, Harold receives a kick from a passing paper boy.

The use of a practical joke to achieve humor is another example of the persistence of more primitive forms that were used extensively by Sennett, Chaplin, and Lloyd in the 1910's. Even though this type of humor is well motivated in this incident and employs the addition of a comic reversal, the incident is not as ingenious as other comic incidents in the film. It may be considered one of the weakest moments in this work.

Harold's efforts to get the policeman away from the building to keep him from detecting Bill are fruitless. Once more the policeman sets up his vigil. Bill tells Harold in Title 74, "There's only one way out. You climb to the second floor, an' duck through the window. Then I'll put on your coat an' hat, an' go the rest of the way. They'll never know the difference." Reluctantly, Harold accepts Bill's plan. Harold has reached the "point of no return"—the crisis of his career. He must take over the role of human fly or lose his chance for success.

This portion of the film is linked with the following sequence, the climactic sequence. A great deal of time is taken to build the situation up to this crisis in which Harold is forced to climb the Bolton Building.

The Freshman

The sequences precipitating the climactic sequence in Lloyd's *The Freshman* are less clearly linked to the plot development than are the corresponding sequences of *Grandma's Boy* and *Safety Last*. This does not mean, however, that these sequences in *The Freshman* are not linked to the central idea of the film. Harold Lamb's desire for social recognition promotes the action of this portion of the work. In the sequence which will now be analyzed, realization of his failure at the Fall Frolic promotes a final decision by Harold to try his best in a football game. Linkage between sequences seems weaker in this portion of the film because it is based more on character than on plot complication. By this point in *Grandma's Boy*, the Boy is chasing a tramp to test his courage, and in *Safety Last*, Harold is trying to institute a promotional stunt. Harold's actions at the Fall Frolic in *The Freshman* are indirect, and his goal is not without realization. He is forced into the position of preserving his dignity, so that he is not furthering his social position but trying merely to preserve what he has—which is very small indeed.

Despite their lack of direct action, the sequences which lead to the climactic sequence are replete with successful comedy. The opening sequence, sequence XI, establishes the comic tone immediately. As host of the Fall Frolic, Harold wants to make an impression with a new tuxedo. Title 75 reads, "The host—how he hoped to look for $38.50." This is followed by a drawing of a handsome man in a rigid, debonair pose, wearing a neat, well-fitted tuxedo. This picture of an advertisement (shot 437) is dissolved into a shot of Harold in the same pose dressed in a sweater and slacks as a tailor measures him for a suit. The result of these two contrasting pictures is risible because of Harold's previously established naiveté and his pretensions.

Since Harold is in a hurry to get to the Fall Frolic, the tailor has time only to baste the suit. It is also established that the tailor has dizzy spells which can be cured by a drink of whiskey or brandy. To avoid any mishap, the tailor, with thread and needle in hand, accompanies Harold to the party.

As he arrives at the party, walking stiffly to avoid ripping the suit, Harold has his first accident with the suit. A series of accidents follow in sequence XIII, "At the Fall Frolic," each one more complicated and more comic than the preceding one.

As Harold enters a crowded ballroom in the Tate Hotel, he is hailed by his fellow students from Tate College. Harold raises his arm to return the welcome and a rip appears under his arm. He smiles weakly when he realizes the nature of the mishap and lowers his arm. The embarrassed smile, as this study indicates, is one of Lloyd's best comic assets. This incident and incidents which follow capitalize on Lloyd's effective facial reactions to his many mishaps. The editor uses many reaction shots of Lloyd to emphasize the comedy.

This first mishap is the beginning of what Henri Bergson described as the "snowball effect" of many comic episodes.[12] The "snowball" of accidents continues as Harold sees his date waving at him. He takes a handkerchief from his coat pocket to wave to her, and the pocket comes off with the handkerchief. After waving, Harold tries to place the handkerchief in the pocket near his lapel and discovers that the pocket material has fallen on the floor. A close-up (shot 477) reveals the material at his feet. With one foot Harold lifts the edge of a rug and shoves the material under it to avoid embarrassment. Then Harold tries to insert the handkerchief in the side pocket of his suit, but again the basted material gives, and the handkerchief appears through the bottom

12. Bergson, p. 112. One incident promotes another in cumulative fashion. Like a rolling snowball, the comedy grows.

of the pocket. He finally succeeds in finding a place for the handkerchief in his pants pocket. The mishap is, of course, minor. But as the sequence progresses, accidents with the suit become increasingly critical and cause greater embarrassment to the comedian.

Another comic incident follows immediately and shows the audience that even greater trouble is in store for the hapless young man. Harold places his thumbs at the edge of the tuxedo's vest to survey the party at which he is host. This dignified gesture is cut short when the whole front of his vest folds down and forward. Frantically, Harold grasps the vest front and tucks it behind the lapels of the coat, tugging at the lapels to hold the vest in place. A quick cut (a reverse angle shot) to the back of Harold's coat reveals the result of his action. A large rip runs up the middle of the coat. Then a cut to a close-up of Harold's face (shot 480) reveals a horrified reaction which is an excellent example of a "comic take"—an overstated emotional reaction. Lloyd begins to execute even broader "takes" as his difficulties and embarrassment mount.

As in the previous incident, editing is functionally effective. It shows the necessary details of the mishap and emphasizes the emotional reactions of the comedian to the mishap.

The tailor, who has been following Harold by ducking around corners and hiding behind potted palms, comes to his rescue from a concealed position and sews up the rip in the back of the coat. In this way, the third accident with the basted suit is resolved by temporary repairs.

A greater hazard, however, immediately confronts Harold when his flighty date pulls him onto the dance floor. The tailor now hides in a curtained alcove with a service bell in case any part of Harold's garment should fall apart. Harold registers extreme frustration when a service bell is rung from one of the tables at the edge of the dance floor. As his girl friend breaks away and dances in a solo routine—an improvised dance with much hip and shoulder movement—Harold also executes a solo dance and looks himself over for rips as he dances. The parallel movements of the girl and the comedian are especially effective because the comedian looks himself over in time to the dance. Comic ingenuity, a trademark in Lloyd's work, comes into play. This incident (the fourth in this series) is concluded when the tailor signals Harold that he is not the one ringing the bell.

The fifth accident actually develops into a series of incidents because it elaborates on one accident with detail. Harold and his

In the party sequence of **The Freshman,** the tailor (Joseph Harrington) sews up Harold's coat from a concealed position.

flighty companion stop dancing, and Harold withdraws his hand from her waist. As he does, his suit sleeve catches on the ornamentation at the back of her dress and pulls off. Clapping for the orchestra, Harold is unaware of his accident. The tailor in the alcove is then revealed hitting the service bell vehemently. A cutback to Harold in shot 514 shows him still clapping, not realizing his predicament. Only after the dance floor is cleared and Harold leans on a pole near the bandstand, does he see his sleeveless arm. The execution of this discovery helps create the comedy. As the comedian surveys his party with a proud smile, he nonchalantly looks down and sees his sleeve. A violent, startled expression (a "comic take") replaces the casual air which he had before. The preceding incident which was a false alarm has given him confidence which is now erased.

Feigning nonchalance, Harold goes after the girl to unfasten his

A casual expression of nonchalance soon to be erased by seeing the lost sleeve in **The Freshman.**

The "comic take" of horror that follows—see previous photo.

sleeve from the back of her waist after he has substituted a black cloth trombone cover for his sleeveless arm. The cloth encasement, however, has only one opening, and his hand is necessarily enclosed in the covered end. With a forced calmness, Harold pursues the giddy girl as she wanders through the crowd showing people a clown doll which has been given to her by an admirer. After several attempts to loosen the sleeve from the girl's dress, Harold sees his opportunity to get it when a group of college students circle about her looking at the doll. Harold yanks the sleeve from the dress and runs off. Indignantly, the flighty girl turns to the man standing closest to her, the College Cad, and slaps him. The College Cad stands startled, his cheek smarting, as the offended young lady walks away angrily. The butt of this gag, interestingly enough, is Harold's adversary. He is the victim of two other gags in this sequence. While Harold has received punishment from the College Cad in previous sequences, the tables are now turned for the moment.

This incident concludes the comic elaboration on the accidental loss of Harold's coat sleeve. Lloyd, however, blends this situation into another series of incidents. Harold is stopped by a young couple as he goes to the curtained alcove to have his sleeve repaired. He is forced to present his unusual college greeting. He executes his little jig and extends his hand which is still covered with the trombone cloth. Harold quickly retracts his arm. An elaborate gag is then set up when shot 525 shows the tailor in the curtained alcove taking the cover from Harold's arm and sticking his arm out through the curtain to substitute for Harold's. Harold repeats his jig and appears to extend his hand to shake hands with the girl. It is, as shot 525 indicates, the tailor's hand.[13]

The incident which follows elaborates on this unusual comic routine. The College Cad comes to Harold and asks, "Speedy, old pal, can you let me have ten dollars?" (Title 85). The description of the following shot indicates the unusual nature of this comic routine:

529 MS Harold appears to scratch his head with his right hand. In reality, it is the tailor's hand. A slight upward shift of

13. Theodore Huff (in *Charlie Chaplin*, p. 96) points out that Lloyd's use of this routine was like Chaplin's "puppet sequence" in *A Dog's Life* (1918) when Charlie, from behind a curtain, deftly manipulates the hands of a knocked-out crook in order to deceive the second crook who does not realize that his colleague in crime is unconscious.

Harold's eyes to see the hand scratching his head reveals the
true nature of the action. The hand from the curtain behind
Harold moves down into his pocket, and brings out a ten-
dollar bill. The Cad takes it, stuffs the bill in his vest pocket,
and pats Harold's shoulder in appreciation. The tailor's arm,
substituting for Harold's arm, pats the Cad's shoulder. At
this moment, unknown to the Cad, Harold's sleeveless arm
comes from behind the curtain and takes the bill from the
Cad's vest pocket. The Cad leaves as Harold turns to enter
the alcove.

This routine displays an unusual type of comic ingenuity on the
part of the tailor and Harold. It places the sixth series of incidents on a high level. As Theodore Huff indicates, the routine
may have originated in the routines of circus clowning.[14] It is a
type of comic pantomime that demands a deftness and exaggeration of movement. The substitute arm, hand and fingers move in
a way that is not normal and, consequently, in a comic way. The
routine adds variety by presenting a type of pantomime seldom
used in the motion pictures.

Harold once more meets his date, a light-headed young lady
who is always urging him to dance. Nervously, Harold protests
and absent-mindedly pulls a thread on the seam of his trousers.
The whole side of Harold's pants leg splits open from the knee
down to the end of the trousers. To cover up this accident,
Harold urges his girl friend to sit down at a table next to the alcove. A cut-away shot (shot 544) reveals Harold's position as he
"sits down." Harold places his leg through the curtain of the alcove so that the seam may be repaired, and he rests his elbows on
the table to appear as if he were sitting in a chair. As the tailor
experiences a dizzy spell (an affliction which was established in
the previous sequence), his hand slips and sticks the needle into
Harold's leg.

Shot 548 reveals Harold reacting to the prick of the needle. He
yells in pain, but quickly covers it up with a strained laugh and a
finger pointed to the water in a glass before him, as if it were the
offender. Once more the tailor, in his faint condition, jabs
Harold's leg. This time Harold yells painfully in a wolflike howl,
but he cuts the howl short, in his concern with maintaining social

14. *Ibid.*

grace, with a quick, forced smile. Then, he grabs his tie as if it were choking him. Once more the comic character is shown trying to maintain his dignity at all cost. Harold's desire to maintain social grace is a key to the comedy of this whole sequence. He pretends that all is well even under the most distressing conditions.

A recent work by the skilled French comedian, Jacques Tati, *My Uncle* (1958), shows the leading comedian at a garden party. He accidentally punctures a pipe leading to a fountain and, by many manipulations, attempts to cover up the stream of water from the ground without being discovered. This type of material is, therefore, still important in the modern comic film. Jacques Tati uses "sight gags" (visual comedy) extensively; he uses some of the same material as the silent-screen comedians used.

The final complication of this ninth series of incidents is culminated when the tailor faints and collapses on Harold's leg. According to Arthur Knight, this develops "the finest gag of the picture" by the "skillful placement of the camera."[15] Knight describes the results of this incident:

> Harold sits at the table with his girl, his chin resting on his hands, his legs extending out to the tailor behind him. But the tailor is subject to sinking spells, and chooses just this moment to faint dead away across Harold's legs. The camera moves around front to show Harold sinking lower at the table, still chatting, still smiling and desperately pretending that it is all the most natural thing in the world.[16]

As Knight's description indicates, the camera assists greatly in the emphasis of this comic incident. Also his description indicates the extent to Harold's obsession to maintain his dignity.

Harold gets out of this situation and finds a flask of brandy to revive the tailor. No sooner has he revived him than an accident befalls Harold that is beyond the scope of the tailor's needle. The back buttons on Harold's suspenders give way. Forced by his giddy date to dance, Harold finds that his plight becomes more distressing:

596 MS Harold's date pulls one of his arms as she forces him into a fast dance. He reaches back for his pants and the girl grabs the arm he is using to hold up his pants. Harold finally gets her to look at someone across the dance floor while he frees both arms in a desperate effort to keep his pants from falling.

15. Knight, p. 122.
16. *Ibid.*

597 CU With both hands Harold twists his suspenders and tries to tie them to a fold in the back of his pants.

598 CU The strain from the tying is too great—the front suspender buttons fly off.

599 MCU Harold's eyes pop in horror as he realizes what has happened.

These four shots, in combination, illustrate the way editing can effectively create a comic situation by emphasizing all the details of the incident. Harold's frustration is emphasized by the close-up of his horrified expression in shot 599.

As Harold struggles to hold up his pants, his loose suspenders catch on the legs of a girl dancing by. Feeling the snap of the suspenders against her legs, the girl, with a horrified expression, stoops to gather what she thinks is her garter belt under her dress and makes a hasty exit.

Harold sees her action and is crestfallen. He realizes that he cannot recover his suspenders, and in desperation, he dances with his girl to a table, grabs a fork, and attempts to pin his pants to his shirt tail with a fork. Unfortunately, he pins a tablecloth to his pants in his efforts. The tablecloth is pulled onto the floor and dragged behind him as he dances with his date. A high angle, long-shot (shot 610) emphasizes his plight and reveals many dancing couples stopping to view the tablecloth dragging behind Harold. A waiter gathers up the glasses and plates which have fallen to the floor as Harold moved off with the tablecloth, and he also pulls the tablecloth from Harold. As he does so, he takes the back part of Harold's pants. Harold is puzzled by the reaction of the people who stare at him because the front part of his pants still remain intact. He turns around and sees the back part of his pants being dragged along with the tablecloth by the waiter. At that moment, the front part of his pants falls, and Harold is left in formal attire from the waist up—only his striped underpants, stockings, and shoes cover the lower part of his body. Frantically he runs toward the door of the ballroom, a ridiculous-looking figure as he wildly jumps over a table to get out of the ballroom as fast as he can.

The crowning gag of the whole sequence is an old gag which even at this time was a cliché. When a comedian desired a laugh in vaudeville, all he needed to do was lose his pants. The resulting loss of dignity and embarrassment provokes laughter. The more dignified the comic character portrayed, and the more dignified

Shot 610 shows Harold losing his pants as the final gag of the party sequence of **The Freshman.**

the dress, the bigger the laugh.[17] This old gag, however, has been calculatedly developed and motivated so that it presents a fresh version, using old material, in *The Freshman*. Even today, an observer of the film can see a great deal of sophistication in the building and execution of this old comedy device.

It should be noted at this time that even Lloyd thought this type of material was too hoary with age and use. To him it was a form of low comedy which he had abandoned when he left the Lonesome Luke series in 1917. "The easiest laugh in the world is to rob a man of his pants in public," Lloyd wrote, "so easy that we were above it."[18] After previewing the picture, Lloyd and his staff

17. This is not meant to be a formula, although this relationship exists. The reaction of the comedian to the embarrassing situation is, of course, a strong factor.
18. Lloyd, *An American Comedy,* p. 174.

discovered that they could not merely unravel his coat and produce laughter. "At each preview," Lloyd wrote, "the audience demonstrated that it was looking forward eagerly to the pants following the coat, and, when they did not, made its disappointment so manifest that, after the lapse of a month, we had to redress the set, call back the cast, including many extras in the ballroom scene, and unravel the trousers."[19]

The results Lloyd and his staff achieved in using this ancient material must not be deprecated. The ingenuity in developing this final gag of the sequence comes from fertile minds. In the same year *The Freshman* was released, Chaplin was toying with this same material; he used the threat of his leading comic figure's pants falling in *The Gold Rush*. This situation occurred, interestingly enough, when the little tramp was dancing with a girl.

The following sequence, sequence XIV, leads up to the climactic sequence. After Harold has grabbed a pair of pants from a bellboy in the hotel, he catches the College Cad making passes at his girl friend, Peggy, who is working at the hotel counter. Harold knocks the cad down. Angrily rubbing his jaw, the College Cad tells Harold what people really think of him: "You think you're a regular fellow—why you're nothing but the college boob!" (Title 88). At first Harold is crushed by this revelation, but through the encouragement of his girl friend Peggy, he resolves to put up a good fight in a football game to show the college crowd his true mettle.

Although this scene is necessary to the plot development, its use of serious emotion is strained. Lloyd attempts to touch his portrait of Harold Lamb with the so-called pathos which Chaplin used in his feature works. Robert Sherwood finds this incident too heavily handled, especially when the temporarily crushed Harold Lamb weeps.[20] I concur with Sherwood in this view. Lloyd's attempts at sentiment go awry in this brief scene. It is one of the few moments in the film when the comedian does not handle his material effectively.

The revelation by the College Cad provides the "point of no return" for Harold. He must take action to counter the attitude which the college set has toward him. This crisis departs from the

19. *Ibid.,* p. 175. Buster Keaton also previewed his works and found that he could not disappoint the audience. In his attempt to refurbish an old gag in *The High Sign* (1921), he had his comic character miss slipping on a banana peel on a sidewalk. Keaton detected audience disappointment in this version of the gag and reshot the scene, adding a second banana peel which tripped up his comic character. (*My Wonderful World of Slapstick,* p. 134.)

20. Sherwood, "The Silent Drama," *Life* 58 (October 15, 1925): 24.

predominantly visual crises of *Grandma's Boy* and *Safety Last.* While visual reactions of Harold and Peggy are important, a great deal of the content is conveyed by verbal means. This verbal crisis is a short sequence which builds to a high point of the crisis without direct assistance from a previous part of the film. The previous sequence in the ballroom is not strongly linked to this crisis.

This unusual treatment of the crisis in *The Freshman* leads this study into several generalizations on the handling of this portion of the plot development in the three films. A great deal of time is taken in *Safety Last's* sequence XIII, "More Trouble with the Law," to prepare and build a crisis. This film has strength in its clarity of direction at this point of the story development. *Grandma's Boy* and *The Freshman,* on the other hand, do not spend time building to a crisis. As it has been explained, a short sequence is used in *The Freshman* to create the crisis. The sequence is used solely to develop the crisis. *Grandma's Boy* blends the crisis and climax into one sequence. The longest sequences which are the core of this part of the film in *Grandma's Boy* and *The Freshman* seem set apart from the crisis. The sequence in *Grandma's Boy* which shows Harold chasing and capturing the tramp, and the sequence in *The Freshman* which shows Harold's difficulties with a basted suit at the Fall Frolic directly precede but do not directly link with the crisis.

This part of each work is important to the total film, however, for it remains linked with the central idea. The coherence of the works may suffer from the lack of direct connection between sequences, but this weakness does not destroy the overall unity of the works. Many film stories with episodic structure may achieve unity by their link with a strong central idea. Siegfried Kracauer has overgeneralized when he writes, "Such stories as the silent film comedy advances have merely the function of interrelating somehow their gags or monad-like units of gags. What matters is that the units follow each other uninterruptedly not that their succession implements a plot. To be sure, they frequently happen to develop into a halfway plausible intrigue, yet the intrigue is never of so exacting a nature that its significance would enroach on that of the pieces composing it."[21] While the structure of many silent film comedies is loose, Kracauer's generalization cannot be applied to Lloyd's three films. An overall design can be seen to be

21. Kracauer, p. 253.

at work. A central comic idea produces unity in each of these three works.

While each work calls upon the medium to assist in creating the comedy, particularly in this portion of the film, the elaborate routines of the comedian in the early portions of *Safety Last* and *Grandma's Boy* illustrate the importance of the leading comedian. *The Freshman* is especially effective in the development of comedy through editing, but the comedian always remains the principal creator of the comedy. His execution of reactions in the close-ups and his broad bodily actions are essential to the comedy of the Fall Frolic sequence. The camera and editing assist him.

In Lloyd's three films, variety in achieving humor is maintained in this portion which leads to a crisis. The chase sequence of *Grandma's Boy* employs exaggerated action through the use of accelerated motion. Working with this device is the use of comic ingenuity which backfires, thus creating a comic reversal of many of the comedian's attempts to catch the tramp. Comic ingenuity which backfires is also an important comic device in *Safety Last* when Harold tries to lure the policeman from his post by deception. Occasionally, comic ingenuity is employed in the Fall Frolic scenes of *The Freshman,* but extensive use of this character facet would not fit the character of Harold Lamb. In the early part of this sequence in the work, much of the humor is achieved by the comedian's attempt to cover up the many minor mishaps with his suit; his struggle to avoid detection involves the expenditure of a great deal of effort over minor problems with minimal results. As the embarrassments become greater, the type of humor turns to a form of degradation.[22] Harold's mishaps with his basted suit soon provide a form of comic humiliation which is stronger than the type of comedy James Agee calls the "comedy of embarassment."[23] The peak of this comic degradation occurs when Harold loses his pants; it is a debasing situation which is obviously too humiliating to be categorized under the "comedy of embarrassment."

The presentation of comic material which shows a link with the slapstick comedy and the genteel comedy traditions is also evident in this portion of the films. A change of emphasis from the midpoint of the development can be observed. In the development

22. This term (often used to indicate an Aristotelian definition of comedy) may be used to refer to humor which is obtained by inflicting some impropriety on a person.
23. Agee, p. 11.

toward a crisis, it may be expected that more and more lively slapstick material will be used. However, the main comedy sequence of *The Freshman,* sequence XIII, "At the Fall Frolic," shows an interesting blend of the two traditions. Much of the comedy which is derived from the comic character's desire to retain his dignity at all cost, fits into the genteel comedy tradition. The minor problems which Harold experiences with his basted suit are similar to the problems which the Boy in *Grandma's Boy* has when his finger gets stuck in a vase while visiting his girl friend, an incident which occurs in the preliminary development of the work. However, these embarrassments at the Fall Frolic eventually lead to humiliation and to an older form of humor. They culminate in the comedian's loss of his pants—a gag that was stock in trade for the comedians of vaudeville.

Both *Grandma's Boy* and *Safety Last* are more closely linked with the older tradition even though they have elements of the genteel tradition in this portion of the films. *Grandma's Boy* demonstrates an obvious link with the one- and two-reel comedies by using chase material. Lloyd has, however, sophisticated his chase sequence in this work. This chase does not deal in the general mayhem of many of the early chases by the Keystone Cops. The comic hero engages in a hectic and concentrated effort to capture the tramp by all means at his disposal. The chase is placed in a more realistic framework—the implausible is not the main ingredient used to achieve humor as it was in the early Mack Sennett films. *Safety Last* draws upon a primitive form of humor—the assault on the human posterior. Lloyd uses the old practical joke whereby one places a sign on another person's back reading "Kick Me." Though this use of a timeworn joke lags in invention, Lloyd fully refurbishes it when Harold, squatting on a runningboard of an automobile to escape a policeman, gets burned on the rump by a blowtorch. *Safety Last,* it is interesting to note, clearly alters its type of comedy from that employed in the previous portion of the movie, the midpoint of the development. In this last section, Harold's clever deception to make his girl friend believe that he is a boss rather than lowly clerk in a department store, follows more closely the genteel tradition.

From the point of decision, the crisis, we now move to one of the most interesting portions of the comic film—the climax. In each of Lloyd's three films, the climax is handled in a single, exciting, gag-filled sequence.

7

The Climactic Sequence

In 1914 Mack Sennett took a giant step by producing and directing a feature-length comedy, *Tillie's Punctured Romance.* This work, starring Charles Chaplin and Marie Dressler, employed many scenes of delightful comic violence which had been the forte of Sennett's one- and two-reel motion pictures in the formative age of the comic film. One elaborate sequence toward the end of this motion picture depicted the Keystone Cops engaged in a frantic rush to arrest violators of the law. It is a lively, exciting part of the film—it is a sequence which shows the comedy chase at its best. Just as this early feature-length work employed an action-filled final sequence, so did many comic features of the twenties use a climactic sequence with excitement and thrills in it.

Grandma's Boy

Having exploited and refurbished traditional chase material in the sequences which lead up to the crisis of *Grandma's Boy,* Lloyd uses a fight for the climax of the work. Robert Sherwood does not mention this fight between the Boy and the Rival in his résumé of the plot; instead he tells of the chase sequence and dismisses the triangle situation by writing, "His final conquest, of course, was the girl."[1] James Agee also lauds the chase sequence in this film and fails to mention the fight sequence.[2] Both critics were evi-

1. Sherwood, *The Best Moving Pictures . . .,* p. 11.
2. Agee, p. 228.

dently captivated by the well-conceived and well-executed chase material used in *Grandma's Boy*. It is, of course, necessary that this study investigate every portion of Lloyd's three works. The fight sequence, while it does not have the appeal of the chase sequence, will be described and analyzed.

At the beginning of this climactic sequence in *Grandma's Boy*, a hint of a forthcoming clash is achieved by the first four shots (shots 479-482). A possible conflict is indicated by the screen direction of the walk of the Boy and the Rival. They are shown moving toward each other progressively in shots 479, 480, and 481.[3] Then shot 482 shows them meeting face to face. The Rival provokes the fight by pulling off the Boy's tie in a manner similar to his taunting action at the beginning of the story. The Boy calmly takes off his coat and lays it down; he places a chip of wood on his shoulder and dares the Rival to knock it off. Instead of hitting the chip, the Rival hits the Boy squarely on the jaw with his fist. This action by the Rival produces the first strong gag of the sequence. It features the surprise twist which is often found in comedy. The startled reaction of the Boy as he is bowled over by the Rival's punch also helps create the comedy. The Boy is amazed to find out that his magic charm has not protected him.

When Grandma arrives at the scene of the fight, she gets caught up in the contest. Empathetically stirred into action, she urges the Boy on by shadowboxing. Her aggressive behavior is comic because it is in such sharp contrast to her kind, sweet disposition.

Many of the comic effects which follow in this fight may be illustrated by one short excerpt from the scenario:

490 LS The Boy and the Rival wrestle on the ground and then get to their feet. The Boy gets hit repeatedly by the Rival's fist. He goes down six times but pluckily gets up for more.

491 MS Grandma urges the Boy on. She shadowboxes as if she were a fight manager beside a boxing ring.

492 LS The Boy gets hit again by the Rival's strong blows and goes down. He gets up, tackles the Rival, and sends him sprawling. He repeats this unusual method of fighting. For the moment, the Rival is baffled by this attack.

493 MS Grandma urges the Boy on.

3. The combination of these shots is the result of a typical editing device used in serious works. It is commonly used when two forces are going to clash in battle.

494 LS The Boy and the Rival repeatedly hit each other on the jaw with their fists. (Accelerated motion is used.) The blows snap their heads back.

495 MS Grandma shadowboxes at the same fast pace.

496 LS The flurry of punches finally affects the Boy, and he collapses just as the Rival throws a strong punch which hits the side of a shack. The Rival withdraws his hand in pain.

These shots illustrate some of the main currents of comedy which are used throughout the climactic sequence. There is an overstatement of the fury of the two-man combat which parodies the stock fight between the hero and the villain of many of the serious works of the time. As early as 1914, William Farnum and Tom Santschi staged a climactic fight in *The Spoilers.* Just before *Grandma's Boy* was released in 1922, *Tol'able David,* a work directed by Henry King, featured a similar climactic fight.

The physical action of the fight in *Grandma's Boy* is exaggerated by the use of accelerated motion in shot 494. The way each man hits the other is also comic; the flurries of punches are not erratic as they would be in a real-life fight—they are mechanically perfect in timing. An early one-reel comedy, *Just Neighbors* (1919), featured Harold Lloyd and Harry "Snub" Pollard in an altercation which led to a fistfight. The two comedians hit each other repeatedly in a manner similar to the incident in *Grandma's Boy.* Accelerated motion was also used in this one-reel work to assist in making the flurries of punches comic.

One other important comic facet of the whole sequence is revealed in the above shots. When the Boy is shown tackling the Rival, the action is comic because it deviates from the hero's usual method of fighting a villain in a serious film drama. Comedians Charles Chaplin, Buster Keaton, and Harry Langdon also employ unusual means of fighting their foes. Charlie, the little tramp, drops a stove on a bully in *Easy Street* (1917); Buster in *The General* (1927) tries to stop a trailroad train full of Union soldiers by throwing boxes in the train's way; and Harry bombs his adversaries with whiskey bottles as he swings over them on a trapeze in *The Strong Man* (1926). When Lloyd and these other comedians fight their adversaries, they use unusual means of fighting that are comic deviations from a normal fight of a hero. And following the unusual logic of the comic films, these comic heroes win their fights *because* of their unusual methods of fighting.

As the fight continues, the Rival climbs up into the hayloft of a barn to get away from the Boy. The Boy's indefatigable energy outlasts the Rival's strength, and the Rival, realizing this, tries to escape from the young man. The medium comes into operation in order to create the comedy of the incident which follows. The Boy and the Rival wrestle in the hay loft at the edge of a doorway which is used to put hay into the upper story of the barn. The danger of this fight is conveyed by Grandma's horrified reactions (shots 503, 505, and 508). As the two men fall out the second-story door of the barn, the camera tilts with their fall and reveals them falling safely into some hay on the ground. This incident uses a mild form of the comic reversal by revelation. It demands good editing and revelation by the camera. The execution of the material is smooth in this incident, but the material itself is not highly risible. The incident seems to be a parody of the cliff-hanging serials (such as *The Perils of Pauline*) in which an episode which follows another shows that no real danger existed at the end of the former episode after all.

A great deal of the material which follows is repetitious. Shot 513, however, does show the essential feature of this sequence which makes it comic:

513 LS The Rival swings a "round-house" punch as the Boy stands with his hands placed nonchalantly on his hips. The Boy ducks deftly as the Rival's swing throws him off balance and almost sends him sprawling. As the Rival staggers to his feet, the Boy kicks him in the seat of the pants. Angrily, the Rival lunges at the young man and swings wildly once more. He twists around in a complete circle and falls; the Boy catches him before he hits the ground and stands him up. The Rival tries another swing and wearily falls, but the Boy catches him again and stands him against a hay wagon. He places the Rival's hands in a folded position. The Rival recovers slightly, swings, and lunges at the Boy; the Boy stoops, and the Rival flies over him, tumbling onto the ground.

As this illustrates, a great emphasis is placed on the pantomime of the leading comedian. His deftness in dodging the blows of his adversary show a comic way of besting the Rival without using his fists. Lloyd displays this perverse method of combat throughout the six-minute climactic sequence. Comedy is strongly rooted in the comedian's character. The humor lies in the comedian's deviation from the normal man's bravery and the normal man's skill in fighting. The Boy ducks, weaves, and tackles in an unconventional manner. His fanatic desire to excel in the manly art of the fight is an overstatement of the cliché that a man with enough pluck will gain his objective. As it has been pointed out previously in this study, the concept that all turns out well for the "go-getter" is a cliché that had a great deal of popularity in the twenties. It is a concept which the Boy uses in all his endeavors.

The conclusion of this fight features a reversal in which the comedian bests his adversary. This pantomime of this final incident displays a carry-through movement which intensifies the comic effectiveness of the reversal. Playing the gentleman in his victory, the comedian offers his hand to his rival; the Rival extends his hand and brings up a well bucket with his other hand to strike the Boy. The comedian executes his art of dodging once more, strikes the Rival on the jaw, and trips him into the well with his foot. This incident brings the feud between the Rival and the Boy full cycle. The Boy had previously been the butt of the Rival's coarse humor and had been pushed into the same well.

The overall structure of this climactic sequence lacks unity even though a single action is dominant. Repetition and slight variations in the fighting methods of the two men are not enough to hold the sequence together. The battle alternately shows the Rival getting the upper hand, then the Boy getting the best of the Rival.

There are fifty-four shots in this six-minute sequence. This number is small for this space of time because much of the action is photographed at a standard long shot position which displays the fight of the two men. Reaction shots are generally confined to the onlooker, Grandma. While most of the shots are functionally effective, they seldom emphasize or create the comedy here. At times, the camera moves to follow the action, but this method of shooting the scene is limited to a few shots. Editing, also, is merely functional and helps tell the story rather than create the comedy. Without titles, this climactic sequence depends on the actions of the Rival, Grandma, and the Boy to tell the story. A strong focus is therefore placed on the comedian. Lloyd's comic character, the Boy, remains the center of interest, and it is up to the actor to display his ability as a pantomimist in order to tell the story and create the comedy.

The basic type of comedy in this sequence lies in the inversion of fighting methods. The Boy fights best when he is *not* fighting. Instead of landing blows on his adversary, he tackles him or ducks his blows and, consequently, wears him out. Also, much of the comedy reflects the spirit of play when the Boy begins to gain the upper hand. He takes the fight as a game. The fight is also made comic by exaggerated and substituted movements.

Safety Last

Harold Lloyd's *Safety Last* contains a climactic sequence which employs the excitement of a dangerous situation. Assuming the role of a human fly in order to fulfill a promotional stunt, the comedian labors up a high building—a climb that brings both comedy and excitement to the story. Since Lloyd had employed the chase and fight in *Grandma's Boy*, he turned to the potentials of a situation he had exploited earlier, one which had proved effective in one-, two-, and three-reel comedies.

Since the climactic sequence of *Safety Last* uses material in a fresh way and elaborates extensively on this material, it will be necessary to devote a greater portion of this chapter to this film than to the other two works. While the climactic sequence in *Grandma's Boy* is six minutes long, *Safety Last* exploits its material in a climactic sequence that lasts twenty-one minutes. Also, more space must be devoted to this work because more background information is necessary to analyze *Safety Last's* blend of comedy and excitement.

In his autobiography, *An American Comedy,* Lloyd calls any of his works which place him in a perilous position on top a tall building "thrill pictures."[4] He indicates a formula to promote comedy in these works. This formula employs "a laugh, a scream, and a laugh," he claims, and he recognizes the link of this formula with David Warfield's recipe for comedy drama, " 'a laugh, a tear, and a laugh.' "[5] Warfield's formula is, of course, obviously a method for developing sentimental comedy.

Buster Keaton revealed a working method for his comedy films that is not unlike Lloyd's. According to John Montgomery in *Comedy Films,* Keaton declared:

4. Lloyd, *An American Comedy,* p. 145.
5. *Ibid.*

The best way to get a laugh is to create a genuine thrill and then re-lieve the tension with comedy. Getting laughs depends on the element of surprise, and surprises are harder and harder to get as audiences, seeing more pictures, become more and more comedy-wise. But when you take a genuine thrill, build up to it, and then turn it into a ridiculous situation, you always get that surprise element.[6]

While Keaton may be using the term "thrill" more broadly than Lloyd does, there is some indication that his working method was similar to Lloyd's. In his work, *The General* (1927), Keaton used dangerous situations on a speeding locomotive and dangerous situations in war in order to develop comic incidents. Lloyd, how-ever, claims to be an innovator of the "thrill picture" with its use of dangerous situations on top of tall buildings. The three pro-genitors of *Safety Last*—*Look Out Below* (1918), *High and Dizzy* (1920), and *Never Weaken* (1921)—are early works which support his claim. Theodore Huff also gives Lloyd principal credit for ex-ploiting this type of material and points out that Charles Chaplin may have been influenced by Lloyd when he used a sequence showing the leading comedian, Charlie, in a cabin teetering on the edge of a precipice in *The Gold Rush* (1925).[7] And, interest-ingly enough, Chaplin used this situation in the climactic part of this film, thereby following a structural method Lloyd used in his "thrill pictures."

Lloyd's 1921 two-reeler, *Never Weaken,* illustrates that the come-dian was moving toward the more effective handling of climactic material by using "thrill comedy." Toward the end of this film the comic protagonist, Harold, accidentally gets pulled from an office window onto a steel girder which is swinging by a cable—evidently through a miscalculation of a crane operator who is moving the beam onto a construction project. With this given situation *Never Weaken* affords a good example of an earlier handling of material similar to that used in the comedian's 1923 feature, *Safety Last.* On this skeleton construction of a building, consisting mostly of verti-cal and horizontal girders, the protagonist encounters a series of obstacles which present a structural pattern also used in the full-length film. Each of the incidents adds increasing danger and complexity to the problems that face the hapless Harold:

1. He has difficulty keeping his balance on the swinging girder as it moves up toward its destination.

6. Montgomery, p. 155.
7. Huff, p. 188.

With "Snub" Pollard in the first thrill comedy on a building, **Look Out Below,** a 1918 one-reeler.

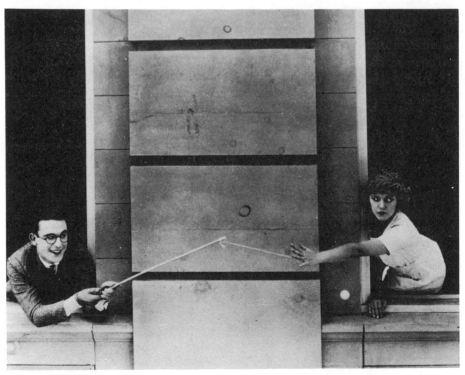

How to catch a woman in an early scene from **High and Dizzy** (1920)—with Mildred Davis.

Problems on a ledge of a high building in **High and Dizzy.**

2. When the girder reaches a potential mooring, Harold struggles with one foot to obtain a safer position on a fixed horizontal beam. He makes the transfer.
3. Moving toward a vertical beam, he finally inches his way around it. Because his vision is obscured, his foot slips as he steps where a horizontal beam should be located.
4. Retracing his footsteps, more fearful than before, he steps on a greased brush used to lubricate pulleys. It was accidentally dropped from above by a workman. He nearly falls over the edge of the beam.
5. He gets up and sees a ladder. Trying to climb it, Harold finds it moving upward, and he is getting nowhere. Two workmen

are shown above, hauling up the ladder with hand-over-hand movements. Harold falls off and onto the beam. He is puzzled by the strange movement of the ladder because he can't see the men above him.

6. Now more horrified by another near fall, he crawls along a beam on his hands and knees. He sits up and leans back on the beam to see where he is. A hot rivet used by construction workers has fallen from above and onto the beam. Burned by the rivet, Harold leaps wildly up toward a vertical girder and grabs it.

7. Since the girder has not been secured and is anchored only by a cable from an unseen crane, it swings away from the horizontal beam. Harold has one foot on the fixed beam, so by shifting his weight, he finally swings back to firmer "ground."

8. Desperately going to a wooden plank which seems to lead to a safer position, the protagonist is confronted by a swinging beam. He manages to duck the first swing of the girder, but is caught by its back swing and falls to a horizontal beam below.

9. Teetering on this precarious perch and about to fall, Harold is hit by another swinging girder. Clutching to the lower edge of the beam, he hangs with his whole body dangling in the air. Paralyzed with fear, he closes his eyes.

10. The girder swings over a construction elevator; Harold falls onto it just as the platform of the mechanism begins to descend.

11. Believing he is still on the top of the building as the elevator reaches the ground, he crawls from the platform onto a girder which is resting firmly in the construction yard. Shaking with fear, he still has his eyes closed.

12. As he crawls along on the metal beam, he still doesn't realize what has happened. Two workmen and a policeman observe his odd behavior. As Harold reaches the end of the girder (his eyes still closed) he grabs the policeman's legs. He opens his eyes, looks around, and finally realizes he has nothing to fear.

As it will be shown in a thorough examination of *Safety Last,* a series of increasingly complicated obstacles, such as those just described, became a fixed design for the "thrill comedy" of Harold Lloyd. While he used material in the 1920 *High and Dizzy* which showed a frightened man trying to get to safety on top of a high

In **Never Weaken** (1921) the comic protagonist gets caught on an iron beam.

building, it was not until a year later in *Never Weaken* that the pattern was fully developed with strong inventive gags for each incident. As indicated above, eleven clear-cut incidents show a build-up of humorous and thrilling complications, with a concluding (twelfth) "topper gag" for the end of the total sequence.

Released two years after its two-reel precursor, *Never Weaken*, Lloyd's best "thrill comedy," *Safety Last*, has a climactic sequence that takes up more than a fourth of the running time of the film. It is composed of many incidents which are clearly linked and integrated into one major action—the climb up a twelve-story building. Each incident presents an obstacle to the comedian's labored ascent.

It is evident that Lloyd has not completely divorced himself from the chase material that he so successfully exploited in *Grandma's Boy*. The chase, however, is subordinate to the climbing of the building. The chase begins at the crisis of the fourteenth sequence when an old animosity is renewed between the professional steeplejack, Bill, who has been engaged to climb the building, and his pursuer, a policeman. The policeman discovers Bill is a man who has formerly eluded him to avoid arrest. Bill is forced to flee, leaving Harold without a qualified person to carry on the human fly attraction which has been promised to the crowd. This forces Harold to take Bill's place until Bill can elude the policeman. Harold is forced into a role in which he is painfully inadequate at the crisis of this work.

Throughout the climactic sequence, three integral actions provide the development. The policeman chasing Bill provides one action; Harold's climb provides another; and the activity and reaction of the crowd provide the third. Both the chase and the urgings of the crowd motivate Harold's climb. The struggle of the comedian, of course, remains the focal point—the main action. The crowd, it should be noted, is not used merely for comic reaction. Members of the crowd urge Harold on, warn him of the danger, and interfere in the climb itself. The interplay of these three actions, therefore, is important to the development of the sequence.

The staging of this part of the film must also be considered before specific incidents may be discussed. Each of the three simultaneous actions takes place in a separate location; they are actions which are linked in continuity through careful editing and shooting procedures. Harold remains outside the building during the entire climb; the policeman chases Bill up the stairs inside the building; and the crowd watches in the street below or in windows of the building. A trained observer of the motion pictures can detect the fact that the majority of shots showing Harold outside the building were staged with motion-picture sets (unlike *Grandma's Boy* in which the entire climactic sequence was shot with "actualities" on location), while some long shots of the climb showed a double, a professional human fly, climbing a real building. According to the *Literary Digest* of July 1923, a dummy structure of a building was constructed on the roof of a real building in order to provide the necessary illusion. The proper camera angles were also used to provide the illusion of height.[8] In his autobiography,

8. "Safety First Stuff in *Safety Last*," *Literary Digest* 58 (July 14, 1923): 45.

Lloyd points out that this same method was employed for the one-, two-, and three-reel comedies of this genre.[9]

The operation of Lloyd's "thrill" and laugh combination as a formula for comedy may be investigated by looking at the overall pattern and specific development of the sequence. An examination of the sequence reveals a series of obstacles placed in the comedian's way. These barriers which thwart his climb promote the "thrill" or excitement. Lloyd encounters six key obstacles in his climb: (1) pigeons, (2) a tennis net, (3) a painter's board, (4) a clock, (5) a mouse, and (6) a weather gage. Each of these obstacles examined in detail should reveal Lloyd's working method for creating the comedy in this sequence.

Lloyd's first obstacle is encountered as he goes from the second to the third story of the twelve-story building. When a small boy who is watching the bungled human fly performance tips a bag of popcorn over Harold from a window, the climber is besieged by pigeons. The beating of the pigeons' wings in Harold's face almost causes him to lose his balance. The "thrill" part of the incident is established.

The staging of this incident is not, however, the only factor at work. The use of editing makes it possible to give animal life (pigeons, in this case) direct, specific actions and characteristics. As it has been pointed out in Chapter 6, a shot of a duck peeking around a corner in juxtaposition to a shot of a crowd peeking around a corner at a ferocious tramp is a product of editing in *Grandma's Boy*. The duck is given human characteristics; and, in the case, the humans are given animal-like traits. Cats in *Grandma's Boy* and *The Freshman* also are given specific actions which plague the comedian almost to the degree that the pigeons interfere with Harold's efforts in *Safety Last. Safety Last,* however, blends danger and comedy—both factors being promoted by the actions of the pigeons. In each of the three films used in this study, a combination of shots showing the activities of animals creates actions which could be staged only with a great deal of difficulty. In short, animals in Lloyd's films are shown engaged in unusual activities through the medium's editing process. At first Harold is bothered by only one pigeon, but once this one is frightened away he brings back his friends to eat the popcorn that has been spilled on Harold. A combination of the correct shots of the pigeons is necessary to convey this idea.

9. Lloyd, *An American Comedy*, pp. 145-46.

A pigeon, followed by his friends, plagues Harold as he starts his long climb in **Safety Last**.

While comic ingenuity of the comedian seldom comes into play during the climb sequence, the incident just described concludes with this way of gaining humor. By grabbing the popcorn sack which has prompted his difficulty, blowing it up, and popping it against the side of the building, Harold manages to scare away the pigeons. Comic ingenuity is used a great deal in the department-store sequences, but the comedian, in this dangerous situation, is more a victim of chance—he does not control his destiny in the climb. Lloyd's bout with the pigeons, therefore, is the only moment in which the comedian displays a cleverness which seems typical of some of the best moments of the film.

Harold's second obstacle, a tennis net, affords the comedian the opportunity to display broader pantomime skills. Looking for a means of support, Harold absent-mindedly clutches a tennis net which has been thoughtlessly draped over a window sill of the department store's sport shop. He is immediately entangled in a web of cord and is unable to free himself. He struggles with the net in a dancelike fashion; he slips it from his head only to have it catch on an arm or leg. The routine is reminiscent of the circus clown's routine with sticky taffy or flypaper. In this case, though, the routine has the added excitement of the danger that is created by this dance of frustration on a narrow ledge above a city street.

Seeing this unusual predicament, a drunk in the crowd below provides one of the few comic understatements of the whole sequence. In Title 78 he suggests, "Why don'tcha take that net off? It's in your way!" With the aid of a young woman watching him from a window, Harold is able to get the net from his arm. The net falls down into the crowd and ensnares the drunk who thrashes about in an attempt to escape. The actor playing the role assists in creating comedy from this situation by broad movements of frustration. He is revealed in the resolution still sitting on the sidewalk trying to figure a way out of the net, obviously hampered by his drunkenness.

Under the constant urgings of Bill, who is still trying to escape arrest, Harold is forced to conquer another obstacle. As he reaches a window ledge, he is knocked on the chin by a large board being used by painters who are shifting furniture around in an office building. Clutching desperately to the board, hanging far out over the street, Harold is shown in even greater danger than he has previously experienced in the climb. An attempt to build tension and excitement with each new obstacle is evident in this third obstacle, but no clear alternation of danger and comedy, as indicated in the Lloyd formula, is at work in this material. Comedy and danger go hand in hand as Lloyd receives a blow from the painter's board. The ludicrous nature of the incident with the comedian's overstated reaction produce the comedy of this incident. Harold's dangerous plight has also been strengthened by the use of a title eight shots before this third incident. An elderly lady is shown standing at a window in the building and scolding him by saying, "Young man, don't you know you might fall and get hurt?" (Title 81). Again, the comic understatement of a title adds variety and the counterpoint to a situation which deals with overstatement.

Rescued by the painters, Harold must continue his climb. He is urged on once more by his friend Bill. Harold, his tight smile now faded, climbs to his fourth obstacle. He has another narrow escape as he climbs up the outside casement of a window. When

Approaching the clock (normal angle) in **Safety Last.**

Bill opens the window to see how far Harold progressed, Harold is tipped onto the push-out window. He slips from the window and grabs frantically onto the edge of the huge clock on the corner of the Bolton Building. Harold cannot hold onto the edge of the clock and desperately clutches the big hand which reads two forty-five. Unfortunately, the hand moves down with his weight to half past two. As Harold attempts to pull himself up by grabbing the small hand, the crowning development of this incident occurs—the whole face of the clock springs outward and down. The complications of this incident do not stop, however. Bill throws Harold a rope which hangs just out of reach. The audience viewing the film is informed that Bill, frightened away by the policeman, has not tied the rope to the leg of an office desk as he had intended. A close-up provides this information with

The hand comes down before the face of the clock breaks away.

A high angle shot (compare with two previous stills) emphasizes Harold's plight.

sharp impact. In the next shot Harold is shown desperately trying
to reach the rope. Then, as he grabs the rope, Bill returns just in
time to snatch the other end of the rope before it flies over the
window sill. Since this last-second rescue employs accelerated motion, Bill's unusually fast dive for the rope is placed on a
superhuman and comic level. This is the only use of accelerated
motion in this sequence.

This situation reaches the fantastic proportions of an early
Mack Sennett one-reel comedy. It is an incident which fans its
comic fire with the unusual and the impossible. The last-second
rescue shows the use of overstatement. A close-up of Harold's

A rope temporarily assists Harold in avoiding the death plunge.

face as he dangles on the end of the rope supports the comic nature of this highly dangerous situation. His expression is one of

wild horror; his eyes pop behind his shell-rimmed glasses. Each action and reaction shot emphasizes the situation and promotes the comic overstatement. The "thrill" element exists in this incident, but the overstatement of the situation prevents it from dominating the comic. Lloyd's formula is again revealed at work. When the viewer is caught up in the danger of the action, a fantastic twist produces a laugh.

Again a title reinforces the dangerous yet ludicrous position of the leading comedian. His antics are considered by some onlookers as merely tricks of his trade. To these spectators, the whole human fly act is good showmanship. As Harold is rescued from his near fall, a fat, jolly onlooker yells to him from a window, "Great! You got the right idea, kid. That's the best one you've pulled yet!" (Title 83). Harold nods vaguely and smiles in his attempt to fulfill his obligation as a would-be performer. The smile, however, is more in the spirit of a whimpering child being encouraged by an adult to do an impossible task.

Saved from this perilous incident, Harold is hurried upward by the presence of a vicious dog leaning out a window. As he climbs over a ledge to another floor in order to escape the dog, a mouse runs up his pants leg. In his attempt to shake the mouse from his pants leg, he performs an antic dance on the narrow ledge. Through the use of effective editing a shot of an applauding crowd is introduced immediately after this action. While the movie audience knows the truth, the crowd in the street interprets the action as typical of a human fly's devil-may-care spirit. These two views of the action are, of course, essential to this comic incident. The ability of the close-up to reveal the true nature of the situation assists in developing the contrast between these two views. As the movie audience comprehends Harold's dangerous predicament, the interpretation of the crowd is injected to provide the comic twist on the situation. Once more, Lloyd's formula is shown at work.

After the comedian has got rid of the mouse, he is hurried on once more when he opens a window to give up his role as a human fly. Inside the building a commercial photographer is taking a picture of an actor who is posed as a criminal with a gun. Harold meets face to face with the actor just as the flash powder of the photographer explodes. This terrifying experience sends Harold hurriedly up the side of the building to his final mishap.

As is now obvious, each obstacle not only provides increased peril for the comedian, but it also provides a more ludicrous situation. The final incident is an attempt to top all previous incidents. There is also a calculated delay and a consequent heightening of the tension of this incident. As Harold pulls himself to the top ledge of the twelve-story building, his girl friend, Mildred, calls to him from the story below. He remains lying on the ledge as he calls down to her and urges her to come up to the roof to meet him. He starts to straighten up, but is held back by his conversation with her. It is obvious to the movie audience that when he straightens up, he will be hit by a large revolving wind-speed indicator just above him. Two times he is called back by Mildred and is stopped from standing up.[10] Finally he stands up and is nearly knocked unconscious by the wind gage. Dizzy from the blow, he staggers along the top ledge of the building in a drunk-like dance, teetering backward and forward.

The final spectacular predicament develops from this staggering teetering pantomime. The comedian's foot catches in the rope of a flag pole, and he is hurled out head first in a pendulum swing over the city street twelve stories below. The full force of the medium comes into play to assist the staging of this spectacular finish. Editing takes over to produce the desired illusion:

764 LS A double for Harold Lloyd is shown swinging by his ankle next to the building in a pendulum-like fashion from right to left frame (4 seconds).

765 MLS The flag pole alone is shown as it bends with the swing to the right and back to the left (3 seconds).

766 LS "Harold" is shown in another swing to the right and back toward the left (4 seconds).

767 LS Mildred stands on the roof of the building with outstretched arms. Harold swings up on the rope and into her arms. They embrace (1½ seconds).

The last shot, shot 767, when placed with the preceding three shots, depicts a complete carry through of an action with an unusual comic twist for a conclusion. The perilous swing through the air ends in safety and security. It is, in short, an unperceived conclusion—an effective comic reversal. As it has been pointed out in this chapter, the climactic sequence of *Grandma's Boy* uses a

10. Agee (*Agee on Film*, pp. 11-12) sees this "delay-technique" as particularly effective. To him, this technique is an effective way to build to the final, spectacular gag.

Going over the top in **Safety Last**, the comic protagonist soon meets another obstacle, a wind speed indicator.

Swinging into the arms of Mildred. Similar (but posed in this photo) to shot 767 in **Safety Last.**

comic reversal with a carry through of several actions which blend into one when the Boy trips the Rival into a well. A type of concluding action which features a stronger switch at the end is Chaplin's use of a balletlike swing at an enemy, which is turned into a whirl and an embrace of the woman he rescued in *Easy Street* (1917).

The final reversal in *Safety Last* depends on editing to achieve the correct rhythm of the swing and the cut to the all important final shot which shows the embrace. It seems that this last shot could only be created by the reversal of the action. In other words, during the filming of this shot, the action must start with the comedian embracing the girl and falling away from her. By presenting this shot in reversed action, the all-important comic twist is created when it is combined with the shots of the man swinging on a flag pole.[11]

As in the other sequences of *Safety Last,* the pictorial elements of the climb are straightforward—they function in the way that will tell the story best. Since the action on the building is generally broad, there are many long shots in this 217-shot sequence; even the medium shots are not tightly composed—they tend toward a classification which may be called "long-medium-shot." Those shots which are called "extreme long shots" are also more numerous in this sequence than in any other sequence of the film. Of significance to the development of the sequence is the angle of the shot and its relationship to other shots. Few low-angle shots are employed; instead, there are many sharp, high-angle shots to emphasize the height of the building which the comedian is climbing.

Also significant is the great amount of cutting from one action to another. While the amount of intercutting does not equal that in *The Freshman's* climactic sequence, this method of editing presents sharp contrast among the three locales and the various characters involved in the sequence. The juxtaposition of these shots of varied content not only follows the strong plot development; it also creates a faster pace. The number of frames per shot rarely aids in creating a faster pace; however, both the clock and weather gage incidents benefits from using very short shots.

How all these facets of the medium affect the comedy is, of

11. This is the only example of this technique in the three films used in this study. A more obvious use of reverse action is used when a long line of cars chase Laurel and Hardy (in the two-reel work, *Two Tars,* produced in 1928) into a railroad tunnel and suddenly back out when a train comes.

course, one of the central issues of this discussion. The editing and camera work show an interesting relationship to the development of Lloyd's "thrill" concept of comedy. Besides the contrast in shot content, there is contrast developed by altering the distance of the camera from the object being photographed. Long shots and close-ups are used in sharp contrast. The comic hero's difficulties with a mouse, for example, show the use of a "big close-up" followed by a long shot. While the use of these two shots is largely functional (that is, they carry necessary information to the viewer—such as the fact that a mouse has run up Harold's leg), it is also a method of enforcing the comic. Not only does this contrast assist in making the comic point, it also emphasizes the danger of Harold's wild dance on the ledge of the building.

From an analysis of the content of this climb sequence, it becomes apparent that overstatement is one of the strongest comic devices used. When Harold encounters the six obstacles, he slips, nearly falls, and clings by his fingertips many times during the climb. At all times, the camera work and the editing assist in emphasizing this perilous situation. Everything happens to him; he encounters obstacles which no human fly would encounter in a life time of his profession. An effective counterpoint for these ludicrous incidents is the use of understatement in the titles. Remarks from individuals in the crowd occur two times after narrow escapes from death, and one time, only eight shots before a near fall. These remarks also fit into Lloyd's working pattern, "A laugh, a scream, and a laugh."

One of the standard devices operating in the creation of comedy is the sudden change from one line of thought to another. Many verbal jokes employ this switch or reversal. Harold's encounter with a weather gage is an incident which illustrates this device applied to pantomime. His dizzy, upside-down swing through the air, as has been pointed out, ends in an embrace. The dangerous swing is suddenly switched to an accidental "rescue" and complete security. The transfer of the tennis net from Harold to the drunk operates in a similar way, but has many of the qualities of a simple substitution. Harold's encounter with the painter's board is a different matter. It is an incident which seems to lack a reversal phase. All other obstacles which confront the comedian use a type of reversal to conclude the comic incident. Reversal, therefore, generally provides the comic high point of an incident and concludes the action. As has been pointed out, the entire sequence depends on its main comic situation—Lloyd must assume a role that is far beyond his abilities. Since Lloyd is an ordinary sales clerk in a department store, his adoption of the human-fly role may be considered a comic "reversal of roles." At all times, this situation provides the central comic idea which is at work throughout the sequence.

Probably one of the best features of the comedy of this sequence is the use of two emotional attitudes by the leading comedian which operate simultaneously. As Harold climbs the building in terror and agony, he affects a smile and a tip of the hat to please the crowd. His face reveals his true feeling in a close-up; his features even reveal these two attitudes by alternating a patronizing smile with a gasp of fear.

While the comedian's whole plight is far removed from the custard-pie comedy which became the forte of the Keystone one- and two-reel comedy, it nevertheless is a plight filled with many abuses. Figuratively speaking, he receives a pie in the face with each obstacle he encounters. Pigeons, a tennis net, a painter's board, a mouse, a weather gage heap upon him a variety of abuses. There is, of course, a sophistication of this comic degradation. No longer is the slapstick applied to the ample bottom of the clown. All of the comedian's misery accrues by accidents. Even pratfalls exist in this sequence, but they are clearly motivated by the situation.

Harold Lloyd's activities as a comedian in this sequence are integral to a series of incidents which rely heavily on situation for comic effect. The comedian's facial expressions are very important. Most of the shots in *Grandma's Boy* reveal broad actions; reaction shots are seldom used. *Safety Last,* on the other hand, allows the comedian to react to the discomfort of his situation by many such shots and, thereby, gains more comedy from Lloyd's expressive face. There are few moments which show the camera giving the comedian "center stage" to work out a pantomime routine. Lloyd depends a great deal on the staging in this sequence; the building assists him greatly. The farm yard and the football field of the two other works do not affect the comedian in the same way that the building affects him in *Safety Last.* Consequently, the actions of the comedian himself in *Grandma's Boy* and *The Freshman* become relatively more important as means of gaining humor. The building in *Safety Last* nearly takes on the aspects of an antagonist—a second actor.

Lloyd's formula for comedy in this sequence indicates that emotional involvement on the part of the audience is desired. Henri Bergson's insistence on the necessity of intellectual detachment on the part of the recipient of comedy hardly seems to be supported by Lloyd's practice.[12] Lloyd clearly follows a design which attempts to play upon the emotions of the audience. A degree of detachment, however, is necessary or the excitement may dominate the comic. Robert Sherwood evidently thought the audience would be too caught up in the excitement of *Safety Last* because he found the toying with acrophobia a little overbearing. The empathy of the audience, he claimed, would be so strong in seeing this work that they would try to laugh "but only succeed in gurgling."[13] The mouse incident would send the audience into a "maudlin state of gibbering hysteria."[14] The emotions of the critic, Sherwood, if not those of the audience, were closely captured by Lloyd's building-climbing sequence. Sherwood's evaluation of an audience's reaction may be journalistic overstatement; there is some question as to how involved the audience gets when the comic twist on each new danger brings them back to the comic quality of the situation. Nevertheless, Sherwood has a point. Lloyd's "thrill" comedy has within it the problem of getting too involved with the "thrill" part to the detriment of the comedy.

Safety Last, according to Lloyd, was one of his best and most popular works.[15] The popularity of the "thrill picture" prompted him to put into two of his sound films *Feet First* (1930) and *Mad Wednesday* (1947), sequences which show the comedian in a dangerous prediction on a tall building. Whether the audience found that the greatest appeal of these works came from the shudder or the laugh, is unanswerable. It is more likely that their main reaction was laughter.[16]

The Freshman

The reviewer for *Variety*[17] and Robert Sherwood for *Life*[18]

12. Bergson, p. 63. Bergson's evaluation of comedy was widely accepted in the early part of this century. More recent, psychologically oriented theories have modified this detachment concept. Emotions are important in comedy, and comedy plays upon the emotions of the audience.
13. Robert Sherwood, "Silent Drama," *Life* 81 (April 26, 1923): 24.
14. *Ibid.*
15. Lloyd, *An American Comedy*, p. 145.
16. Private showings of *Safety Last* by the author reveal the audience more inclined to laughter.
17. Review of *The Freshman, Variety* 79 (July 15, 1925): 34.
18. Robert Sherwood, "The Silent Drama," *Life* 76 (October 15, 1925): 24.

Feet First (1930), Lloyd's second sound feature, illustrates a return to thrill comedy material.

found the climactic sequence, the football game, in Lloyd's *The Freshman* one of the best parts of the film. Paul Rotha, in his history of the movies, also found the incorporation of the last reels of the game in the 1947 Lloyd work, *Mad Wednesday* a "brilliant" piece of comedy.[19] Rotha concludes with the remark that the remaining part of the sound picture lagged behind the reels of Lloyd's 1925 work.

The climactic sequence in Harold Lloyd's comic thesis on college life is certainly one of the most interesting parts of the film. It is understandable that critics favor it. It is full of well motivated and well developed gags. Unlike the climactic parts of the other

19. Rotha, *The Film Till Now*, pp. 499-500.

Grave problems on a ledge once more, in his last movie, **Mad Wednesday** (1947).

Even a friend, Jimmy Conlin, has trouble as he comes to the rescue in **Mad Wednesday.**

two films, this sequence has a complete story development that is almost independent of the previous sequences. It could exist as a short film and might conceivably be called "Harold's Big Day." It contains the exposition and the development that is similar to the period of the comedian's two-reel works. The sequence runs, in fact, almost as long as a two-reel work—eighteen minutes in all —just a few minutes short of the standard two-reel work.

The overall structure does not have the unity and coherence of the climactic sequence of *Safety Last;* nevertheless, it is carefully worked out. The excitement of a contest, while it is pale material beside a fight between adversaries or a climb up a twelve-story building, provides an emotional basis for this sequence. Harold's drive to win the game and prove his mettle also provides strong forces to build up this part of the film.

The exposition sets up a situation which evidently was familiar to the audiences who viewed the football films of the day.[20] There are only a few minutes to go in the football game and the home team, Tate College, has suffered a serious setback—Union State has a lead of three points, leaving Tate scoreless. A comic over-statement of the brute strength of Union State is revealed by a shot which shows four battered Tate players lying on the ground like wounded gladiators. A title just before this shot (shot 682) provides an understatement from the crowd which contrasts with the visual overstatement. Peggy's mother remarks, "I'm afraid Union State is too heavy for our boys—they've knocked out al-most the whole Tate team." A visual comment on Harold's value to the team is also soon established in the exposition. When he is asked to lend his football sweater to a player who has damaged his uniform, Harold is shown with a huge zero on his football jer-sey.

When no other substitute is available, Harold is allowed to enter the game. But it takes a great deal of pleading to convince the coach to make this move. The coach informs Harold of his posi-tion on the team in Title 105 by saying, "Why we've just been kidding you—you're only the water boy." Momentarily, Harold is emotionally crushed by this revelation. He sits down as if to give up, but he rises again, angrily throwing down his football helmet and declaring, "You listen now! I wasn't kidding! I've been working—and fighting—just for the chance—and you've got to

20. Charles Ray's *Two Minutes to Go* and Ernest Truex's *Little, But Oh My!* used this type of material before Lloyd—in 1921.

The coach in **The Freshman** doesn't send Harold Lamb into the game until he is the last man.

give it to me!" (Title 106). The coach is surprised by Harold's anger, but does not give in until an official says that he must send in a substitute or forfeit the game. In desperation, the coach sends Harold in.

When Harold enters the game, the comedy of *The Freshman* begins to build to the final, winning touchdown. The brilliant visual humor of Lloyd comes fully into play. A series of mishaps and mistakes develops this part of the film effectively even though the structure of these incidents is not as unified as that in the climactic sequence of *Safety Last*. A good portion (85 shots—about a third of the sequence's running time) has, by this time, been used to build up the basic situation of the football contest and Harold's desire to get into the game.

Harold's first moments in the game are marked by a series of mishaps which result from his overeager spirit and his faulty knowledge of the fundamental of the game. In Title 107 Harold urges his teammates on by shouting, "Come on, you old women! Are you afraid of mussing your hair? Don't you know how to fight?" The members of the Tate team are surprised by his enthusiasm and are, for the moment, caught up with Harold in their eagerness to play. As the men line up, Harold tries to encourage them as if he were a leader. It will be recalled that the Boy in *Grandma's Boy* displayed some of the same enthusiasm as he went to battle with the tramp. The mock-heroic gestures of a general leading his men into battle in this earlier work are similar to the gestures displayed here in the football game. A comic twist results after this enthusiastic build-up. Shot 747 presents the first gag in a series of upsets which frustrate the efforts of the comic hero:

747 ls Harold jumps into a playing position by leaping over several men. All keyed up with enthusiasm, he raises his hand as if he were holding a sword and leading an army into battle. He squats down into playing position and then rises again in the same pose of a general leading his army. Suddenly, the play starts, catching him off guard, and he is smashed between two lines of players. A big pile-up results with Harold on the bottom. The players unpile, and Harold is revealed on his back—unconscious.

A comic reversal is evident in this incident. Harold has gone to battle as a lion and ends up the lamb. He is upset and knocked out on the first play without even "fighting" as he has advocated to his teammates. A reaction of the coach on the players' bench is shown in shot 748. With a gesture of disgust, his face seems to reveal his thoughts: "Wouldn't you know. . .!"

Harold is not defeated, however. As he is carried off the field on a stretcher, he regains consciousness, jumps up, and goes back into the game. His ability to play, however, does not match his pluck or enthusiasm. In the moments that follow, a series of incidents further reveals his ineptness:

1. He gets tramped underfoot.[21] (shot 754)
2. Harold is pushed into the line by a teammate who tries to get him to remain in the proper position. He ends up crushed

21. A mock-up shot that shows Harold's face and chest being ground under the feet of both teams. An effective comic overstatement of the punishment Harold receives.

between both lines, with his legs sticking straight up in the air. (shot 755)

3. Still dazed by the mauling he has received, Harold is pulled out of the way by an opposition guard; he rolls up field and accidentally catches a pass at the end of his roll. (shots 759-765)

4. Harold runs out to catch a pass. He mistakes a bowler hat which has been thrown from the crowd in the excitement of the game for a football. He runs across the goal line before he discovers his error. (shots 774-785).

5. Urged on by the sneers and taunts of the College Cad, Harold takes it upon himself to grab the football from the fullback. He is tackled but refuses to stop at the official's whistle. Finally, he is halted by the physical efforts of the officials. (shots 787-295)

6. Harold looks for the football which has just been kicked by the opposition only to see what looks like five footballs in the air. A balloon vendor has tripped and lost his wares, sending a group of his balloons sailing over the football field. Harold gets hit on the head by the real football as he stands puzzled, open-mouthed, and open-armed, trying to decide which object in the air is the true football. (shots 811-813)

Each of these incidents shows the comedian as inept at football as he is at climbing a building in *Safety Last.* As in *Safety Last,* he is the object of our laughter in these incidents; and also as in *Safety Last,* this sequence shows gags building to broader, more fantastic comic situations. But the main comic idea is quite different. Harold is not placed in the position of changing his normal role for another. While he is not a good football player, he at least considers himself so. At no time in the climactic sequence of *Safety Last* does he begin to believe he is a human fly.

The next developments also point up the difference between the comic idea of *Safety Last* and that of *The Freshman* in their climactic sequences. The pattern of mistakes and mishaps changes at this point. Harold switches to his own brand of football and finds out that the switch brings results. As in *Grandma's Boy,* he is more successful when he fights with his own odd set of rules and impromptu actions. Comic ingenuity becomes the unifying pattern for the remaining comic incidents in the climactic sequence.

When Harold retrieves the football once more, he is horrified at the sight of a huge, bestial Union State player bearing down on him. He displays his first clever method of avoiding capture. He unlaces the ball, places it on the ground, and yanks it away as the brute dives for the ball. Harold pulls the ball up and into his arms as if he were operating a yoyo. Having avoided one man, Harold runs down the field only to see several Union State players charging him. He slows down to a nonchalant walk and hides the ball behind his back. The players are easily deceived and run past him.

These two incidents show the use of comic ingenuity—a trait which seems to be a part of the breezy, brash side of Lloyd's comic character. Harold's cleverness has a temporary setback in the next incident, however. He has been told to stop running when the whistle sounds. As he is running with the ball once more, he stops at the sound of a train whistle and throws the ball down just short of the goal.

It is only a temporary setback, however. Harold manages to make one more run. The final, big run by the comedian comes with only a minute left in the game. In this run, it is not merely Harold's odd behavior on the field that befuddles the opposition and wins the day. An almost superhuman effort is exercised by this eager young man. After Harold has stolen the ball from a Union State player the final, action-filled moments of this sequence begin:

849 LS Harold runs furiously. (Accelerated action begins with this shot—the action shown in a travel shot.) He is almost tripped. Men dive for him from the right and the left and from the front of him. They all miss him.
850 MLS Tate's coach yells "go" excitedly.
851 LS (A travel shot) Harold straight-arms a man and jumps over two men on the ground who are in his way, as if he were running a hurdle race. A player tackles Harold and he falls flat, but he does not stay on the ground long. He jumps up, loses the ball, but picks it up again. Then he gets caught by the ankle, and men swarm down on him. He escapes from them, but a player grabs his pants and delays him. (The last accelerated motion shot)
852 ELS Harold struggles up to the goal post in the foreground. One man holds onto his pants as another charges up to him.
853 LMS Harold is shown dragging two men. A player comes up

A posed shot for **The Freshman** that shows the last-minute run toward the goal—similar to shot 853.

behind him and knocks him toward the goal line. (A high-angle travel shot)
854 MS The timekeeper shoots his gun.
855 MS The coach for Tate yells "Oh!" as if he were shot. He closes his eyes in agony and speaks to a man next to him:
Title 115 "I can't look! Is it over the line?"
856 MS The coach waits for a sign from the official.
857 LS There is a big pile of men at the goal post. They start getting up. (A high-angle shot)
858 MS A man draped over Harold's head gets up. Another gets up from his stomach. Harold's head is down in the turf. As Harold lifts his head, a huge white line (lime from the goal line) is shown running straight across his face. He blinks and looks down at the football which is over the line. He smiles broadly through the white line across his face.

While the spectacular run in this sequence requires a great deal of description to convey what happens visually, the actual screen time is short. The run itself is only thirty-three seconds. It is, as the scenario indicates, an incident crowded with many actions. Much of the humor depends on the overstatement of Harold's uncanny pluck and eagerness to get across the goal line. The overstatement of the number of men who try to tackle him also makes the wild run laughable. Most of the comedian's actions are comic because they are substitutions for normal actions. Harold allows no obstacle to stop him as he dashes to the goal. He will not weave around the players who have been knocked in front of him; instead, he jumps over them as if he were engaged in a high hurdle race (shot 851). When he grabs the ball, Harold rolls upon it and is up again in one deft motion. Everything he does is wrong according to the fundamentals of football. But it works —and that is the fantastic luck of the comedian. The logical world is turned topsy-turvy. It is a distortion which creates some of the finest moments of the silent screen comedy.

Part of the distortion of logic is achieved by the use of accelerated motion. There is some of the same excitement in Harold's big run as there is in the chase in *Grandma's Boy*. The run, in fact, is nearly a chase. Men are pursuing Harold, and Harold is trying to escape them. The distortion of all logic in this run is, however, more like the final fantastic moments of Harold's climb up a building in *Safety Last*. The comedian's accidental swing into the arms of his girl friend has no equal in *Grandma's Boy*. *The Freshman*, however, shows a winning touchdown that exists in a unique world—the unusual world of the comedian where almost anything can happen.

The overall structure of *The Freshman's* climactic sequence shows a logical, planned progression similar to that of *Safety Last's* climactic sequence. A series of incidents is set forth in a way that places the more risible situations at the conclusion of this part of the work. The broader, more fantastic situations provide a build to a climax. There is also a wide variety of material used in this part of the film. *Grandma's Boy*, on the other hand, lacks this variety. Humor comes from only one onlooker in that film, while *The Freshman* uses not only the football coach but the spectators for comic reactions.

Most of the shots used in *The Freshman's* climactic sequence are not outstanding. They are pedestrian in the early part of the sequence even though they are functionally effective. Toward the end of the sequence, however, the variety and quality of the shots improve. The spectacular run by Harold is well photographed. The use of travel shots as Harold runs increases the excitement of the moment, and the use of high-angle shots (853 and 857) at the end of the run displays to greater advantage Harold's last struggling steps to the goal.

Editing assists in creating the urgency of the football contest and increases the pace of the sequence's closing moments. Many cut-away shots showing the timer with his raised gun (e.g., shot 846), the coach writhing in the agony of uncertainty (e.g., shots 855 and 856), and the cheering of the crowd add to the development of the excitement. The sophistication of *The Freshman* in the use of cut-away shots shows a development in the ability of the filmmakers that is superior to the editing of *Grandma's Boy* and *Safety Last*. The blending of crowd reaction with the game operates as an effective counterpoint to the actions of the comedian.

While *Grandma's Boy* uses no titles in its climactic sequence, *Safety Last* uses eight, and *The Freshman* uses nineteen. Most of these titles are needed to convey information about the progress of the football game and to indicate verbal reactions from the crowd and the coach. Only a few titles can be classified as humorous. On the other hand, *Safety Last's* eight titles are all humorous.

The main comic idea of the climactic sequence in *The Freshman* is the inversion of the concept that the most skilled person in a game wins. Harold wins because of his lack of skill. He uses his own strange method in winning the game. His combination of pluck and comic ingenuity is evident in the winning touchdown. Before this time, most of the humor is achieved by comic degradation. The comedian is shown in a series of mishaps in which he is knocked out, crushed, and tumbled over. A more primitive form of humor, this type predominates throughout the sequence.

While it might appear to the reader that Lloyd abandoned the climactic chase during the period of three of his best silent screen features—a period of four years—from 1922 to 1925, he also produced another full-length work which exploited this material. In 1924 he created a feature which showed that he could develop the chase (or, correctly in this film, a "race to the rescue") into a highly satisfactory, inventive work even though similar material had been used by so many other comedians for the climax of a film. When he returned to a traditional placement of the chase sequence at the climax of *Girl Shy* (1924), he provided a range of gags not found in the chase of the tramp which he used prior to the climactic fight scene in *Grandma's Boy*. Use of a variety of means to obtain a goal (in this case, the race is undertaken to prevent a wedding of a sweetheart) can produce a wealth of comic detail. When the comic hero, Harold Meadows, is forced to take various types of vehicles in his race to stop the wedding, gag potentials are increased. A brief account of the basic actions will reveal many opportunities for comic invention:

1. Harold Meadows runs to catch a train as it leaves the station but misses it when a woman's shawl blows from the train and covers his head, obscuring his vision.
2. Forced to hitchhike, he is repeatedly turned down by passing automobiles. Ingeniously, he blows up a paper bag and pops it. This trick stops a driver who thinks he has a flat tire. Harold, however, is refused a ride. Desperately, he jumps onto the car and clings to the running-board, concealed from the driver's vision. His attempt to steal a ride is fruitless, however. The car goes only a few feet and pulls into a garage.
3. He tries to thumb a ride from a woman who is receiving driving instructions. Since she has so much difficulty with this minor skill, she starts and stops several times. Harold believes he is repeatedly being accepted and then rejected as a rider. He finally grabs onto the rear spare tire of the automobile, only to be crushed against a telephone pole when the novice driver spins around in circles and backs into the pole.
4. In desperation he steals a car from a young man and woman who are picnicking by the side of a road. Forced to travel on a detour that is replete with huge bumps, his car, evidently receiving broken springs from the detour, continues rocking and shaking ludicrously until Harold abandons the vehicle with a gesture of disgust.
5. He jumps into another automobile and is trying to start it when he discovers the car is attached to a tow truck and is being pulled backwards.
6. When two streetcar conductors do not heed Harold's plea to take him to his destination, he absconds with their car and races it wildly down the street, causing many accidents as the streetcar rushes through intersections and around sharp

Dangling on the pole of a streetcar in the climactic sequence of **Girl Shy** (1924). Lloyd's use of "a rush to the rescue" material.

curves. When the trolley's swiveled pole becomes disengaged from the overhead electrified wire, Harold climbs up to replace the pole. The streetcar starts and races wildly on. As the streetcar rounds a bend in the tracks, Harold, still holding onto the pole, swings out from the car and dangles over an automobile. Unable to hold onto the pole, he falls through the roof of the automobile.

7. Harold forces the unwilling driver of the car to go faster by pressing his own foot on the accelerator. The car is stopped for speeding by a police officer on a motorcycle.

8. As the police officer writes out a ticket for the hapless driver, Harold gets out of the car and escapes with the motorcycle. He causes further consternation as he roars madly down the street and through an open-air market. He finally runs the

    motorcycle through a ditch and crashes on top of a pile of
    dirt.
9. Harold sees a wagon with a team of two horses nearby. He
    snatches it and drives the horses at furious pace. When a
    wheel falls off the wagon he jumps onto one of the horses
    and continues his mad dash without interruption. He rides
    up the steps of the estate in which the wedding is taking
    place.
10. Jumping from the horse, he breaks into the house and
    dramatically stops the wedding by carrying off the bride.

Such elaboration on traditional comic material was the typical treatment which comedians gave to chase sequences when the silent-screen comedy reached the peak of its development in the twenties. The above description has many comic details that have been left out of this limited study for the sake of brevity. Actions numbered 2, 3, 5, 6, 7, and 8 contain many more comic incidents. Gag follows gag in a strong cause-and-effect relationship. Each incident builds to a final, more laughable incident. Such an accumulation and variety of comic detail was rare in the early one- and two-reel chase comedies. While *Girl Shy*'s chase sequence relies on accelerated motion in a way similar to that in which the early works used it, this dizzy, fast movement of objects and people is only one means of achieving the comic. In order to obtain a comic effect, the chases of the one- and two-reel comedies depended greatly on this photographic technique; they relied heavily also on the pratfall and fights between the adversaries engaged in the chase. In short, comic invention was slight.

Except for the 1924 production, *Girl Shy*, Lloyd seemed to be seeking a variety of ways to handle the climactic sequence in his works. He used a fight, a dangerous climb, and a football game for his material—material which would give him swift, intensified action and an opportunity to gain a full range of comic incidents.

Other major comedians turned to similar material after exploiting the chase. Buster Keaton used chase-rescue material in both *Our Hospitality* (1923) and *Sherlock Jr.* (1924), but in the 1924 *The Navigator*, he developed a lively, gag-filled fight with natives who board his ship for the climax of the film. His 1926 *The General* employed the chase as a pattern of development for most of the picture, but it turned to a climactic sequence which featured a comic version of a Civil War battle. Another comedian of note, Harry Langdon, struggled in the chaos of a tornado for the climactic portion of *Tramp, Tramp, Tramp* (1926) and, in the same year, little Harry in *The Strong Man* engaged in an elaborate tavern brawl, bravely fighting a mob of angry men by swinging over the crowd on a trapeze and bombing them with whiskey bottles.

In his 1925 *The Gold Rush* and 1928 *The Circus* Charles Chaplin moved toward the "thrill comedy" used by Lloyd in *Safety Last* for the high point of his pictures. But the famous comedian used less elaborate gags. In *The Gold Rush,* Charlie was caught in a miner's cabin after a storm moved the dwelling to the edge of a precipice. The little cabin teetered on the edge of this cliff so precariously that a sneeze or cough of its occupants would send it into the abyss below them. Forced by love to be daring, Charlie was shown trying to imitate the feats of a tightrope walker in *The Circus.* On the high wire, Charlie performed reckless and dangerous stunts when he was plagued by escaped monkeys who crawled over his face and tore off his trousers while he was trying to maintain his balance. New material such as this was constantly being sought, or old material was being given a fresh twist. In works by Lloyd and Chaplin, however, the chase still provided the comic spice for other portions of their films.

Some of the characteristics of Lloyd's handling of that portion of the silent-screen comedy which often provides the best laughs and the most excitement can be summarized. For extensive development, both in amount of incidents and number of gags, his climactic sequences have an equal only in the works of Buster Keaton. The author has viewed the majority of Keaton's silent features and found them to contain a great deal of innovation. At times they seem to be presenting the same material that Lloyd used—a parody of the success theme. Buster yearns to be a soldier in *The General* and proves himself in battle, just as Harold gets into the game in *The Freshman.* Buster desires to be a famous detective in *Sherlock Jr.* and a hero in athletics in his 1927 *College.* While the two comedians differ greatly in their comic characters, success by unusual means is burlesqued in the climactic portions of their films.

Both Lloyd's *Grandma's Boy* and *The Freshman* achieve some of the comic tone of their climactic sequences through burlesque.

The Freshman, as this analysis has revealed in preceding chapters, firmly establishes burlesque situations early in the film. When Harold patterns his behavior after a movie version of a campus hero, burlesque begins to develop. The climactic sequence follows along this same path. The fight in *Grandma's Boy* is not clearly motivated as burlesque in the early part of the film, but the intrigue of the fight achieves a comic tone by exaggerating some of the clichés of a serious fight between a hero and a villain.

The use of the medium to gain humor becomes important in both *Safety Last* and *The Freshman. Grandma's Boy,* on the other hand, does not call on the medium extensively to produce comedy in the climactic sequence. *Safety Last,* as this analysis has explained, depends a great deal on the staging of this part of the film as well as the techniques of camera work and editing.

The comedian's execution of pantomime is important to the development of each comic incident in *Grandma*'s climactic sequence. While the comedian's reactions are also important in *Safety Last,* the intrigue and the comic incidents are often strongly supported by the medium. In *The Freshman,* both the medium and the comedian work hand in hand to create the comedy. It is difficult to determine when the contribution of the comedian dominates.

Intrigue and comedy reach their highest point in the climactic sequence of Lloyd's work. Only one more step in the creation of a dramatic story remains—the story must be resolved.

8
The Resolution

The resolution or conclusion of a dramatic work presents the solution to a dramatic problem. It brings about a restoration of equilibrium from a state of unrest or conflict. Unlike life with its situations and complications that are often never completely resolved, the drama attempts to reconcile its situations and complications in a definite conclusion.

In *Grandma's Boy*, the Boy, according to the dramatic question and previously established situations, should gain manly courage and win the girl; in *Safety Last*, Harold should attain success in the business world and get the girl; and in *The Freshman*, Harold Lamb should gain social acceptance and win the girl. Obviously, Lloyd has observed one stock conclusion in these three works —the comedian must win the girl. Through the resolution, he does.[1]

Grandma's Boy

There is a strong verbal element in the resolution in *Grandma's Boy*. All the necessary information to reveal the deception in Grandma's method of promoting courage in the Boy is revealed in four titles:

Title 54 [The Boy] "It was your wonderful charm that did it, Granny—it wasn't me."

1. Chaplin used this stock plotting device in *Easy Street* (1917) and *The Gold Rush* (1925), but altered his ending in *The Circus* (1928) so that the little tramp does not get the girl—he is shown going sadly away alone.

Title 55 [Grandma] "There was no charm, Sonny. It was all
   you—nobody but you. Granny knew her real boy better than
   he knew himself."
Title 56 [The Boy] "But the charm saved Granddaddy?"
Title 57 [Grandma] "Bless your heart, Sonny. That story was all a
   fib—just a little white fib."

Some elaboration, of course, is visual. The charm, it is revealed
in a close-up, is only an old umbrella handle. In shot 537,
Grandma places the carved wooden object, which Harold believes
is the charm, on an old umbrella. It fits the umbrella perfectly. In
shot 542, the Boy finally realizes the impact of Grandma's words
and of her action of placing the carved wooden handle on the
umbrella. He is amazed and overjoyed when he realizes that he
has possessed courage without the aid of a charm, and expresses
his feelings in pantomime.
   A strong, humorous touch follows the Boy's realization that he
has conquered his cowardice. Shot 543 harks back to shots 46 and
48 at the beginning of the story. The Rival is viewed peering over
the edge of the well into which the Boy has dumped him after an
intensive fight with him. The situation parallels the Boy's predicament at the inceptive action of the drama when the Rival had
thrown him into the same well. The tables are now turned. The
wheel has now come full circle—the comic hero has conquered
the comic villain.
   Only one more situation must be resolved. The triangle must be
broken—the Boy must get the Girl. This situation provides a
light, comic touch. The Girl remains aloof; the Boy, forgetting his
manliness for the moment, pleads with her in a manner that he
used before he proved himself a man. He even grabs the umbrella handle once more to help him; then, he realizes that he is
in error and switches to his newly found role. He demands of her
in Title 59, "WILL YOU MARRY ME?"[2] She nods meekly and
the Boy adds, "RIGHT NOW?" in title 60. He sweeps her off her
feet and carries her away in his arms.
   A final comic touch is added in the last shot of the film:

560 ʟs The Boy carries the Girl across a brook, stepping on
   stones as he goes. What looks like a stone turns out to be a

2. H. M. Walker's titles use capitalization to indicate the authoritative voice the Boy
uses. The Boy's exaggerated manliness becomes comic in this situation.

pig. It rears up when it feels the weight of the Boy and the Girl and upsets them into the water. Too engrossed with each other to be disturbed by this accident, they embrace each other as they sit in the water, and the disgruntled pig waddles up the bank of the brook.[3]

These three comic incidents provide the most interesting moments in the conclusion of the film. The comic villain, cowering after being pushed into the well, presents a type of humor which plays upon the delight an audience receives in seeing the cocky bully receive the same punishment as he has dealt out to others. The love play of the Boy and the Girl is also a stock situation which audiences appreciate. The naive lovers who desire a declaration of devotion provide material for light comedy. The Boy absent-mindedly slips back into a former mode of behavior (much to the audience's delight) and then, once more, places his recently realized role into operation. The Boy, in his effort to win the Girl, puts forth a bold front that is too innocent in its execution to be severe—it is more like a child playing at being an adult.

The final gag of the picture is an effective comic reversal. From a highly romantic pose, the lovers are upset by a pig and thoroughly soaked in the brook. Unfortunately, the medium does not support this gag effectively. The incident is presented entirely in a long shot. Details important in emphasizing the comic incident are not clear. A close-up of the Boy stepping on the pig, with a follow-up medium shot of the lovers falling into the brook, would have helped emphasize the comedy of the situation. In content, the gag is effective, but the execution of the gag neglects possibilities.

Although the concluding sequence of *Grandma's Boy* does not deal with fresh material, it provides a suitable resolution to the story. The acting in this part of the work provides believability and makes this portion acceptable. The actors exhibit a skill in the final scenes which gives freshness to old material. The high point of the action, the fight between the Boy and the Rival, has been passed, and a strong gag sequence is not necessary. The work is pleasantly and humorously rounded out by the resolution.

3. Buster Keaton uses a similar gag in *The General* (1927). Catching the Confederate flag from the flag boy's dying grasp, Buster holds the flag aloft in a heroic pose by placing his foot upon a "rock." He is upset when the "rock" turns out to be a Confederate officer crouched behind a cluster of gray rocks.

Safety Last

While *Grandma's Boy* takes a little over two minutes to resolve its story, *Safety Last* rushes to a swift close in less than a minute. In this brief time, several parallel actions are tied together. Harold's success, however, is assumed and not demonstrated. Since he has climbed the building, the audience is called upon to assume that this promotional stunt will make Harold a success in the business world.

At the beginning of this short resolution, Harold is comforted by Mildred after his weary, nerve-shattering climb. This action is followed immediately by an extreme long shot showing Bill, only a tiny figure on top of a distant building, still being chased by the policeman. Very small print in an iris frame in Title 86 indicates his distant call: "I'll be right back—soon as I ditch this cop." Then a third action is added. The drunk is shown on the street below still tangled in the tennis net. He registers extreme desperation as he tries to disentangle himself. Finally, the action is switched back to Harold and Mildred as they embrace; then:

778 MLS They walk away hand in hand. In the background, men are tarring the roof. Harold, all of his attention of Mildred, walks through the freshly applied tar, and his shoes get stuck and come off. Not realizing what has happened to his shoes, he keeps walking arm in arm with Mildred. His socks come off in the tar. Too engrossed in his girl friend, he walks away with her in his bare feet.

Each of the above actions produces a gag. Bill's attempts to escape the policeman have taken on characteristics of a running gag. Throughout the climb up the building, Bill has assured Harold that he would take over the climb when he could shake the policeman. At this point in the story, there is no need for Bill to take over the climb, but he is still striving to escape the law officer. His promise in this situation, coupled with his obsession, has become comic. The drunk struggling with the net which had snared Harold is another comic obsession. This action, as well as Bill's, reveals the fact that while Harold is out of danger, others are still "suffering" from the results of the climb. The drunk's actions are comic to us because they present the actions of a man temporarily incapacitated by alcohol so that he is reduced to childlike behavior. In a strained way, he tries to reason out his predicament, but becomes frustrated and flails away in the net like a child in a temper tantrum.

The final embrace of Harold and Mildred and their walk away from the camera hand in hand strike a romantic pose which is shattered in a way similar to the way in which the final gag in *Grandma's Boy* is produced. The lovers' walk away from the camera is a standard shot which has become a cliché. Often, a sunset is added to this type of final, romantic scene. An accident mars the sentimental direction of this incident and turns it to comedy. This gag, like the final gag in *Grandma's Boy,* suffers from the lack of emphasis. A close-up of the specific nature of the loss of the shoes and socks would assist the execution of the gag.

Three parallel actions are presented in this short resolution. Harold embraces his girl friend and their future is assumed to be bright; the policeman is still chasing Bill; and the drunk is still engaged in a frantic effort to get out of the tennis net. These three actions continue the three basic actions of the climactic sequence of the film; one action is concerned with Harold's fate, a second with Bill's, and a third deals with reactions from the crowd. Unfortunately, *Safety Last* is not clearly resolved. Harold's success in the business world is assumed; there is no dramatization that suggests his success through this daring enterprise.

The Freshman

The action of the climax is blended into the resolution in this film. After Harold makes his last-minute touchdown, the victory is re-emphasized by showing the score board in shot 862—Tate wins 6 to 3 over Union State.

The excitement and jubilation of the crowd become an important part of the resolution. Harold is lifted onto the shoulders of his teammates and carried to the Tate locker room. Harold's acceptance by the college set is revealed mostly by visual means. Only a note from his girl friend Peggy expresses verbally the significance of Harold's victory. She writes a note on the side of a football program and hands it to Harold as he passes by her on the shoulders of his teammates: "I knew you could do it—I'm so proud and I love you." This message is revealed in an extreme close-up of the program in shot 885.

The small-town boy becomes the football hero in **The Freshman.**

The best presentation of Harold's victory, which is the best visual gag in this part of the film, is shown earlier than the verbal evaluation of his success:

882 LS Outside the window of the locker room, a student shows three of his friends Harold's jig and handshake. Tate's coach steps up and demonstrates the correct way to do it. With great enjoyment, others imitate the coach until a whole crowd of students and the coach engage in the jig and handshake.

Harold's greeting has become a running gag. Throughout the film story, he has been called upon to demonstrate his jig and handshake. It has been a way for the student body to laugh at

Harold behind his back and to ridicule him before other students. Now, instead of an action that is derisively imitated, it is an action to be emulated. It is a sharp reversal of a running gag and a clever comment on the changing attitudes of people who will use an action for ridicule one day and for emulation the next.

One final gag rounds out the resolution of *The Freshman*. Harold goes into the shower room where he can read his note from Peggy without being disturbed by his teammates' congratulations. In shot 887 he reads the note and smiles broadly, then leans against the wall of the shower room in a heavenly trance. As he leans against the wall, he accidentally leans against a shower handle and turns on the water. Still in his football uniform, he is too entranced with the sentiments which Peggy has written to notice the water pouring down on him.

This simple, final gag in *The Freshman* shows once more the comedian's engrossment with love. When love comes to Lloyd's comic character, he is as moon-struck as Pierrot in the French pantomime. His love for a girl is very intense so that the world around him is not noticed. In each of the three films, some variation on the comedian's behavior when he is engrossed with thoughts of the girl he loves is used. Even though the final shot of *The Freshman* presents the last comic incident in a long shot, there is no need for editing or closer camera shots to bring out the details of this action. The action is much broader than the final, detailed pantomime in both *Grandma's Boy* and *Safety Last*. The action can be fully realized in a long shot.

The concluding sequence of *The Freshman* effectively resolves the story of a young man's struggle for social acceptance. Structurally, it is stronger than the other two conclusions, and it links more directly and clearly with the climactic sequence immediately preceding it.

Both *The Freshman* and *Grandma's Boy* use serious material in their resolution sequences. Since *Safety Last* does not base its story on a sociological or psychological problem of the leading comic character, no serious note is presented. Serious matter used in the resolution of the other two works, however, is lightly handled with comedy in the vein of the genteel tradition. Victory for the leading character is not a subject for serious contemplation; it is a subject for gaiety. Nor does Lloyd sentimentalize the endings of these two works. The final gags are directed at the romantic or sentimental pose.

The concluding sequence in each of the films has the virtue of brevity. The longest, in *The Freshman,* lasts only two and a half minutes. *Safety Last,* as I have said, suffers from incompleteness, however. Harold's success could have been explicitly presented in this part of the film.

In each of these works, the focus remains on the leading comedian. He is shown as the man who has won a victory. And there is, in all three works, a strong emphasis on the comedian's ability to create and convey the comedy of the resolution. The techniques of the medium, which have assisted strongly in emphasizing the comic and at times have even created comedy without assistance from the leading comedian, become secondary; the comedian is king of the comedy in the concluding moments of the film.

One observation that can be made about Lloyd's work in films is that his resolutions improved markedly from the 1918 through the 1920 one- and two-reelers. The 1919 one-reelers such as *The Chef* and *Chop Suey and Company* have forced and uninteresting endings. Even a good "topper gag" seems to be absent. By the end of the 1920's better structure becomes evident in *Get Out and Get Under.* By 1921 *Never Weaken,* the thrill comedy precursor of *Safety Last,* has a clearly motivated resolution with a good "topper"—Harold and his girl almost get carried up on a girder attached to a cable as they sit down on it to express their love for each other. Evidently Lloyd and his gag writers became more concerned about the resolutions of their films on the eve of the comedian's move to feature length films. This concern, fortunately, was carried over into the creation of Lloyd's major works of the twenties.

9
Overall Observation

Lloyd's Use of Material

Three practices of Lloyd are most significant to the discussion of
his use of material: (1) his use of the success story, (2) his blend of
slapstick and genteel traditions of comedy, and (3) his use of stock
comic material. These practices, it will be revealed, are interre-
lated and are linked to the other areas of investigation which are
being discussed in this final chapter.

In general, Lloyd uses a variation on the success story which
can most readily be identified with the writings of Horatio Alger,
Jr.—such works as *Ragged Dick* and *Luke Larkin's Luck*, for example. Lloyd, of course, does not use a serious treatment of the
rags-to-riches theme as Alger does. *Safety Last* fits some of the
qualifications which Russel Crouse, an editor of a collection of
Alger's novels, sets forth regarding Alger's success story. According to Crouse, the hero of this type of story "is always the same
young man. He is poor; he is honest; he is manly; he is cheerful;
he is ambitious. He always starts at the bottom and ends up at the
top."[1] Alger's work was, unlike Lloyd's, a direct plea to youth
which "told them to be honest and persevere. It told them to
work and win. To be more exact, it told them to have pluck and
they would have luck."[2]

While many of the attributes of the Alger hero can be applied
to the comic character Harold in his struggles in *Safety Last*, there

1. Crouse, *Struggling Upward and Other Works* (New York, 1945), p. viii.
2. *Ibid.*, p. xiii.

202

are marked differences. Obviously, the greatest difference is in the comic treatment presented by Lloyd. Alger's serious treatment does not promote more fully developed characterization than Lloyd's treatment. Alger is too obsessed with situations that promote commonplace truisms. Many situations in his stories end with elaborate platitudes; he does not use situation to develop character.

In *Safety Last* Lloyd's comic character, unlike Alger's, satisfied many of his wants by using harmless deceptions. A character in an Alger story would not use such devices. He is a plodding soul who gains his success by persistence and not by the straightforward aggressiveness of Harold in *Safety Last*. Lloyd also does not allow his comic character to reach his goal merely by luck. Lloyd's comic hero in *Safety Last* is a manipulator who often falls victim to his own schemes. As Crouse points out, Alger's hero achieves success by convenient accidents. The actions of the hero are incidental to the final success.[3] However inept the comic hero in Lloyd's work, he still determines his own destiny with some assistance from good luck.

Both *Grandma's Boy* and *The Freshman* are stronger deviations from the standard success story. They take one phase of the success story—personal and social success—and exploit it fully. *Grandma's Boy* places emphasis on the Boy's personal triumph over cowardice, while *The Freshman* stresses Harold Lamb's struggle to gain recognition from a particular social group, the college set. Both films show the young man working directly to obtain his goal. Lloyd, therefore, gives his comic character some of the go-getter spirit that was used by Johnny Hines and Douglas MacLean in their feature-length genteel comedies of the period.

It may be concluded that Lloyd's treatment of the success story is a mild burlesque of the basic material. In *Grandma's Boy,* the Boy wins his fight against the Rival through his unorthodox way of fighting—a way of fighting which is not in the manly tradition of the Horatio Alger story. He gains the courage of a lion through a ruse and captures a tramp. The comic character in *Safety Last* is forced to play the role of a human fly; through a series of hair-raising accidents, he is goaded to the top of the building and to the success he desires. And in *The Freshman,* Harold Lamb wins the game and the admiration of the college set

3. *Ibid.,* p. viii.

by his own interpretation of the rules of the game. In short, because of the protagonist's character and his approach to his goal, all three portraits are comic deviations from the common success story.

In his treatment of the success story, Lloyd incorporates an interesting blend of genteel and slapstick comedy. The overall pattern of this blend shows the story framed, through the introduction and conclusion, in the genteel comedy tradition. The basic problems and solutions of the Boy in *Grandma's Boy* and those of Harold Lamb in *The Freshman,* as presented at the beginning and end of the works, are especially in the genteel tradition. There are sentimental overtones throughout these works which are typical of this tradition. *Safety Last,* on the other hand, minimizes this tradition, with only the love affair of Harold and Mildred in the beginning and ending of the story displaying the genteel comedy tradition. The leading comic character's efforts to gain success are not sentimentalized in this work. *Grandma's Boy*, however, sentimentalizes slightly the Boy's efforts to be a brave man. Harold Lamb's strivings to be socially accepted in *The Freshman* also receive this same emphasis. The core of these two works, in contrast to *Safety Last,* is sentimentally directed.

The basic comedy sequences, the parts of the films which are filled with the most comedy, lean toward the older, slapstick tradition. This investigation has revealed four main comedy sequences in *Grandma's Boy,* three in *Safety Last,* and four in *The Freshman.* Only one sequence in each of these three films reflects an emphasis on genteel comedy throughout the complete sequence. The Boy's embarrassments at the Girl's party, sequence VI in *Grandma's Boy;* Harold's attempts to appear successful to Mildred while working in a department story, sequence X in *Safety Last;* and Harold Lamb's speech before the student body, in sequence V of *The Freshman,* are part of Lloyd's work which concentrate on genteel humor. The Fall Frolic sequence of *The Freshman,* sequence XIII, in which the leading comic character experiences embarrassments and eventual humiliation, presents an interesting blend of both the genteel and slapstick traditions.

An important pattern may therefore be observed: Lloyd uses genteel humor in the frame and plotting of his stories, but employs humor in the slapstick tradition for the strongest parts of his comedies. This observation, a basic one in this last chapter, needs qualification: the slapstick comedy Lloyd uses in these three films is often a modified, milder version of the slapstick comedy used in the one- and two-reel comedies of the formative period of silent-screen comedy. Also, genteel comedy sequences used between these slapstick sequences affect the overall work so that a greater range and a greater variety of comic incidents are produced.

In the execution and development of his basic material, Lloyd employs comic materials that have been handed down from the past. He modifies such standard comic material as disguise for comic intrigue, odd clothing for comic effect, the pratfall, comic beatings, the chase, and stock comic characters. Most of the alteration in this type of material comes from the blend of the two comic traditions and a clear cut design in the plotting which integrates this stock material into a strong story line.

Lloyd's use of disguise for comic intrigue is not extensive in these three works. *Grandma's Boy* uses this device in the Civil War flashback when Grandpa, as a seemingly incompetent spy for the Confederates, disguises himself as a servant in the Union army headquarters. The only direct comedy created from this disguise develops when Grandpa is easily detected because his Confederate trousers can be seen beneath an apron which he has draped over them. *Safety Last* capitalizes on the comedian's disguise as a female mannequin. Harold uses this ruse to gain entrance into his place of employment without being counted late to work. A mild use of this device which does not employ the risqué often accompanied the intrigue developed from a man disguised in woman's clothes in the one- and two-reel comedies of the 1910's.

Odd attire and faulty clothing assist in creating comedy in *Grandma's Boy* and *The Freshman*. In *Grandma's Boy*, the Boy is shown in a ridiculously shrunken suit after he has been pushed into a well by the Rival, and the Boy dons an ancient suit which brings him embarrassment at a party. *The Freshman* not only shows Harold Lamb in a ludicrous football uniform; it features the comic hero's many difficulties with a suit that a tailor has had time only to baste. Lloyd's use of comic clothes and disguise, therefore, generally produces mild humor, with one notable exception that occurs when Harold Lamb loses his pants in the Fall Frolic sequence of *The Freshman*. Lloyd, therefore, normally uses clothing in the genteel tradition in much the same manner as comedians Johnny Hines, Douglas MacLean, and Charles Ray. His horn-rimmed glasses, straw hat, and dark suit do not follow the older tradition of the clown habit which Charles Chaplin, Buster Keaton, and Harry Langdon used even in the 1920's.

In contrast to Lloyd's use of clothing, his use of pratfalls and comic fights reflects the characteristics of the older tradition. Harold Lamb's fall from a speaker's stand in *The Freshman* shows the pratfall in its simplest form with some sophistication of the device through the handling of the camera and the editing. *Safety Last* presents a comic fall from a streetcar which is similar to the many falls which the Keystone Cops took from a speeding patrol wagon; and many of the slips and falls which occur while Harold is climbing a building in the same picture are like the violent actions in the early comic films. The difference between Lloyd's works and the early works can be explained in one word —motivation. In early one- and two-reel films the pratfall is often developed from unmotivated fights between comedians and from incidents which feature such happenings as an accidental slip on a banana peel. There is, for example, little motivation for the police patrol boats and the patrol wagons in *Tillie's Punctured Romance* (1914) and *Fatty and Mabel Adrift* (1916) to periodically throw policeman into the water or onto the street.

Just as the pratfall is more clearly motivated, comic fights in Lloyd's work are carefully integrated into the action of the story. The Boy's long, exhausting fight with the Rival is an outgrowth of the basic triangle situation. His battle with the tramp is also similarly motivated by the plot development. Football practice and the big football game itself in the climactic sequence of *The Freshman* retain many of the features of a comic fight of the early comic films, displaying these features with clear-cut motivation.

From the early comic film Lloyd also draws chase material for one of the best and most elaborate sequences in *Grandma's Boy*—the one in which the Boy pursues the tramp. A chase is used again in *Safety Last* when the policeman pursues Bill, the steeplejack. In both cases, the improbabilities of the early chase sequences of Mack Sennett's Keystone Cops are not the main ingredient of the comedy. The chases are generally handled on a more realistic basis with most of the gags featuring actions that are probable in real life.

Lloyd uses an abundance of stock comic characters as material for his comedies. The girl friend in his three films is always a trusting, pretty, naive young girl. A stock antagonist or comic villain, such as the Rival in *Grandma's Boy* and the College Cad in

The Freshman, creates opposition for the comic hero in a direct and relentless way. Stock portraits of the comic drunk who is a great nuisance, and the stupid policeman with a sternly official, humorless air are used in *Safety Last. Grandma's Boy* features Grandma, a "Mrs. Fixit," who helps solve the Boy's problems. Only in Lloyd's character does a degree of dimension in a comic character exist—a subject that will be discussed in detail later in this chapter.

On the whole, then, Lloyd's use of comic material shows a strong heritage from the past. He generally achieves freshness in handling this stock material by elaborate, careful motivation with a fresh twist in the use of the material at the end of an incident or sequence. The last-second touchdown in *The Freshman,* for example, features a superhuman run with many chaselike features which concludes with a pile-up of men at the goal line. It is then revealed that Harold has made the winning touchdown when he is shown with his face covered with lime from the goal line. A fresh twist of the comic fall is also created in *Safety Last* when the comedian gets tangled in a flagpole rope and swings out over the street twelve stories below. Such effective and fresh treatments of his material made Lloyd an outstanding comedian in the motion pictures of the twenties.

Lloyd's Organization of His Materials

Harold Lloyd uses a strong, tight construction in the development of his comic film story. Paul Rotha's concept that Lloyd's films are "entirely contrived out of a series of comic situations"[4] is not valid. Episodes or sequences with an extensive use of gags in a series do exist, but Rotha's view underrates the overall design of Lloyd's works. In each film, the larger units (exposition, primary development, midpoint of development, etc.) contain at least one extended sequence which is intensely filled with a series of gags. These series of gags spring from logical developments of the story. Sequences of this nature are surrounded by linking sequences which present information, and of situations that give the work coherence. Episodic structure exists to a degree; but episodic development exists in many films, serious and comic.

4. Rotha, p. 214. Bardèche and Brasillach also have expressed this opinion (see p. 292 of their work), but Joe Franklin and Robert Sherwood praise Lloyd's construction of his films.

Some of the characteristics of the overall organization of the three films in this study may be seen by examining the number, arrangement, and nature of the sequences. The works break down into a similar number of sequences: *Grandma's Boy,* seventeen; *Safety Last,* sixteen; and *The Freshman,* sixteen. Four transitional sequences[5] assist in the story development of *Grandma's Boy. Safety Last* uses two transitional sequences which assist in setting forth Mildred's concern for Harold and her desire to join him in the big city; it also has one transitional sequence which helps set up many of the situations for the building-climbing sequence. *The Freshman* employs a total of four transitional sequences; three of these are used in the early part of the story development, and only one is used in the last part of the film to establish the conditions for the Fall Frolic. On the whole, *Safety Last* is more successful than the other two works in blending exposition with plot development.

Another design can be detected in the use of sequences which are filled with a great deal of comic material. These sequences form major portions of the work and present the most interesting episodes in the films. In *Grandma's Boy,* this type of sequence is used four times. These sequences with their total running time (in minutes and seconds) are: VI, "The Party at Mildred's House" (9:08); XI, "Grandpa's Civil War Adventure" (7:48); XIV, "The Boy Pursues the Tramp" (6:19); XVI, "The Great Battle Between the Boy and the Rival" (5:50). *Safety Last* presents a similar pattern, with one less major comic sequence and an extension of running time: IV, "Trouble Getting to Work" (9:01); X, "Harold's Dual Life" (16:17); and XV, "Harold's Big Climb" (20:45). *The Freshman* features four major comic sequences: V, "Before the Student Body" (9:37); VIII, "Football Practice" (15:14); XIII, "At the Fall Frolic" (16:52); and XV, "The Great Game" (17:30).

Each work features the climactic sequence as the last major comic sequence. As the numbering of the sequences indicates, a pattern of location is similar. These major comic sequences indicates, a pattern of location is similar. These major comic sequences are strategically placed: stronger comedy in greater amounts occurs in the latter part of the works as the development reaches a climax. For example, in *Grandma's Boy,* two major comic

5. As has been explained, the transitional sequence is used for the purpose of exposition. Situations are usually established which are used in major actions later in the story development. Comedy is mild or even absent in Lloyd's transitional sequences.

sequences, XIV and XVI, are in the last third of the work. *Safety Last* places one strong comic sequence, X, well past the halfway point; and sequence XV, the climactic sequence, runs until the last minute of the work. This climactic sequence is the longest major comic sequence of the three works and presents greater elaboration on one situation than do any of the other major comic sequences. *The Freshman* follows a pattern similar to that in *Grandma's Boy,* with comic sequences XIII and XV in the last third of the work.

The material in the later sequences of Lloyd's films, as this analysis indicates, is progressively humorous. Lloyd builds to a climax by placing the strongest comic material toward the end of the film. While this may seem to be an obvious method for developing a comedy, the amount of comic material used is high. Not all comic works feature such an intensive amount of comic material in this part of the drama.[6]

After a detailed study of *Grandma's Boy,* it may be concluded that the comic treatment of the regeneration theme is unified by the central comic idea. As Chapter 2 pointed out, even in synopsis form this unifying comic idea can be detected. The whole idea of the complete about-face or transformation of a cowardly, incompetent person into an extremely brave, heroic character assists in unifying the dramatic story. *Safety Last* also presents a central comic idea which makes this film effective structurally. It presents a comic hero who is a pretender to success—a man who gets caught in his own manipulations. Both works, therefore, are structurally bound up in comic reversals that affect the total pattern of the story development. *The Freshman,* in the final analysis, is more complex. There is a reversal that occurs when the college boob becomes the college hero—Harold Lamb then achieves social success. The work is not, however, unified by an overall comic idea that affects the total pattern of the story development as it does in the other two films. This study, therefore, must conclude that structurally, *The Freshman* does not use a main comic idea as a unifying agent. This accounts for some of the weaknesses of the story development, especially in the development that leads to a crisis, an observation which has been discussed in Chapter 6. This

6. Of the major comedians, Buster Keaton is second to Lloyd in the placement of gag-packed sequences toward the end of his works. Many of his features—for example, *Our Hospitality* (1923), *Sherlock, Jr.* (1924), *The Navigator* (1924), *The General* (1927) and *Steamboat Bill, Jr.* (1927)—employ many gags to develop an episode in this portion of the films.

sequence is poorly related to the total design of the work even though it is related to the comic hero's strivings toward a goal.

Another way of achieving unity is also evident. Unity is achieved in the comic films of Harold Lloyd not only by having a story revolve around one character, but by displaying a strong interrelationship or integration of plot and character. A great deal of emphasis is placed on the central character and his drive for success. Both *Grandma's Boy* and *The Freshman* have a plot development which springs from the leading character's personal problem. While character seems less strongly related to the plot development in *Safety Last,* the basic drive of the leading figure is evident throughout the film. Only in the degree of emphasis is the character less strongly applied in the plot development of this work. Unity is achieved, therefore, by the obsession of the leading character and the actions which result from this obsession. The Boy in *Grandma's Boy* craves courage; Harold, in *Safety Last,* wants success in business; and Harold Lamb in *The Freshman* desires social acceptance.

Unity in Lloyd's work is greater than in many of the important silent-screen comedies. Mack Sennett's *Tillie's Punctured Romance* (1914) lacks unity because the leading comic figures, played by Charles Chaplin and Marie Dressler, do not have clear-cut goals. Chaplin's little tramp in *The Gold Rush* (1925) does not possess a clear-cut goal. He is too much of an outcast from society to be interested in some of the same goals that a Harold Lloyd comic character might seek. The little tramp's desire for friends is a goal which helps unify the film, but the little tramp can only weakly pursue this goal. Harry Langdon presents a similarly weak, pathetic creature in *The Strong Man* (1926) as he is dominated completely by a circus strong man. Buster Keaton's comic character in *The General* (1927) is placed in a situation where he might develop a drive similar to that of a Lloyd comic character. Buster is very depressed when he is rejected from serving in the Southern army in the Civil War. He does not take the necessary steps to get into the war as a Lloyd character might, however. By accident, Buster gets involved in the war and carries on a one-man battle against Union forces. Unlike Harold Lloyd's comic character, Buster fights with a stoic air—he is caught up in the current of the conflict without being greatly disturbed. Consequently, his goal or goals are never clear.

Strength in Lloyd's work is achieved, therefore, in a comic character that is more directly related to reality—a young man who has the same goals as average young men. Chaplin, Keaton, and Langdon present a traditional clown type—an outcast who is similar to the European clown. While Lloyd's character is an outcast at the beginning of both *Grandma's Boy* and *The Freshman*, he has the potentials that eventually help him to gain social acceptance. The tramp-clowns created by Langdon, Keaton, and Chaplin are rejected lost souls who have characteristics which make them unacceptable to society, regardless of their brave deeds and successes. They bear the stamp of the rejected and cannot alter their manners and deficiencies. They are sadly lacking in the will to succeed—a trait that Lloyd's character has in abundance. Lloyd's character follows a more realistic, American tradition. The drive of this Yankee clown gives the plot sustenance—imparts unity to the whole plot development.

With this observation, another major conclusion is reached in this study. The importance of character in the development of the dramatic story line is not realized by the critics who have evaluated Lloyd's works. Such critics as James Agee, Paul Rotha, C. A. Lejeune, and Joe Franklin are unaware of the importance that character plays in the development of Lloyd's films. They express views which maintain that Lloyd depends mostly on plot and comic situation, and they fail to see the comic character operating within the situation. This is an understandable first impression because the mechanics of Lloyd's plotting are, at times, noticeable. His cleverness is not always disguised. His cleverly executed gags often fall into a pattern. The critics, however, do not find this an objectionable feature of his works. While they overlook the importance of character in unifying the plot, they are impressed by Lloyd's inventiveness in developing the comic situation.

The Character of the Leading Comedian

An analysis of Lloyd's use of character in his works shows that plot and character are strongly integrated. Even though he has used many strong situation gags which stand out, and has therefore produced comic incidents which seem to be based more on situation than character, the importance of the leading character is evident throughout the work. Lloyd uses character as the basis of plot development.

The key to understanding the comic character developed by Lloyd lies in the leading figure's zeal. The enthusiasm of this comic character gives it distinction. Leading comedians of the time—Chaplin, Keaton, and Langdon, seldom used this trait in their comic characters. Lloyd, on the other hand, uses this trait as the basic facet of his character. Some of the best comic moments of the films occur when Harold's zeal leads him to situations which backfire. In *Safety Last,* for example, Harold is forced to live two roles—one to impress his girl friend that he is a success, and the other to maintain his position as a lowly clerk in the department store. His desire to make a promotional stunt succeed forces him to assume the role of a human fly. Throughout *The Freshman,* Harold Lamb's eagerness to be socially accepted makes him a boob in the eyes of the people he is trying to impress. He becomes a ridiculous figure because he attempts feats he is ill-equipped to handle: he tries to make a speech before the student body, and he struggles pathetically to play the game of football. In *Grandma's Boy,* his enthusiasm to display his courage backfires many times as he pursues the tramp. In each case, however, the fault that gains the comedy is also the virtue that wins the victory. His zeal drives him to conquer his obstacles in a variety of unusual ways. Victory is achieved, it must be pointed out, with the assistance of luck.

By developing a comic character whose fault and virtue lie in his zeal, Lloyd has developed a comic type which is closely related to one phase of our national character. He has developed "an American comedy." We are a nation that has accomplished much through the philosophy and zeal of the "go-getters." Progress has been our battle cry since the nineteenth century. Lloyd has, of course, shown this zeal in a humorous light. In our eagerness we bungle; we plow into situations without reflection; and often our eagerness and haste make us comic to the Old World with its more stoic demeanor. In a gentle way, Lloyd allows us to laugh at ourselves; and he is consequently moving some of the great tensions which result from a culture which is strongly motivated by a philosophy of progress and success.

While Lloyd allows us to laugh at the struggles of his comic hero, he does not permit satirical elements to enter into the

A brash young man in **Why Worry?** (1923), a character that sometimes dominated the total story.

makeup of this laughter. In his attempt to gain sympathy for the leading comic character, he, unfortunately, is not so successful in blending serious and comic materials as Charles Chaplin and Harry Langdon were. Serious incidents which intend to invoke sympathy for the comic character are introduced momentarily in Lloyd's works when the Boy in *Grandma's Boy* breaks down and weeps. These moments are not effectively handled; there is not the underplaying of the serious situation which made Chaplin and Langdon successful in handling this type of material.[7] There are moments, however, in which Lloyd captures the audiences with a blend of the serious and the comic. In the early part of *Grandma's Boy*, the plight of the Boy who has been pushed into the well by the Rival is effectively demonstrated. There is also a touch of tender comedy in *The Freshman* when Harold Lamb is innocently mauled by teammates as he assumes the role of a tackle dummy for a football practice session. Dazed by this gueling punishment, the young man collapses wearily on the shoulders of the coach who has given him the assignment. Pathetically, he slides to the feet of the coach and, like a faithful dog, remains devoted to his master who glares unsympathetically down at him. It is one of Lloyd's best blendings of the serious and the comic.

Lloyd's character also reveals a blending of two comic traditions. In the final analysis, it seems more firmly based on the genteel tradition of comedy. However, his character moves in an unusual world in which many things can happen to him. He can get into situations that force him to fight, climb a tall building, or chase an outlaw. In such situations, broad, slapstick comedy seems to reign. In the shadows of the most frenzied activity that grips this character, however, lies the basic sentimentalized figure. This is the young man who is striving to get ahead. Many of his setbacks, the milder moments of Lloyd's films, reveal the genteel comic character in embarrassments that are too tame for the slapstick tradition. But his character undergoes a rapid metamorphosis in dire circumstances. Only a hint of the genteel character remains; nevertheless, it is always there. When Lloyd's comic character struggles the hardest (a trait in the genteel tradition), many of the facets of the older clown overshadow the newer. When the comic character fights the tramp and the Rival, strug-

7. The most successful integration of sympathetic moments in Lloyd's films can be seen in the 1927 *The Kid Brother*. The comedian's underplaying of these scenes is superior to the enactment of similar material in his other works.

gles up a building, and makes a spectacular run in the football game, the slapstick character of the past springs forth in full bloom.

Harold Lloyd's Acting

Just as the handling of the story material and the development of the leading comic character display a blend of two traditions, so does Lloyd's acting style. Many moments in Lloyd's work show the actor playing his part broadly as if he were a vaudeville comedian who needed to emphasize his reactions to the back row of the theater. This is especially noticeable in *Grandma's Boy* but is not evident in *The Freshman*. Since many long shots are used in *Grandma's Boy*, the actor must often point up the comic business without a great deal of assistance from the camera or editing. The duration of the shots in this film shows that editing and special set-up shots are not being employed to any great extent. Consequently, Lloyd's performance reflects the older one- and two-reel method of action. Lloyd's use of this older style is highly effective, however, in the routines of *Grandma's Boy* when the Boy gets his finger stuck in a vase and, later, when he accidentally swallows a mothball. The comedian's reactions are broad and are directed to a camera which remains in a neutral position. This same acting style can be seen in the routine which shows Harold trying to enter the boss's office in *Safety Last*. In this routine the comedian screws up his courage many times to try to accomplish this simple task. While this type of pantomime reflects the older style of film acting, many of the reactions of the comedian in *The Freshman*, especially in the Fall Frolic scenes in which the comedian has trouble with his tuxedo, are less broad and are not so strongly directed to the camera.

Other characteristics of Lloyd's acting may be seen in his handling of broad pantomime, simple pantomimed business, facial reactions, timing, and special skills.

The critics have noticed Lloyd's skill in pantomiming broad comic actions. Gilbert Seldes points to his athletic skills;[8] and Buster Keaton, who is noted for his unusual gifts in this type of movement, credits Lloyd with a great deal of acrobatics in his

8. Seldes, *The Movies Come from America* (New York, 1937), p. 42.

comedy.[9] As the Boy in *Grandma's Boy,* Lloyd exhibits his acrobatic skill in his fight with the Rival; his pursuit of the tramp is likewise filled with acrobatics. As Harold Lamb in *The Freshman,* he also illustrates this skill by tumbling, jumping, and running in football practice and the game. And, probably most notable of all, the comedian's antics as a would-be human fly on a high building in *Safety Last* prove his ability to execute broad comic movements with deftness.

Broad pantomime is, however, not enough to sustain a feature-length film. A skilled performer must be able to handle simple pantomime material, because much of the story development of a comic film depends on minor problems and frustrations which are commonplace and similar to the everyday experiences of the motion picture audience. Lloyd uses such material in *Grandma's Boy.* Varying degrees of comic shyness are shown when the Boy sits on the bench with his girl friend and the Rival. His efforts to court the Girl are frustrated when he discovers that he has been holding hands with his rival in love. Forced to live out his lie that he is an executive in a large department store, the leading comic figure of *Safety Last* undergoes the anxiety of near discovery by his girl friend or the boss. Lloyd displays comic nervousness by pulling at his collar and straightening the contours of his suit. In both of these illustrations of his handling of simple material, Lloyd is especially adept in masking his true feelings by the use of disarming smiles directed toward the actress portraying his girl friend while, at the same time, he reveals to his movie audience his discomfort in the situation. Deftness in timing accomplishes this change in attitude. Slight gestures and facial reactions are executed cleverly to achieve the comedy in these situations.

Many of the incidents in sequence XIII, "At the Fall Frolic," in *The Freshman* also depend on very simple reactions by the leading comedian. Each embarrassment requires an attitude from the comedian which is conveyed by slight bodily movements and facial reactions. The handling of this type of material requires the talents of a skilled performer. The material itself is not as comic as that involving more elaborate situations; the comedian's execution of the pantomime creates the comedy.

One of the strongest assets of the motion-picture comedian is his ability to register effective facial reactions. This skill is evident

9. Keaton, *My Wonderful World . . . ,* p. 127.

in Lloyd's three films. His ability to register comic emotions with a smile is outstanding. As James Agee wrote, Lloyd has a "thesaurus of smiles."[10] In *Grandma's Boy,* he displays the meek, shy smile of a young man who is more a mouse than a man when he greets a woman. When he goes to battle with the tramp in the same work, and when he bends all his energies to clerking in a department store in *Safety Last,* he presents the smile of an overeager young man. When he is confronted with a dangerous situation as he is teetering on a ledge of a building in *Safety Last,* Lloyd reveals the nervous smile of a man who is afraid but is trying to cover his fear with a smile. In *The Freshman,* as Harold Lamb, a young man with social pretensions, the comedian displays a smile to cover up the embarrassment of having his clothes unravel at a public dance. In all three works, Lloyd shows the broad, doting (almost simpering) smile of a young man engrossed in his girl friend's charms. In short, Lloyd's smile is one of his most distinguishing assets. He makes it a strong part of his comic character in each film. It helps set him apart from the other major comedians of the twenties. Buster Keaton never smiled; his comic character was stoic in love and battle; his face remained as expressionless as if it were hewn of stone. Both Charles Chaplin and Harry Langdon used a variety of smiles, but they did not use them extensively.

Lloyd's work also demonstrates his ability to execute effective "comic takes." Lloyd, however, seldom uses the more contrived pantomimic gesture of the "double take"—a realization which demands a delayed-action "take." A "take" is a sharp, exaggerated, comic reaction that is often used in moments of anger, fear, determination, frustration, embarrassment, and humiliation. Lloyd exhibits his aptitude in registering such comic attitudes when he is climbing the building in *Safety Last.* His range of emotional attitudes is extensive. His "comic takes" which show a growing fear with each struggling step up the building are effectively controlled. He also shows a variety of emotional attitudes which range from mild embarrassment to utter humiliation when he has problems with a faulty tuxedo in the Fall Frolic sequence of *The Freshman.*

Each of the pantomimed gestures which Lloyd executes in his work depends on a good sense of timing. This facility is well developed in Lloyd's acting. As most skilled pantomimists realize, a

10. Agee, p. 10.

The shy smile of the meek soul in **Grandma's Boy.**

The con-man smile in **Why Worry?**

joke cannot be effective unless the action is carefully timed. This ability of Lloyd's is most evident when he is handling simple material such as the incident in *Safety Last* in which he fails repeatedly to screw up enough courage to knock on his boss's door. Each effort to knock must be extended only so long, and the reaction to failure also must be held the correct length of time to gain humor from the incident. It is a skill, moreover, that can also be witnessed in broader pantomime.

Comedians often have special skill in juggling, dancing, and mimicking people or animals which helps them in their comic routines. Such skills are not so marked in Lloyd's work as they are in the works of Charles Chaplin, Buster Keaton, and W. C. Fields. Nevertheless, at times, Lloyd exhibits his ability to execute these special skills. In *Grandma's Boy*, as the Boy pursues a tramp who is wanted for murder, Lloyd assumes the role of a cowboy lassoing a steer as he comes near the tramp in an automobile. He skillfully swings the rope as he drives the car with his feet.[11] Lloyd also lapses into a fencing routine in the bargain sale sequence of *Safety Last*. He fences, yardstick in hand, with the aplomb of a master to ward off an indignant woman who pokes him with her umbrella. Yelling in pain after being stuck by a needle in *The Freshman,* he imitates the howl of a wolf for comic effect.

In general, Lloyd demonstrates superior pantomime ability. He has a wide range of comic facial expressions and bodily attitudes which he uses within the scope of his material. He seems to have followed his policy of not adding an irrelevant gag. He is quoted on this matter by John B. Kennedy: "All my pictures were to be full of gags, but the stunt was never to subordinate the story, and not a laugh was to be made unless it had a basis in logic."[12]

The Characteristics of Lloyd's Use of Comedy

After examining the comic incidents in Lloyd's three films, I find that the overall characteristic which predominates is the spirit of the comedy. Lloyd's comedy is permeated with the spirit of play; the derisive spirit seldom takes over a comic incident. The play spirit, taken in its broadest sense, calls upon the audience to take everything in the spirit of good fun—it provides a light, comic touch that does not hold personages in the drama up for ridicule. While the leading comic character in Lloyd's films is subject to many abuses, such as the trials of the Boy in the early part of *Grandma's Boy,* and the grueling punishment of Harold Lamb during the rough game of football in *The Freshman,* the improprieties directed toward the comedian do not result in a high degree of derisive comedy. There are situations in which the particular attitudes present in derisive laughter and those present in sympathetic laughter are not distinct. By blending two comic traditions, the slapstick and the genteel comedy. Lloyd has created a comic drama that has thrived on this combination. While the derisive spirit of the older slapstick tradition at times assumes the major emphasis—especially during fights and other physical im-

11. Camera work and editing assist in creating the full impact of this gag. Nevertheless, the special skill Lloyd has in handling a rope is evident in this action.

12. Kennedy, p. 28.

proprieties (such as Harold's loss of his pants in *The Freshman* and his burn on the rump from a blowtorch in *Safety Last*)—this spirit is not strong in the total design. Abuse of the stupid policeman in *Safety Last,* and the tramp and the Rival in *Grandma's Boy,* do not make up the bulk of the comedy in these works. In short, by blending the slapstick and genteel traditions, Lloyd has softened the improprieties of the slapstick he uses and still retains some of the strong, lively action of this type of comedy. Most of Lloyd's comedy is gentle; the bulk of his humor is in fun—in the spirit of play.

To create comedy, Lloyd uses specific devices such as comic ingenuity, overstatement, understatement, reversal. Comic ingenuity is one of the most interesting devices for achieving comedy. Each leading character in his films employs this unusual way of solving some problem. The device is directly related to character and situation. Harold in *Safety Last,* for example, uses comic ingenuity more often than the Boy and Harold Lamb in the other two works. It is part of the essential cleverness of the young man in *Safety Last,* but it is only used by the Boy and Harold Lamb when they are exerting all their efforts to gain their objectives; ordinarily, they are too shy or naive to use their wits in this way. The Boy and Harold Lamb often use a childlike comic ingenuity; they solve their problems by engaging in an "act of play"—they fight for their objectives as if they were merely playing a game.

Harold, in *Safety Last,* has an aggressive facet to his character which prompts him to apply his unusual logic in order to get himself out of many difficulties. Sequence IV, "Trouble Getting to Work," shows Harold trying to get to work on time by attempting many schemes; and sequence X, "Harold's Dual Life," features his feigning success before Mildred by using various tricks. The former situation reveals more of the "game spirit" of the child while the latter displays a cleverness that is adult. When he climbs a building, however, the situation softens his ingenuity. He is too afraid to apply his wits to the majority of the obstacles which lie in his path.

Unlike Harold in his successful use of comic ingenuity in *Safety Last,* the Boy in sequence XIV, "The Boy Pursues the Tramp," in *Grandma's Boy,* finds many of his clever schemes backfiring on him. At times Harold Lamb, in *The Freshman,* employs comic ingenuity on an adult level. In a couple of incidents in sequence

Romance was always important in the plot. Lloyd's leading lady, Jobyna Ralston, appeared in seven features from 1923 through 1927.

The tender heart was often a part of his character—in **Hot Water** (1924).

XV, "The Great Game," he uses his wits to escape a tackler as he carries the football. *Grandma's Boy* and *The Freshman*, however, do not extensively use this method of achieving comedy.

On the whole, *Safety Last* presents some of its best comic moments when comic ingenuity is displayed. This method of achieving comedy is especially effective because it often promotes strong visual gags; it reveals the character of the leading comedian; and it provides comedy that illustrates strong invention on the part of the leading comedian. All major comedians, Chaplin, Keaton, and Langdon, as well as Lloyd, use this method of achieving comedy.

Most of the strongest incidents of humor in Lloyd's works follow the pattern of the earlier one- and two-reel comic films, with many sophistications in the handling of material. Incidents are made comic by an exaggeration or overstatement of a normal situation. The climb up the building in *Safety Last*, for example, uses more obstacles than would be encountered in the lifetime of a professional human fly. More things happen to Harold Lamb's faulty tuxedo in *The Freshman* than could possible happen in a real-life situation. Plausibility is constantly sought, however, by the careful planting of motivating causes; development follows a strong cause-and-effect relationship.

Overstatement of the leading comic character's traits is an important comic device which operates throughout the films. The overstatement of Harold Lamb's naiveté is basic to the development of the character's humorous actions in *The Freshman*; *Grandma's Boy* presents excessive meekness in the Boy that is comic in its exaggeration; and *Safety Last* (and *The Freshman*, to a degree) presents an overeager young man who is constantly leaning forward, smiling, ready to go. Harold Lamb does not possess the same aggressive spirit as his counterpart in *Safety Last*, but his eagerness reflects some of the same spirit.

At times, the type of humorous device used is understatement, but these times are rare. More often, understatement is manifested in the verbal humor of the titles. When a motherly lady leans out of a window and warns Harold, "Young man, don't you know you might fall and get hurt?" as he struggles in his climb up a building in *Safety Last*, understatement is clearly used. Of the three films, *Safety Last* uses this device most often.

While comic understatement is seldom employed, comic reversals are often used. Reversals which utilize the motion-picture medium are the most spectacular way of gaining humor in Lloyd's

Automobile troubles in **Hot Water** (1924)—an elaboration of material used in one-reelers.

films. Each film, as this study has shown, employs an elaborate comic revelation in the early part of the story; this revelation displays a sharp comic reversal. More common types of reversals are freely used throughout Lloyd's works. The reversal is often used to conclude an incident and also to conclude a comic sequence. *Safety Last's* climactic sequence show this pattern clearly—each incident is concluded by a sharp reversal, and the final incident produces the most spectacular reversal.

By far the most important comic reversals, however, are those that affect a large portion of the plot development. *Grandma's Boy* is based upon the comic transformation of a meek lad into a fearless hero. *The Freshman* also reveals the most incompetent player on the football team, Harold Lamb, winning the game without the assistance of his proficient teammates.

In **The Kid Brother** (1927) Lloyd used a chase and fight climax. For the moment he gained advantage, since a snake (unknown to Harold) had coiled itself around his weapon.

The running gag (which usually combines repetition with a final reversal) is seldom used by Lloyd. The best example of this device in Lloyd's work is in *The Freshman*. Harold Lamb repeatedly executes a jig and a handshake as a college greeting throughout the film. The policeman's pursuit of Bill in the building-climbing sequence of *Safety Last* also has many features of a running gag. Although this comic device is seldom used, its use shows the wide range and the variation of devices which Lloyd employed. The running gag always works hand in hand with overstatement and reversal.

In general, there is a great deal of variety in the devices used to gain humor in Lloyd's work. A major comic sequence uses many devices to avoid monotony and to make the most of its basic material. Only two devices seem to fall into a definite pattern. The reversal in each of the three films is often used to conclude an incident, a sequence, or to conclude the whole drama. Overstatement also is an overall controlling device which throws the material with which Lloyd is dealing into a comic vein.

Lloyd's Use of the Techniques of the Motion Picture Medium

Throughout the main body of this study a description and analysis of the techniques of the motion picture medium have been presented with the full realization that Lloyd molded his dramatic story material by using the techniques of the medium. All the photographed material, the actions of the actors in their scenic environment (both in the studio and "on location"), are controlled by these techniques. As an evaluator, I must disengage these techniques from the film, dissect them, and still leave the reader with the understanding that the dramatic presentation and the tools of the art are inseparable in the final art object—the film drama.

Though they are sparingly used in Lloyd's three films, titles serve an important function in the development of silent screen comedy. Expository material is often easily established verbally. Lloyd uses titles sparingly for both exposition and humor; the greater part of his comedies is developed by the pantomime of the actors. Verbal humor in *Grandma's Boy* and *The Freshman* is usually confined to a comment on the situation or on the characters of the drama. This type of narrative comedy functions as a comic aside by the title editor. *Safety Last*, on the other hand, incorporates a great deal of verbal humor in the dialogue. Verbal humor is used extensively in Harold's dialogue in sequence X, "Harold's Dual Life," when the young man tries to impress his girl friend in the De Vore Department Store. During the climactic sequence, XV, "Harold's Big Climb," comments from the crowd as they view the actions of a bogus human fly account for some of the best verbal humor in the film. This type of humor is especially important because it provides contrast with the visual comedy. It provides greater variety and increases interest by often developing a counterpoint to the visual.

Lloyd uses a technique of the medium that is a carry-over from the formative days of the motion-picture comedy—accelerated motion. Accelerated motion in the chase and fight sequences of *Grandma's Boy* is, at times, the main factor used to create comedy; but this distortion of normal action often receives support from the basic situation which exists before the technique is applied. Furthermore, it is difficult to determine how much the pantomime of the actors contributes to the comic situation. Since the fast movements of the actor are created and distorted by this mechanical means, the action which results (such as the overstatement of running and fighting) disguises the actor's contribution.

The technique of accelerated motion is used more sparingly in *Safety Last* and *The Freshman* than it is in *Grandma's Boy*. Moments in the policeman's pursuit of Bill employ accelerated motion. *The Freshman* features a climactic sequence with only a third of its thirty-three-second touchdown run by Harold in "fast" action. The use of accelerated motion in Lloyd's feature works clearly shows the decline of this technique from the early one- and two-reel works which often employed this device for a comic chase or a comic fight.

Lloyd generally uses a wide variety of shots in his films. Long shots, medium shots, and close-ups assist greatly in telling the story and emphasizing the comic situation. Of the three films, *Grandma's Boy* uses the least variety. It employs standard long shots and medium shots with only a few close-ups. The close-up in this work generally functions merely as a device for revealing some detail that will help tell the story. For example, a close-up of a sheet of music reveals the lyrics of the song that the Boy's girl friend is singing. Reaction shots which show the impact of some frustrating or terrifying situation in *Grandma's Boy* are seldom used. *The Freshman,* in sharp contrast with this work, uses many effective reaction shots to point up the embarrassing and frustrating situations which confront Harold Lamb. This is especially noticeable in the Fall Frolic sequence in which Harold is threatened with the loss of his pants when his suspender buttons snap off. Close-up reaction shots of dismay and terror are also important to convey the comic character's plight in the building-climbing sequence of *Safety Last*.

All three films, moreover, use the long shot with skill. *Grandma's Boy* exhibits many excellent long shots (often with a traveling camera) in the chase sequence of the film. In its building-climbing sequence, *Safety Last* uses many extreme long shots to convey the dangerous plight of the comic character in his pathetic attempt to play the role of a human fly. The climactic sequence of *The Freshman* also employs good long shots and a traveling camera in the last-second touchdown by Harold Lamb.

Lloyd seldom uses unusual composition of shots. Asymmetrical framing of the objects being photographed is rarely employed. A shot in *The Freshman* illustrates that Lloyd deviated from his straightforward compositional style when he handled unusual material. In this shot, the comic character's shadow is shown on the sawdust pit where he has been repeatedly tackled by his teammates. Most of Lloyd's shots, however, are presented in a conventional framing of the objects being photographed—objects are generally framed symmetrically. Furthermore, the material Lloyd uses allows this simple, straightforward treatment.

It may be concluded that the shots in each of Lloyd's films are generally more effective during the portions of the film in which the most activity is presented. Shot-wise, however, *The Freshman* is also a work of skill in its less active moments. Comic facial reactions are recorded by clean-cut, well-composed close-ups.

The most effective use of camera angle also seems to be in the portions of the film with the greatest activity. The angle of the shot helps to emphasize the situation. As I have pointed out in chapter 7, *Safety Last* uses strong contrast in angles by switching to a high-angle shot to emphasize a particularly dangerous moment in the comic character's climb up a building.[13] When the character slips and grabs for the hands of the clock, a sharp, high-angle shot is employed to emphasize the dangerous height at which the young man is dangling over the city streets. One of the best uses of camera angle in all three of Lloyd's works is featured in *The Freshman*. Comedy is created when Harold Lamb gets up from a hard tackle in football practice and looks down at his leg. His leg appears to be grotesquely dislocated or broken; but in reality, the leg is from a tackle dummy. Because the proper angle and length of shot are used, the audience can see the damaged tackle dummy in the background.

These examples of Lloyd's effective use of camera angle are, of course, selected from many shots which are more conventional. The majority of Lloyd's shots, as in many motion pictures, are

13. Editing must, of course, come into play to establish this contrast. The high-angle shot in itself, however, conveys the situation with strong impact.

taken from an angle similar to the way we view objects in everyday life. These shots may be said to approximate an eye-level view. Nevertheless, the times when Lloyd does depart from this conventional angle show his awareness of the values of using this technique of the medium.

Lloyd also shows his ability to control and emphasize his material through the use of editing. When the comic character accidentally swings on a flagpole rope in *Safety Last,* editing creates the proper illusion by linking a mock-up shot of the comedian dangling head down on this rope with a shot of a stunt man swinging on the rope from a real building. This spectacular incident relies heavily on editing, special effects, and camera work to create this ludicrous situation. Editing sophisticates the age-old comedy device of the pratfall in *The Freshman.* A series of different angles coupled with long, medium, and close shots prolong and build up Harold Lamb's teetering on a speaker's stand (on which he has climbed to rescue a cat) and his eventual fall. Editing is especially effective in the development of this comic character's embarrassments in the Fall Frolic sequence. Close-ups of his disintegrating tuxedo are coupled with close-ups which show the young man's reactions to his plight.

All these examples show the importance of editing in both telling the story and emphasizing the comic content of the incident. At times editing takes on the special function of creating the joke itself. In *Grandma's Boy,* the juxtaposition of crowd reaction and the movement of a duck create comedy. Two actions which are not in themselves comic have been placed side by side to obtain humor. The crowd reactions in the climactic sequences of both *Safety Last* and *The Freshman* are handled in a similar way. When Harold breaks into a frantic dance to shake a mouse from the inside of his pants leg as he clings to the high ledge of a building in *Safety Last,* a shot is shown of the crowd below him clapping. This juxtaposition of shots conveys the idea that the crowd believes Harold is merely showing his devil-may-care attitude as a human fly by "dancing" on the ledge. While not as direct as this example from *Safety Last,* the crowd reactions and the reactions of the football coach in *The Freshman* to Harold Lamb's bungling attempts to play football reveal the editor both creating and emphasizing the humor of this situation.

Both camera work and editing are often used to create some of the best comic moments in Lloyd's works. The most effective comic incidents in the early portions of his films are developed by revelation. Information is withheld by the use of a particular, limited shot; then, another shot or camera movement reveals the true nature of the incident. In *Safety Last,* the opening shot establishes a misconception which leads the viewer to believe that Harold is in prison; a second shot reveals that he is merely looking through the bars of a gate in a railway station. In *Grandma's Boy,* editing assists in establishing the misconception that the Boy is cranking a car to get it started. A shot is shown of his girl friend asking him if he needs help. Then another shot reveals the Boy cranking. A pan and a dolly-back of the camera reveal that he is merely laboring to make ice cream with a hand-cranked freezer. The revelation gag in *The Freshman,* however, receives little assistance from the film editor. An irised shot opens to reveal that Harold Lamb is not leading a crowd in a football cheer, but is merely practicing in front of his bedroom mirror.

This revelation device creates strong comic incidents at the beginning of each film. Consequently, this use of the techniques of the medium provides an excellent springboard to the total comic development. Superior gags are created early in the films. Thus, the techniques of the medium are highly important to the beginnings of the stories as well as to the portions of the works with the most action in them.

Special effects are not used extensively by Lloyd to achieve comedy. Dissolves are the most frequently used special effects in his works. More often used as a way to show the thoughts of a character, they are rarely used to create comedy. For example, *Safety Last* uses this technique in showing the comic character thinking about a past incident. This earlier occurrence is injected by a dissolve into the past action; when the brief action is completed, another dissolve returns to the present. In *Grandma's Boy,* however, a comic comment is created by a superimposition. The Boy's grandfather is shown pouring several bottles of whiskey into some punch. The strength of the punch is indicated by a superimposition of a mule kicking. Such a use of special effects by Lloyd is, however, rare. He uses them more often as a storytelling device.

Three generalizations may be made in concluding these observations on Lloyd's use of the tools of the film medium. The latter third of each film depends more on the techniques of the medium than the first two thirds. The change is brought about generally by the increasing complexity of the material and the increasing pace of the story development. There is also a progressively greater sophistication in the use of these techniques in the three films from the first, *Grandma's Boy* in 1922, to the last, *The Freshman* in 1925, which indicates Lloyd's growth in making the most of his material by using the techniques of the medium more extensively and effectively. As a third observation, I would like to point out that Lloyd realizes the potentials of all the techniques of the medium. There is never a self-consciously clever use of these techniques. Lloyd uses them in a straightforward, practical way. He does not use unusual pictorial composition or inject spectacular special effects. Lloyd uses these techniques to emphasize, create, and control the comic incidents in his films. To realize how important the techniques of the medium are to Lloyd's feature works, one need only view some of his early one- and two-reel films to see the vital role that these techniques play in developing a more effective comic work. The early works have a flair—a zest that is intriguing, but they often fail to exploit their material fully. Many gags are lost through an inadequate emphasis on comic detail. Lloyd's feature works show the techniques of the medium gripping the basic material effectively and exploiting it fully.

Lloyd's Place in the Development of the Comic Film

The reviewer of the reissued 1932 *Movie Crazy* in *Time* magazine of July 1949 stated: "Compared with most recent film comedies, it sparkles like vintage champagne."[14] Reviewing Lloyd's last picture, *Mad Wednesday*, critic Hollis Alpert revealed his admiration for the comedian's abilities:

> Of course, if you're contemplating taking the children to see "Mad Wednesday," some prior indoctrination will be necessary for them, and they'll probably still lag behind you, as you drag them toward the movie house, casting anguished glances toward the marquee proclaiming the latest Bob Hope picture. No use to tell them that they will have a comic experience far more rich and satisfying than anything Mr. Hope or Danny Kaye could give them; and apprising them of the

14. Review of *Movie Crazy*, *Time* 54 (July 18, 1949): 76.

232 / THREE CLASSIC SILENT SCREEN COMEDIES

Difficulties with the top of a convertable car in **Movie Crazy** (1932) as he tries to help a girl, Constance Cummings.

fact that Harold dangles from a ledge fifteen stories above the street may only cause them to express doubts about the humor of such goings-on. Just sit them down, though, and tell them to be patient, and be assured that Harold will come through for you.[15]

This colorful way of relating a view that Lloyd could provide "a comic experience far more rich and satisfying" than the leading comedians of the forties and fifties does indicate the respect and even the homage paid to one of the kings of the silent-screen comedy. And it now becomes more evident that even in the sound era, Lloyd could make successful movies.

Jumping into sound pictures with all the gusto of the "aspiring young man" that he portrayed, Lloyd reshot a good portion of

15. Alpert, "The Middle Years of Harold Diddlebock," *Saturday Review of Literature* 33 (November 4, 1950): 26.

With Helen Mack and Adolphe Menjou in **The Milky Way** (1936).

Phyllis Welch looking for a fugitive archaeologist, who happens to be just out of view—from **Professor Beware** (1938).

the silent *Welcome Danger* for its 1929 sound release. He renovated thrill material by showing his protagonist once more struggling to reach safety on a high building in his next film, *Feet First* (1930). He then slowed his production of feature films to every other year: *Movie Crazy* (1932), *The Cat's Paw* (1934), *The Milky Way* (1936), and *Professor Beware* (1938). Fortunately, all of his films retained much of past tradition. He excelled in the visual moments but proved he could handle dialogue more effectively than other major silent-screen comedians, Keaton and Langdon, who tried to make the transfer to sound.

Two examples of how well he handled dialogue can be found in his last picture. A screening of the 1947 *Mad Wednesday* before a film society audience in 1973 provided testament on the comedian's ability to handle two long monologues. As the character Harold Diddlebock, he delivers a long explanation to Miss Otis (Frances Rensden) of his love for all six of her older sisters, and he further explains that it was always his fate to miss marrying one of them. When this protagonist consumes a special drink concocted by a bartender (Edgar Kennedy), Lloyd reveals how the character switches from a standard meek-mannered person to an aggressive "fireball." Diddlebock launches into an elaborate, wacky speech by calling for a bucket of the drink which has transformed his character. He verbally attacks a policeman who enters the bar because he thinks the officer has maligned his friend Wormy (Jimmy Conlin). Eventually, Harold plunges into a pompous oration on "our forefathers," the pioneers. But in this movie, as in most of his other sound comedies, he returns to the lively visual comedy of the past. In the climactic sequence Harold Diddlebock ends up entangled in the leash of a huge lion, while dangling over a ledge on the fifteenth story of a building.

Lloyd's contribution and his status as a creator of comedy film will probably not be measured by his sound pictures even though many of his works of the thirties and forties are superior to the average movie fare of the period. *Grandma's Boy, Safety Last,* and *The Freshman* measure up to the best of Buster Keaton's creations, *Sherlock Jr.* (1924) and *The General* (1927), for example. Lloyd's best films are even a match for Charles Chaplin's *The Kid* (1921) and *The Gold Rush* (1925). Structure-wise Lloyd's films may even be considered superior. The question of his comic character's uniqueness and the position it plays in developing his films may still be open to question even though this study has attempted to show

A youthful-looking, studious, middle-aged man in **Professor Beware.**

The last picture, **Mad Wednesday** (1947). A publicity still with Frances Ramsden. The lion's name—Jackie.

the protagonist's function in the total film. James Agee's tribute focuses on this issue: "If great comedy must involve something beyond laughter, Lloyd was not a great comedian. If plain laughter is any criterion—and it is a healthy counter-balance to the other—few people have equalled him, and nobody has ever beaten him."[16]

Much of the preference for one comedian over another is a matter of taste, but several points may be made to illustrate Lloyd's place among his contemporaries. "Plain laughter" is the major criterion; otherwise the purpose of the comic drama is not realized. Nevertheless, there is dimension in the portrayal of a great clown that goes beyond the techniques of the stand-up comedian who gets laughs from a series of gags. This dimension lies in the character created, as well as in the consummate skill of the comedian. Critics have no argument with Lloyd's skill and rank him high; nevertheless, there is something about his character that seems too close to home to be realized. If the critic looks for a Chaplinesque "pathos," he will seldom find it in Lloyd's work. The comedian's portrait is infused with the spirit of Harlequin the Happy, not Pierrot the Sad. His comic character brings the audience that gaiety of all clowning as if he were bringing us bushels of sunshine. Herein lies the strength of Harold Lloyd's character. He brings us a fuller measure than Chaplin did, although the Harlequin in Charlie is more frequent than the Pierrot. In this respect both Lloyd and Chaplin outstrip Keaton and Langdon—the spirit of gaiety and fun being much stronger in their works. Furthermore, Lloyd's character achieves its uniqueness because he comes closer than the other three to some comment on the American scene. There is an exploitation of a type of character that has been an important part of our life—a gentle lampooning directed at the roots of our attitudes so that we can laugh at our dreams of success.

16. Agee, p. 12.

Appendix A
A Listing of the Sequences
in Lloyd's Three Films

Grandma's Boy

I	The Early Life of the Boy	(shots 1-13)
II	The Feud of the Boy and the Rival over the Girl	(shots 14-49)
III	The Boy Goes Home Defeated	(shots 50-54)
IV	The Boy Fails Against Another Foe—the Tramp	(shots 55-77)
V	Getting Ready for the Girl's Party	(shots 78-104)
VI	The Party at the Girl's House	(shots 105-177)
VII	The Sheriff Forms a Posse (Part A)	(shots 178-184)
VIII	The Tramp Kills a Merchant (a flashback sequence)	(shots 185-196)
VII	The Sheriff Forms a Posse (Part B)	(shots 197-218)
IX	The Boy Runs Away from His Duty	(shots 219-233)
X	Grandma Finds a Remedy for the Boy (Part A)	(shots 234-250)
XI	Grandpa's Civil War Adventure (a flashback sequence)	(shots 251-328)
X	Grandma Finds a Remedy for the Boy (Part B)	(shots 329-339)
XII	The New Man Goes to Battle	(shots 340-357)
XIII	The Boy's One-Man Battle with the Tramp	(shots 358-404)
XIV	The Boy Pursues the Tramp	(shots 405-475)
XV	News of the Boy's Bravery Spreads	(shots 476-478)
XVI	The Great Battle of the Boy and the Rival	(shots 479-533)

Appendix B
Filmography

Although enough data is available to provide a month-by-month listing of Lloyd's films, the accuracy of such a system with the early one- and two-reelers can be questioned. Any listing of dates according to reviews may produce a date later than the actual release of the movie. Hal Roach's Rolin Film Company did not copyright any film before March 16, 1917. Copyrights, when available, give a more accurate date since the film was often registered just before its release. Using this concept as a guide, this filmography steers a middle course by listing movies in the approximate position within the year that the films became available for distribution. Most early, short works are one-reel movies, therefore only films of two or more reels receive a note of their length. Brief indication is also given to significant landmarks in the history of Lloyd's development.

1912

First film appearance as a Yaqui Indian, a bit role for the Edison Company.

1914

Samson
(Only work with data to indicate Lloyd and Hal Roach appeared as bit players before turning to comedy.)
Willie Work Comedies ⸜
(Produced and directed by Roach; these films were not sold or released.)

1915

Just Nuts
(First released one-reeler with Ray Stewart and Jane Novak, reviewed in the April 21 *Dramatic Mirror*.)

240

Lonesome Luke
  (Earliest use of the character in a title, reviewed June 9, *Dramatic Mirror*.)
Once Every Ten Minutes
Spit Ball Sadie
A Mixup for Mazie

Some Baby
  (According to Lloyd in *An American Comedy* Bebe Daniels and Harry "Snub" Pollard joined the company at this time.)
Fresh From the Farm
Giving Them Fits
Bughouse Bell Hops
Tinkering With Trouble
Great While It Lasted
Ragtime Snap Shots
A Fozzle at a Tee Party
Ruses, Rhymes, Roughnecks
Peculiar Patients Pranks
Social Gangster

1916

Luke Leans to the Literary
Luke Lugs Luggage
Luke Rolls in Luxury
Luke the Candy Cut-Up
Luke Foils the Villain
Luke and Rural Roughnecks
Luke Pipes the Pippins
Lonesome Luke, Circus King
Luke's Double
Them Was the Happy Days
  (An April 26 release according to a Pathé ad)
Trouble Enough
Luke and the Bomb Throwers
Reckless Wrestlers
Luke's Late Lunches
Luke Laughs Last
Luke's Fatal Flivver
Luke's Society Mixup
Luke's Washful Waiting
Luke Rides Roughshod

Unfriendly Fruit
Luke-Crystal Gazer

Luke's Lost Lamb
Luke Does the Midway
Luke Joins the Navy
Luke and the Mermaids
Luke's Speedy Club Life
Luke and the Bang-Tails
Luke, the Chauffeur
Luke's Preparedness Preparation
Luke, Gladiator
Luke, Patient Provider
Luke's Movie Muddle
Luke's Fireworks Fizzle
Luke Locates the Loot
Luke's Shattered Sleep
    (Bebe Daniels and Harry "Snub" Pollard continue to support Lloyd in these films.)

1917

Luke's Last Liberty
Luke's Busy Days
Drama's Dreadful Deal
Luke's Trolley Trouble
Lonesome Luke, Lawyer
Luke Wins Ye Ladye Faire
Lonesome Luke's Lively Rifle
    (Rolin Film Company, working with Pathé, copyrighted the following two-reel comedies, starting March 16):
Lonesome Luke on Tin Can Alley
Lonesome Luke's Lively Life
Lonesome Luke's Honeymoon
Lonesome Luke, Plumber
Stop! Luke! Listen!
Lonesome Luke, Messenger
Lonesome Luke, Mechanic
Lonesome Luke's Wild Women
    (Copyrighted August 8, an August 25 *Dramatic Mirror* review praised this two-reeler.)
Over the Fence
    (The first one-reeler starring and directed by Lloyd using the young man with hornrimmed glasses. Copyrighted August 25.)
Lonesome Luke Loses Patients (two reels)
Pinched
By the Sad Sea Waves
Birds of a Feather (two reels)
Bliss
Lonesome Luke from London to Laramie (two reels)

Rainbow Island
Love, Laughs and Lather (two reels)
The Flirt
Clubs Are Trump (two reels)
All Aboard
We Never Sleep (two reels)
   (The last Lonesome Luke.)
The Tip

1918

The Non-Stop Kid
The Lamb
Hit Him Again
Beat It
A Gasoline Wedding
Let's Go
Look Pleasant Please
Here Come the Girls
On the Jump
Hey There
Kicked Out
Two-Gun Gussie
Fireman, Save My Child
The City Slicker
The Big Idea
It's a Wild Life
Sic 'Em Towser
Are Crooks Dishonest?

An Ozark Romance
Beach Nuts
Bride and Gloom
Step Lively
Follow the Crowd
Pipe the Whiskers
Somewhere in Turkey
Kicking the Germ Out of Germany
Two Scrambled
That's Him
Swing Your Partners
Bees in His Bonnet
Why Pick on Me?
Hear 'Em Rave
Nothing But Trouble

Take a Chance
She Loves Me Not
Ring Up the Curtain
Wanted—$5000
Going! Going! Gone!
Look Out Below
    (Lloyd's first "thrill" picture on a high building.)
On the Fire
Ask Father
Next Aisle Over

1919

I'm On My Way
The Dutiful Dub
Just Dropped In
Crack Your Heels
A Sammy in Siberia
Young Mr. Jazz
Si, Senor
Before Breakfast
The Marathon
Back to the Woods
Pistols for Breakfast
Off the Trolley
Swat the Crook
At the Old Stage Door
A Jazzed Honeymoon
Spring Fever
Just Neighbors

Billy Blazes, Esq.
Chop Suey and Co.
Count Your Change
Heap Big Chief
The Rajah
He Leads, Others Follow
Never Touched Me
Don't Shove
Be My Wife
Soft Money
Count the Votes
Pay Your Dues
His Only Father
Bumping into Broadway (two reels)

(First in a special contract of nine films with Pathé)
Captain Kidd's Kids (two reels)
(Last Film of Bebe Daniels with Lloyd.)
From Hand to Mouth (two reels)
(Mildred Davis's first film with Lloyd.)
His Royal Slyness (two reels)
(Last film of Harry "Snub" Pollard with Lloyd.)

1920

(Two-reel films)
Haunted Spooks
An Eastern Westerner
High and Dizzy
(The second "thrill picture" using a high building.)

Get Out and Get Under
Number, Please
(Fred Newmeyer takes over direction from Hal Roach.)

1921

(Two-reel productions—often released as two-reelers)

Now or Never
Among Those Present
I Do

Never Weaken
(The third "thrill" picture using building-climbing material.)
A Sailor-Made Man (four reels)
(Directed by Fred Newmeyer, with Mildred Davis and Noah Young.)

1922

(Lloyd moves to feature-length films.)
Grandma's Boy (five reels)
(Directed by Fred Newmeyer, with Mildred Davis, Anna Townsend, and Charles Stevenson.)
Dr. Jack (five reels)
Directed by Fred Newmeyer, with Mildred Davis, John T. Prince, and Eric Mayne.)

1923

Safety Last (seven reels)
(Directed by Fred Newmeyer and Sam Taylor, with Mildred Davis, Bill Strothers, Noah Young, and Westcott B. Clarke.)
Why Worry? (six reels)

(Directed by Fred Newmeyer and Sam Taylor, with Jobyna Ralston and Johan Aasen.)

1924

Girl Shy (eight reels)

(Directed by Fred Newmeyer and Sam Taylor, with Jobyna Ralston, Richard Daniels, and Carlton Griffin.)

Hot Water (five reels)

(Directed by Fred Newmeyer and Sam Taylor, with Jobyna Ralston and Josephine Crowell.)

1925

The Freshman (seven reels)

(Directed by Sam Taylor and Fred Newmeyer, with Jobyna Ralston, Brooks Benedict, James Anderson, and Joseph Harrington.)

1926

For Heaven's Sake (six reels)

(Directed by Sam Taylor, with Jobyna Ralston, Noah Young, and James Mason.

1927

The Kid Brother (eight reels)

(Directed by Ted Wilde, with Jobyna Ralston, Walter James, Leo Willis, Olin Francis, and Eddie Boland.)

1928

Speedy (eight reels)

(Directed by Ted Wilde, with Burt Woodruff, Babe Ruth, Ann Christy, and Brooks Benedict.)

1929

Welcome Danger (twelve reels)

(Directed by Clyde Bruckman, with Barbara Kent, Noah Young, Charles Middleton and William Walling. (The comedian's first sound movie.)

1930

Feet First (ten reels)

(Directed by Clyde Bruckman, with Barbara Kent, Robert McWade, Lillian Leighton, Alec Francis, and Noah Young.)

1932

Movie Crazy (nine reels)

(Directed by Clyde Bruckman, with Constance Cummings, Kenneth Thomson, Sidney Jarvis, Eddie Fetherstone, and Robert McWade.)

1934

The Cat's Paw (twelve reels)

(Directed by Sam Taylor, with Una Merkel, George Barbier, Nat Pendleton, Grant Mitchell, and Warren Hymer.)

1936

The Milky Way (ten reels)

(Directed by Leo McCarey, with Adolphe Menjou, Verree Teasdale, Helen Mack, William Gargan, George Barbier, Dorothy Wilson, and Lionel Stander.)

1938

Professor Beware (eleven reels)
(Directed by Elliott Nugent, with Phyllis Welch, Raymond Walburn, Lionel Stander, Cora Witherspoon, Etienne Girardot, and William Frawley.)

1947

Mad Wednesday (also titled *The Sin of Harold Diddlebock*) (eight reels)
(Directed by Preston Sturges, with Frances Ramsden, Jimmy Conlin, Edgar Kennedy, Rudy Vallee, Arline Judge, Franklin Pangborn, Jack Norton, and Lionel Stander.)

1962

Harold Lloyd's World of Comedy (ten reels)
(Produced by Harold Lloyd. A compilation of sequences from the comedian's works from the silent days to the sound age. Features used are *Safety Last, Girl Shy, Hot Water, Why Worry?, Feet First, Movie Crazy, The Milky Way,* and *Professor Beware.*)

1966

Harold Lloyd's Funny Side of Life (eleven reels)
(Produced by Harold Lloyd. The complete feature created in 1925, *The Freshman,* used as the main attraction with sequences from *Why Worry?, Girl Shy, For Heaven's Sake, The Kid Brother,* and *Speedy.*)

Appendix C
June 1965 Interviews
with Harold Lloyd

Probably the best source for a view of Lloyd's working methods may be found in his 1928 autobiography, *An American Comedy,* written in collaboration with Wesley W. Stout. Fortunately, this rare work once more became available when Dover Publications reissued the book in paperback in 1971. This volume also contains a 1966 interview of the famous comedian, which was conducted by Hubert I. Cohen at the University of Michigan in Ann Arbor. *Harold Lloyd's World of Comedy* by William Cahn, constructed in part from interviews, also may be consulted. Of interest, but mostly routine, is Arthur B. Friedman's interview of the comedian which appeared in the Summer 1962 *Film Quarterly* 15:7-13.

The following notes have been edited to avoid repeating Lloyd's views already in print. This transcription must contain personal references, since a great deal of give and take occurred in the meeting. Lloyd had read my dissertation on *Grandma's Boy, Safety Last,* and *The Freshman;* he was interested in any of my recent writings on silent-screen comedy.

June 8, 1965 Since I had obtained Harold Lloyd's unlisted phone number through correspondence with him, I called him as soon as my family and I were settled in the Hollywood Roosevelt Hotel. Mrs. Lloyd (known as Mildred Davis when she starred with the famous comedian) answered and evidently helped screen phone calls for an initial contact.

The phone conversation lasted about twenty minutes. A social visit that included my family was arranged for June 10. Lloyd expressed interest in my dissertation on his works and *Four Great Comedians: Chaplin,*

248

Lloyd, Keaton, Langdon, a work that was in its first draft. He indicated that he had read my dissertation, which I had sent him, and appreciated my thorough analysis of his three films. He added that he would like to read the manuscript of my "present project" and give suggestions—if I were interested in his views on his films and those created by others in the silent period. I learned that he wanted me to see a screening of *Safety Last* and wanted my advice on a new prologue to *The Freshman,* his silent feature that eventually was released under the title *Harold Lloyd's Funny Side of Life.* When he mentioned that the screening of *Safety Last* would feature special organ music created for the movie, I offhandedly indicated that this work was my favorite and that I would enjoy hearing a score as I viewed it. He seemed surprised that I favored *Safety Last.* He told me that he liked parts of the film and appreciated each of his "top grade" movies for different reasons.[1] Since his *The Kid Brother* had been well received at a special screening, he said he'd make sure I got to see it while visiting the area.

Evidently Lloyd was concerned that proper musical accompaniment for his pictures be used. He was disturbed that the Museum of Modern Art had presented some of his movies at public showing with only piano music. Organ music or a full orchestra, he felt, was a necessity to support his comedies effectively. I told him I thought many of the comedy compilations such as Robert Youngson's *Golden Age of Comedy* had been overscored—the music attempted to make comic points or comments on almost every gag. I told him I admired subtler music and the judicious editing of *Harold Lloyd's World of Comedy.* That view he said was "dear to his heart." He had been asked to narrate the "Silents Please" series for television. He was shown a condensed version of *Dr. Jekyll and Mr. Hyde* starring John Barrymore, and Buster Keaton's *The General.* The producer urged him to respond with, "Wasn't it great!" Lloyd said, "I'll talk to you later." Pressed for an answer, the comedian finally replied that he was horrified, because he wouldn't want his own films and those of his friends cut to a half hour. He stressed the "violence" done to a feature comedy work when it is edited to half or a third of its original length. While the version of *The General* that had been cut for this television show retained enough gags to make the version funny, Lloyd observed, "It wasn't *The General.*"

This phone conversation was concluded with a brief discussion of the approach taken by the fan magazine and of scholar's concerns when interviewing a motion-picture actor. Lloyd realized that I was more interested in his creations than his personal life; he was grateful, since he realized the interviews would avoid the "old, tired questions."

1. Lloyd rated *Grandma's Boy, Safety Last,* and *The Freshman* as his best creations. It became increasingly clear in the interviews that followed that comedies with "character based stories," (as he labeled them) were the ones he preferred. His 1927 *The Kid Brother* had just been added to his "best" list.

June 10 The first meeting with the comedian was essentially social in nature. My wife, Joann, two daughters, Marcie and Connie, and I visited the comedian in his fabulous mansion. Seventy-two years of age at the time, Lloyd shared with us some of his hobbies developed in retirement. For example, we looked at his collection of costly, elaborate Christmas-tree ornaments on two huge trees—a year-round, colorful conversation piece. When a brief discussion of comedy did develop with my family in the library of the actor's home, most of the material he introduced was rather typical interview material composed of entertaining anecdotes for a group of admirers. For example, Lloyd related how he took a rather painful fall while rolling down a hill, but when the rushes were screened, the angle of the camera placement made it appear as if the comedian were merely rolling along on a flat surface. Asked to repeat the feat, he flatly refused, indicating by his attitude that even in his early pictures he placed some limits on achieving comedy through the pratfall.

After listening to a stereo-player system, which Lloyd claimed was superior to any movie studio playback audio equipment (it was housed in a large all-purpose room for entertaining and projecting films several decades ago), I gave the comedian a formative, basic chapter evaluating his films, plus two other chapters that dealt with his work, comparing it with Chaplin's, Keaton's, and Langdon's. At his phoned request, I brought the complete manuscript of *Four Great Comedians* to him. This was given to him on the first intensive interview of the 12th.

June 12 Lloyd informed me that he'd like me to attend a screening of *Safety Last* and *The Kid Brother*. He told me the latter work represented a feature which he placed "number four or higher" among his creations. I readily accepted the invitation and we launched into a three-hour exchange[2] that touched on many aspects of the comedian's working methods.

Lloyd seemed somewhat defensive at first. In a chapter of my manuscript I had used a scathing review of his 1915 *Just Nuts*. I evaluated it as a Chaplinesque film using "park comedy" material, labeling it a very disjointed one-reeler. He said that he was using a comedy character closer to a Gloomy Gus or Happy Hooligan. *Just Nuts,* he felt, was more complicated than the type of one-reeler created by "getting a camera, going to a park and trying to be funny"—Lloyd's apt characterization of the weakness of many primitive efforts to produce a comedy. I agreed that some attempt was made to move away from typical park comedies. The second part of the film did move from a park to a dance hall, thereby

2. The nature of our discussion was that of an exchange. We discussed our theories on screen comedy. I was bold enough to correct him when his lapses of memory confused an issue and, at times, I disagreed with some of his evaluations. We were alone and the spirit of our conversation became friendly and personal. We soon addressed each other by our first names.

attempting to introduce more complicated plotting and newer material. But, I maintained, even this commendable effort created two actions that contributed to the disunity. "You've seen the film?" he inquired, more as an observation than a question. I said I had viewed it at the Museum of Modern Art Film Library in June of 1964. He finally admitted that it was a very early step in his development and that he understood I was trying to show his progressive improvement in this portion of the manuscript.

We discussed at length his move to features with *Grandma's Boy,* focusing a good deal of the conversation on his use of a character who had psychological problems. This he believed was an effective means of creating a feature-length comic drama.[3] He noted that I praised the chase of the tramp portion of the film. It was not so strong a sequence as originally created, he claimed. He and his production staff inserted more gags in this part of the film after a preview indicated that people wanted the material more fully exploited. *Grandma's Boy,* according to my evaluation had an overextended flashback—Grandma's elaborate fib about Grandpa's becoming brave through a magic charm seemed tangential. Lloyd had read this view in my manuscript and felt this portion of his picture needed to be this long. The Boy, he maintained, needed the jolt of an elaborate fib to make him accept the fake magical charm. I realized this, I told him, and explained that I was more concerned about structure than the audience. As I critic, I desired more unity in a comic work than did the average viewer. We took up the question of how innovative a critic could label the climactic fight sequence. He felt that an audience in the twenties was more interested in this portion of the film than are people today—that the struggle became a parody of the many fights in the serious melodramas of that age. "Maybe there aren't enough gags in that part of *Grandma's Boy.* When I see my films today," he concluded, "there are many things I'd like to do over." He laughed, and added "But that's impossible, isn't it?"

As we moved to a consideration of *Safety Last,* the comedian revealed a practice I'd never heard of—that of previewing a film with a movie of a rival. He said that *Safety Last* was shown on the same bill as Buster Keaton's *The Navigator* (I interjected that it probably was *Our Hospitality,* since both features appeared in 1923 while *The Navigator* was a year later). Lloyd proudly indicated that of the two, his work received a more favorable audience response. It was a brutal way to see if a feature comedy "had it," he remarked; it was "almost a sink or swim" approach to testing a movie, since the other, rival picture had already been reworked after it had been previewed.

---

3. Our exchange regarding this phase of our examination need not be set down. Many of Lloyd's views on the Boy's character appear in other publications, e.g., *An American Comedy.*

We discussed the nature of the gags in *Safety Last*. Much as others have related, he talked about the building-climbing sequence[4] that had a running gag to hold it together, thereby producing a more effective thrill picture—one that was better than comedy films using similar material. Another film using similar "thrill-laugh" situations, *Mad Wednesday*, was briefly examined. He revealed his struggle with writer-director Preston Sturges as they developed gags for the picture. Lloyd claimed that Sturges didn't understand the more subtle use of comedy situations in the twenties. He seemed to want to recapture the primitive slapstick of Mack Sennett by having eight men dangling over the edge of a building ledge as they held onto a leash tied to an evidently very strong lion. Lloyd was able to trim the number down to two people, comedian Jimmy Conlin and himself. He then embarked on a good-natured, but firm, explanation of Sturges's inability to grasp the nature of the comedian's handling of comic material. Lloyd felt that he was required to do either "idiot or Casper Milktoast" routines—moving in both directions to an overstatement of character. The actor claimed that he had control in his relationship with the director for about a third to half of the picture, but finally gave up. The results, he felt, did not make coming out of retirement worthwhile.[5]

The comedian then observed that he admired my examination of his works and respected my right to look objectively at the strengths and weaknesses in them. He felt, as I did, that critics of the twenties often erected a sacred wall around Chaplin, making him untouchable. He also felt that I was correct in separating his films from Charles Ray's—a link suggested by Gilbert Seldes in his 1924 *Seven Lively Arts*. In my manuscript I had questioned Seldes's view that *Grandma's Boy* could have been done by Ray. This I maintained "would have condemned the picture to obscurity."[6] Lloyd was very severe in his judgment of Ray's work. He said he didn't "admire" his films and felt that the actor could never obtain "depth" in his comic character. "To be blunt about it," he declared, "I had plenty of rivals, but Ray was not even a very good actor."

As the conversation wandered to modern comedians, Lloyd said he admired Jacques Tati, but wondered why such a skilled comedian didn't exploit his material more effectively. By using a "hit and run" approach to a gag, Tati was unable to get variation and a building of the comedy situation.[7] The French actor, he noted in his analysis, had enough gags

4. On pp. 125 and 126 of the appendix "The Serious Business of Being Funny," an interview by Professor Cohen in the republished *An American Comedy*, Lloyd explains his views on this sequence.

5. The picture holds an audience better than Lloyd realized at the time. It is seldom seen, but I witnessed a small movie society crowd enjoying the film thoroughly.

6. McCaffrey, *Four Great Comedians* (London, 1968), p. 159.

7. In Cohen's interview ("The Serious Business . . .," p. 121) Lloyd expressed the view that comedian Jerry Lewis's "greatest failing" was his inability to build gags from one situation.

for many pictures. Lloyd believed that his method of dropping some of the "shotgun gags" and adding more gags on one basic situation had helped his films—a process sometimes executed after a preview.

Lloyd and I talked at length about his use of basic climactic material, which he classified as "1. Chase, 2. Fight, 3. Danger on High Places or Thrill Comedy, and 4. The Haunted House." It was obvious that he, as did comedians and critics of the twenties, used the term *chase* loosely—it also included the rush to the rescue when no actual pursuit took place. He said that much of this material appeared in a simple form in his one- and two-reelers. When he moved to the feature, he explained, he expanded and exploited the material to its fullest extent, only cutting out gags that seem overextensions—those that made the whole episode repetitive.

June 14 While no formal interview was conducted during the screening of *Safety Last* and *The Kid Brother,* some discussion about the use of music for the silent film proved interesting. At the home of Richard Simonton in North Hollywood, a tape for both of these movies had been prepared by organist Gaylord Carter. After viewing these films Mr. Carter and Mr. Lloyd explained how important the proper scores for such films were. The music provided a support for the dramatic action. Since I had studied *Safety Last,* in detail, without a score accompanying the film, I noted the effect of this screening. Even with this small group attending the presentation, I detected a stronger empathic response from the audience as they witnessed the climactic building sequence. Gaylord Carter stated that, by using a theatrical organ, he attempted to develop proper musical support for each scene in a film. As an illustration, he said that King Vidor praised his use of a steady drumbeat in that director's *The Great Parade* (1927) as soldiers were advancing in the woods toward the enemy. Lloyd indicated to me that he felt that serious moments in his own films received support, and probably went over better with an audience, with an effective organ or orchestral background.

June 15 Lloyd treated my family and me to a preview of his 1966 release, *Harold Lloyd's Funny Side of Life.* Since this compilation contained a series of sequences from *Speedy, Girl Shy, For Heaven's Sake, The Kid Brother,* plus a complete feature, *The Freshman,* it illustrated the handling of several variations on his comic character and provided a good sampling of his work to conclude the interviews.

After his 12:30 P.M. showing. Lloyd visited our Hollywood Roosevelt Hotel room for a final discussion. While we had reached the stage when many phases of his working methods were being rehashed, we did touch on a few new items. We discussed his 1934 *The Cat's Paw,* a work the comedian believed was his most genteel creation. This film departed more from the traditional gag-filled film that he had created in his past productions. He described a meeting in which he and director Sam Taylor decided to draw from a hat a slip of paper indicating "new way" or "old way"—their means of deciding how to handle the picture. Since the "new way" slip was drawn, they created a film that put less reliance on an elaborate milking of gags from a given situation. While he expressed the view that it was a successful picture, he admitted that he felt inclined to return to his former working system in 1936 with *The Milky Way* and in 1938 with *Professor Beware*.

I asked him about his bold embrace of the sound medium with *Welcome Danger* in 1929—an action the opposite of that of Charles Chaplin, who produced two films, *City Lights* (1931) and *Modern Times* (1936), that were essentially silent screen films. Lloyd declared that he believed in change and had reshot a good portion of his 1929 film because it was his desire to follow the trend of the time. "I didn't fear sound," he claimed. Many of his supporting actors found the reworking of the picture a distressing experience because many of them had not worked on the stage. Lloyd felt that he had enough stage work to carry him through the transitional phase, but admitted that he faked confidence in the movie's potential success because he was in charge of a plunge that had disturbed the whole film industry. "As we dubbed in some dialogue (when it was possible to use old footage)," he said, "I pretended it was very easy, to give some of my co-workers the feeling that the years of silence had been nothing. But it was a problem. I worried underneath my outward show of confidence."

Lloyd noted that some of the ad lib features of creating comedy from the silent screen sometimes came into being when he worked on a sound picture. The attempts to erect the top of a convertable car in *Movie Crazy* (1932) during a rain storm proved to be more difficult than planned. The struggles he and the girl had with the top were left in the final edition of the film because the action proved to be funny. Sometimes, but very seldom, Lloyd pointed out, the unexpected problems that arose during the shooting of a scene would produce a comic effect. He remembered that in the early one- and two-reel days a streetcar chase called for him to run away from the trolley straight along the track and eventually dodge out of the way. The vehicle jumped the tracks as he attempted to get out of the way—following him in a way he thought would surely kill him. His scrambling was "pure horror," but his actions proved to be very funny and the scene was left in the film.

Since I was interested in pursuing the value of previews, I produced a 1928 copy of *American Cinematographer*,[8] which clearly indicated that Lloyd had used an almost scientific study of crowd reactions for *The Kid*

---

8. P. A. Thomajan, "The Laughograph" *American Cinematographer* (April 1928), pp. 36-38.

Brother. I showed him a graph in the magazine that charted the intensity of the laughter and the number of gags that received a response. He recalled making some notes, but could not recall hiring someone to make this accurate log on audience response.

Trying to get to the core of the character that he created, I asked Lloyd what the glasses signified—how did they give the "boy next door" a quality unlike that of other comedians? He explained by saying that he was not creating someone who was "necessarily a sissy or a dandy." He indicated that the boy was set apart because he had a "serious, basic intent" and might even be studious in the way he went about solving the problems that confronted him. Being more eager than the average person, the character sometimes made a fool of himself. While Lloyd recognized that this portrait came from the popular fiction of the day, he felt that he was more innovative with his character than were the stories. "I could make him more of a shy guy as in *Grandma's Boy* and *The Kid Brother.* On the other hand, he could lean toward the hustler with some smart aleck traits—like in *Safety Last.*" He maintained that he changed his character with each film and realized that he must avoid repeating the same character to avoid stagnation. He avoided doing a carbon copy of a successful comic protagonist as he moved from one picture to the next.

During this discussion, as in previous ones, the comedian occasionally referred to a work as "a Lloyd picture" or used a sentence such as "Lloyd wouldn't use such a gag." Using the third person in this way might have been construed as egocentric, but it appeared that it was his attempt to be objective about his work or it illustrated that he felt his screen portrait of Harold had become a special creation that only he could handle. Furthermore, he expressed the view that his comic films were not "merely burlesques or broad" dramas, but a blend of many types of humor. He claimed he ran the gamut—using "broad, light, farcical, dramatic elements." He, like Chaplin, wanted sympathy for his protagonist and the love of a woman. He maintained that the audience "went along with the boy" as he engaged in various adventures, even though he had "the badge of comedy, a recognized comic character."

We talked briefly about different types of gags. He used terms such as "running gag" and "switch" (for which I used "reversal"). We talked more at length about his use of a "revealing" gag, which he called a "surprise" gag. I noted that he used a set-up to promote such a gag at the beginning of many of his movies—for example, appearing to be riding in the back of a fancy limousine. When we see the car pull ahead, it is revealed that Harold had been seated on a bicycle, riding along on the other side of the automobile.[9] Lloyd remarked that he liked this gag and

9. This gag appeared at the beginning of *Movie Crazy* (1932). I told him that British comedian Norman Wisdom copied it for his *Trouble in Store* (1953) without enough switch in the situation to realize innovative thought.

that it had to be carefully worked out. He said that most of his "surprise" gags did "sell," but occasionally he would take one out if it appeared too self-conscious. The gag that was too self-conscious, he said, was the "fantastic" gag—an impossible feat that sometimes produced laughter. He recalled the attempts to fix his car in *Get Out and Get Under* when he leaned far into the hood of an automobile, so far that he disappeared. "Obviously there wasn't enough room for me in there and it did get a laugh, but I gave that type of thing up in my features." This two-reel film made in 1920 was one of his last to use that kind of gag; he felt that it was a type of gag that was not the best way of achieving humor—it was something for the film cartoon, but not the live-action comedian.[10]

When Lloyd acted as a producer for RKO and created *A Girl, a Guy, and a Gob* (1941) and *My Favorite Spy* (1942), he was most willing to give gags and suggestions on the set. He told me that he worked closely with Richard Wallace, the director, on the 1941 film, giving many tips to Edmond O'Brien and Lucille Ball.[11] He explained that when he worked on a picture he always let what might be called an assistant director by other comedians get full credit as director. While he was not an actor in those two RKO pictures, he continued the practice. In many ways, he confided, he helped build a director's reputation. He said this sometimes worked against him, because a big company "would dangle a lot of money in front of my director and I soon lost him." But in the long run, he felt, his system of giving full credit to the director while doing his films helped the total creation. Since filmmaking demanded so much cooperation from everyone, he declared, "we needed a system that worked best for me." Lloyd realized that as the actor who dominated so many (almost all) of the scenes, he needed someone to give the picture firm control. He and the director thereby were somewhat like co-directors.

We came to a point when we talked about the title of my book, *Four Great Comedians*. He said that Harry Langdon might have been working in some of his pictures instead of signing with Mack Sennett. Lloyd said he saw Harry's vaudeville routine and liked it; he went to see Hal Roach and asked him to get the comedian under contract. Roach viewed the act, but refused to pay him the $100 a week it would take to hire him. Lloyd wondered why. Roach bluntly answered, "He's not worth $100." The question came up in our conversation: Did he deserve to be rated as one of the "Four Great Comedians?" Lloyd tended to agree with my wife (who was present during this interview and occasionally asked him a question) that Langdon was not in the same league with Chaplin, Lloyd,

10. In a June 15 telephone conversation with Buster Keaton, I got a similar reaction. He had used "fantastic" gags in his short works, but tried to avoid them in features.

11. In a periodical of the times, the reviewer gave comedian Lloyd most of the credit for this film. "Lloydian Laughs by Proxy. Comedian-Producer's New Film Leaves Slapstick to Others," *Newsweek* (March 17, 1941), pp. 62-63.

and Keaton. "He wasn't handled correctly, except by Frank Capra," Lloyd said, adding "And he couldn't do his own work." He continued by examining the concept that a master comedian needed to be able to handle all phases of the production to do his best work. "When I felt my control starting to slip, I got out," he declared. He laughed and admitted he was "sucked into" *Mad Wednesday* by Preston Sturges. He reflected: "It's not a bad picture, but it's just not a *good Lloyd* film."

Selected Bibliography

Books

Agee, James. *Agee on Film.* New York: McDowell, Obolensky, Inc., 1958.
Arnheim, Rudolf. *Film as Art.* Berkeley and Los Angeles, Calif. University of California Press, 1957.
Balázs, Béla. *Theory of the Film; Character and Growth of a New Art.* Translated by Edith Bone. London: Dennis Dobson, Ltd., 1952.
Bardèche, Maruice, and Brasillach, Robert. *The History of Motion Pictures.* Translated and edited by Iris Barry. New York: W. W. Norton and Company, Inc., 1938.
Bergson, Henri. "Laughter," *Comedy.* Edited by Wylie Sypher. Garden City, N. Y.: Doubleday and Company, Inc., 1956.
Brownlow, Kevin. *The Parade's Gone By. . .* New York: Alfred A. Knopf, Inc., 1968.
Cahn, William. *Harold Lloyd's World of Comedy.* New York: Duell, Sloan and Pearce, 1964.
Crouse, Russel, ed. *Struggling Upward and Other Works* by Horatio Alger Jr. New York: Crown Publishers, 1945.
Dannenberg, Joseph, ed. *Film Year Book 1922-1923.* New York: Wid's Film and Film Folks, Inc., 1923.
——. *Film Year Book 1925.* New York: The Film Daily, 1925.
——. *Film Year Book 1926.* New York: The Film Daily, 1926.
Eastman, Max. *Enjoyment of Laughter.* New York: Simon and Schuster, Inc., 1936.
Griffith, Richard, and Mayer, Arthur. *The Movies: The Sixty Year Story of the World of Hollywood and Its Effect on America, From Pre-Nickelodeon Days to the Present.* New York: Simon and Schuster, Inc., 1957.
Huff, Theodore. *Charlie Chaplin.* New York: Henry Schuman, Inc., 1951.
Keaton, Buster, *My Wonderful World of Slapstick.* Garden City, N. Y.: Doubleday and Company, Inc., 1960.
Knight, Arthur. *The Liveliest Art:* New York: The Macmillan Company, 1957.

Koestler, Arthur. *Insight and Outlook: An Inquiry into the Common Foundations of Science, Art, and Social Ethics.* New York: The Macmillan Company, 1949.

Kracauer, Siegfried. *Theory of Film.* New York: Oxford University Press, 1960.

Lahue, Kalton C. and Brewer, Terry. *Kops and Custards.* Norman, Okla.: University of Oklahoma Press, 1967.

————. *World of Laughter: The Motion Picture Comedy Short, 1910-1930.* Norman, Oklahoma: University of Oklahoma Press, 1966.

Lawson, John Howard. *Theory and Technique of Playwriting and Screenwriting.* New York: G. P. Putnam's Sons, 1949.

Lean, David. "The Film Director," *Working for the Films.* Edited by Oswell Blackeston. London: The Focal Press, Ltd., 1947.

Lloyd, Harold. *An American Comedy.* New York: Longmans, Green and Company, 1928.

————. "Introduction," *The Laugh Makers* by William Cahn. New York: G. P. Putnam's Sons, 1957.

Mast, Gerald. *The Comic Mind; Comedy and the Movies.* Indianapolis, Inc.: The Bobbs-Merrill, Inc., 1973.

McCaffrey, Donald. *Focus on Chaplin.* Englewood Cliffs, N.J.: Prentice-Hall, Inc., 1971.

————. *Four Great Comedians: Chaplin, Lloyd, Keaton, Langdon.* London: A. Zwemmer, Ltd., and New York: A. S. Barnes and Co., 1968.

————. *The Golden Age of Sound Comedy; Comic Films and Comedians of the Thirties.* New York: A. S. Barnes and Co., and London: The Tantivy Press, 1973.

Meredith, George. "An Essay on Comedy," *Comedy.* Edited by Wylie Sypher. Garden City, N. Y.: Doubleday and Company, Inc., 1956.

Montgomery, John. *Comedy Films.* London: George Allen and Unwin, Ltd. 1954.

O'Dell, Scott. *Representative Photoplays Analyzed.* Hollywood, Calif. Palmer Institute of Authorship, 1924.

Palmer, Frederick. *Photoplay Plot Encyclopedia; An Analysis of the Use in Photoplays of the Thirty-Six Dramatic Situations and Their Subdivision.* 2d ed. revised. Hollywood, Calif.: Palmer Photoplay Corporation, 1922.

————. *Technique of the Photoplay.* Hollywood, Calif.: Palmer Institute of Authorship, 1924.

Payne, Robert. *The Great God Pan: A Biography of the Tramp Played by Charles Chaplin.* New York: Hermitage House, 1952.

Reisz, Karel. *The Technique of Film Editing.* 5th ed. London: The Focal Press, Ltd., 1957.

Rotha, Paul. *The Film Till Now: A Survey of World Cinema.* New York: Funk and Wagnalls Company, 1949.

Seldes, Gilbert. *The Movies Come From America.* New York: Charles Scribner's Sons, 1937.

————. *The Seven Lively Arts.* New York: Sagamore Press, Inc., 1957.

Sherwood, Robert. *The Best Moving Pictures of 1922-1923*. Boston, Mass.: Small, Maynard and Company, 1923.

United States Copyright Office. *Catalogue of Copyright Entries, Cumulative Series, Motion Pictures 1912-1939*. Washington, D.C.: Library of Congress, 1951.

Weaver, John T. *Twenty Years of Silents: 1908-1929*. Metuchen, N. J.: The Scarecrow Press, Inc., 1971.

Articles and Periodicals

Alpert, Hollis. "The Middle Years of Harold Diddlebock," *Saturday Review of Literature* 33 (November 4, 1950): 26-27.

Review of *The Freshman, Variety* 79 (July 15, 1925): 34.

Friedman, Arthur B., "Interview with Harold Lloyd," *Film Quarterly* 15 (Summer 1962): 7-13.

Garringer, Nelson E. "Harold Lloyd Made a Fortune by Combining Comedy and Thrills," *Films in Review* 13 (Aug.-Sept. 1962): 420-22.

Geoffrey, John. Review of *Little, But Oh My!, Dramatic Mirror and Theatre World* (December 17, 1921), p. 890.

Review of *A Girl, a Guy and a Gob, Newsweek* 17 (March 17, 1941): 63.

Hinckley, Theodore B. Review of *Safety Last, The Drama* 13 (September 1923): 361.

Review of *Homer Comes Home, Dramatic Mirror; the Screen and Stage Weekly* 82 (July 3, 1920): 24.

Review of *Just Nuts, The New York Dramatic Mirror* 73 (April 21, 1915): 35.

Kennedy, John B. "It Pays to Be Sappy," *Collier's* 79 (June 11, 1927): 12, 28.

Lloyd, Harold. "The Hardships of Fun Making," *The Ladies Home Journal* 93 (May 1926): 32, 50, 234.

Review of *Lonesome Luke, The New York Dramatic Mirror* 73 (June 9, 1915): 39.

Review of *Lonesome Luke's Wild Women, The Dramatic Mirror of Motion Pictures and Stage* 77 (August 25, 1917): 21.

Review of *Movie Crazy, Times* 54 (July 18, 1949): 76.

Mullett, Mary B. "A Movie Star Who Knows What Makes You Laugh," *American Magazine* 94 (July 1922): 36-39.

"Safety-First Stuff in *Safety Last*," *Literary Digest* 78 (July 14, 1923): 43-44.

Review of *Safety Last, New York Times*, April 2, 1923, p. 22.

Review of *The Sheriff's Son, The Dramatic Mirror* 80 (April 8, 1919): 30.

Sherwood, Robert. Review of *The Freshman, Life* 86 (October 15, 1925): 24.

————. Review of *Safety Last, Life* 81 (April 26, 1923): 24.

Sobel, Bernard. Review of *Burn 'Em Up Barnes, Dramatic Mirror and Theatre World* 84 (September 10, 1921): 389.

————. Review of *One A Minute, Dramatic Mirror and Theatre World* 83 (June 25, 1921): 1083.

Index

261